God Sees Her

365 Devotions
for Women by Women

Our Daily Bread
Publishing™

God Sees Her: 365 Devotions for Women by Women
© 2020 by Our Daily Bread Publishing.
All rights reserved.

Requests for permission to quote from this book should
be directed to: Permissions Department, Our Daily Bread
Publishing, PO Box 3566, Grand Rapids, MI 49501, or
contact us by email at permissionsdept@odb.org.

ISBN: 978-1-64070-004-8

Printed in China
First printing in 2020

Foreword

I remember the painted brick walls, the rows of dented lockers, the sound of teenage laughter bouncing against the low ceiling. As I clutched my textbooks against my chest, I scanned the faces of passing classmates, hoping to find one friend who might make eye contact with me. Smile back at me. Speak my name.

As I grew into my twenties, the longing to be seen by others remained. I wanted to be visible, not invisible. Counted, not discounted. But it seemed the harder I tried to get people's attention, the more they looked the other way.

Only when I came to the end of myself did I discover that Someone has always had His eye on me: The God of all creation. He sees me. Just as He sees you, beloved.

Right from the beginning, "God saw all that he had made, and it was very good" (Genesis 1:31). From that day forth, He has kept His gaze firmly fixed on His own. "For the eyes of the Lord range throughout the earth to strengthen those whose hearts are fully committed to him" (2 Chronicles 16:9).

He doesn't simply look at us; He supports, encourages, and strengthens us.

His special care for women is evident in the story of Leah, whose husband, Jacob, despised her. God saw her sorrow and mended her broken heart with a gift: "When the Lord saw that Leah was not loved, he enabled her to conceive" (Genesis 29:31).

Or consider the story of a widow in Nain, mourning the loss of her only son. "When the Lord saw her, his heart went out to her and he said, 'Don't cry'" (Luke 7:13). He misses nothing, least of all our pain. Even if others don't notice us, we can be certain He does.

After watching a weeping woman anoint His feet with her tears, Jesus asked Simon the Pharisee, "Do you see this woman?" (Luke 7:44). All Simon saw was an nameless prostitute. All Jesus saw was a heart devoted to Him.

As the title and first entry of this book make clear, *God Sees Her*. Sees Hagar, sees Leah, sees the widow, sees you, every minute of every day. He will never grow weary of watching over you. And you will never be less than beautiful in His eyes.

May you see His love on every page, dear sister.

Liz Curtis Higgs

International speaker and author of thirty-seven books, including *Bad Girls of the Bible*

God Sees Her

GENESIS 16:7–14

She gave this name to the LORD who spoke to her:
"You are the God who sees me," for she said,
"I have now seen the One who sees me."
—GENESIS 16:13

My first eyeglasses opened my eyes to a bold world. Without glasses, items in the distance were a blur. At age twelve, with my first pair of eyeglasses, I was shocked to see clearer words on blackboards, tiny leaves on trees, and perhaps most important, big smiles on faces.

As friends smiled back when I greeted them, I learned that to be seen was as great a gift as the blessing of seeing.

The slave Hagar realized this as she fled from her mistress Sarai's unkindness. Hagar was a "nobody" in her culture, pregnant and alone, fleeing to a desert without help or hope. Seen by God, however, she was empowered to see Him. God became real to her—so real that she gave God a name, El Roi, which means, "You are the God who sees me." She said, "I have now seen the One who sees me" (Genesis 16:13).

Our God sees each of us too. Feeling unseen, alone, or like a nobody? God sees you and your future. In return, may we see in Him our ever-present hope, encouragement, salvation, and joy.

—*Patricia Raybon*

Thanks Journal

PSALM 117

Praise the LORD, all you nations;
extol him, all you peoples.
—PSALM 117:1

When I was a new believer in Jesus, a spiritual mentor encouraged me to keep a thanks journal—a booklet I carried with me everywhere.

Taking note of praise items is a good habit. It reminds us of God's presence, provision, and care.

In the shortest of the psalms, Psalm 117, the writer encourages everyone to praise the Lord because "great is his love toward us" (v. 2).

How has the Lord shown His love toward you today, this week, this month, and this year? Don't just look for the spectacular. His love is seen in the ordinary, everyday circumstances of life. Then consider how He has shown His love toward your family, your church, and to others. Let your mind soak up the extent of His love for all of us.

The psalmist added that "the faithfulness of the LORD *endures* forever" (v. 2; emphasis added). In other words, He will continue to love us! So we will continue to have many things to praise God for in the coming days. As His dearly loved children, may praising and thanking God characterize our lives!

—*Poh Fang Chia*

Overcoming Challenges

NEHEMIAH 6:1–9, 15

So the wall was completed on the twenty-fifth of Elul, in fifty-two days.
—NEHEMIAH 6:15

My friend Mary and I met monthly to hold one another accountable to our goals. One of hers was to reupholster her dining room chairs before the year's end. In November she reported her progress from October: "It took ten months and two hours to recover my chairs." After months of finding the hard-to-get material plus carving time out of her schedule, the project took merely two hours of committed work to finish.

God called Nehemiah to a far greater project: rebuild Jerusalem's walls (Nehemiah 2:3–5, 12). As he led the people in the labor, they experienced mockery, attacks, and temptation to sin (4:3, 8; 6:10–12). Yet God equipped them to stand resolute in their efforts—completing a daunting task in just fifty-two days.

Overcoming such challenges requires more than a personal desire or goal. In Nehemiah's case, he knew that God appointed him to the task. His sense of purpose invigorated the people to follow his leadership.

When God charges us with a task, He gives us the skills and strength necessary to do what He asked, no matter what challenges we face.

—*Kirsten Holmberg*

Growing Gratitude

ROMANS 11:33–36

*For from him and through him
and for him are all things.*
—ROMANS 11:36

George Herbert, a seventeenth-century British poet, encouraged readers toward being thankful in his poem "Gratefulness." "Thou that hast given so much to me, give one thing more: a grateful heart."

The Bible declares Jesus as the source of all blessing: "For from him and through him and for him are all things" (Romans 11:36). "All things" encompasses both the extravagant and the everyday gifts in our lives. Everything we receive comes directly from God (James 1:17), and He willingly gives us those gifts out of His love.

To expand my awareness of God's blessings in my life, I'm learning to cultivate a heart that acknowledges the source of all the joys I experience each day, but especially the ones I often take for granted. Today those included a crisp morning to run, the anticipation of an evening with friends, a stocked pantry so I could make French toast with my daughters, and the beauty of the world outside my window.

What is the "so much" that God has given to you? Opening our eyes to those blessings will help us to develop grateful hearts.

—*Lisa Samra*

Cradled in Comfort

ISAIAH 66:12–16

As a mother comforts her child, so will I comfort you; and you will be comforted over Jerusalem."
—ISAIAH 66:13

My friend gave me the privilege of holding her precious, four-day-old daughter. Soon, though, she started to fuss. I hugged her closer, my cheek pressed against her head. I began to sway and hum in a gentle, soothing rhythm. Despite these earnest attempts and my years of parenting experience, I couldn't pacify her. But when I placed her back into her mother's eager arms, peace washed over her almost instantaneously. Her cries subsided and her newborn frame relaxed into the safety she already trusted. My friend knew precisely how to hold and pat her daughter to alleviate her distress.

God extends comfort to His children like a mother: tender, trustworthy, and diligent. When we are weary or upset, He carries us affectionately in His arms. As our Father and Creator, He knows us intimately. He "will keep in perfect peace all who trust in [him], all whose thoughts are fixed on [him]" (Isaiah 26:3 NLT).

When the troubles of this world weigh heavy on our hearts, we can find comfort in the knowledge that He protects us as a loving parent.

—*Kirsten Holmberg*

Being Human Beings

1 PETER 2:11–17; 3:8–9

Finally, all of you, be like-minded, be sympathetic,
love one another, be compassionate and humble.
—1 PETER 3:8

When asked to define his role in a community that was sometimes uncooperative with law enforcement, a sheriff simply explained, "We are human beings who work with human beings in crisis."

His humility—his stated equality with his fellow humans—reminds me of Peter's words to first-century Christians suffering under Roman persecution: "All of you, be like-minded, be sympathetic, love one another, be compassionate and humble" (1 Peter 3:8). Perhaps Peter was saying that the best response to humans in crisis is to be human—to know we are all the same. After all, isn't that what God did when He sent His Son—became human in order to help us? (Philippians 2:7).

Gazing at the core of our fallen hearts, it's tempting to disdain our human status. But Jesus teaches us how to live fully human, as servants recognizing we are all the same. "Human" is how God made us, created in His image and redeemed by His unconditional love.

When we encounter folks in various struggles, let's respond humbly—as fellow humans who work together with other humans in crisis.

—*Elisa Morgan*

It's an Attitude

JAMES 1:1–12

Consider it pure joy, my brothers and sisters, whenever you face trials of many kinds.
—JAMES 1:2

Regina drove home from work discouraged and tired. The day had started with tragic news in a text message, then it spiraled downward in meetings with uncooperative co-workers. After Regina prayed, she thought it best to put the stress of the day aside by making a surprise visit with flowers to an elderly friend. Her spirits lifted as Maria shared how good the Lord was to her. She said, "I have my own bed and a chair, three meals a day, and help from the nurses here. And occasionally God sends a cardinal to my window just because He knows I love them and He loves me."

Attitude. Perspective. As the saying goes, "Life is ten percent what happens to us and ninety percent how we react to it." The people James wrote to were scattered because of persecution, and he challenged them with these words: "Consider it pure joy . . . whenever you face trials of many kinds" (James 1:2).

The joy-filled perspective James talked about comes as we learn to see that God can use our struggles to produce maturity.

—*Anne Cetas*

Priceless Worship

MARK 12:38–44

*"They all gave out of their wealth;
but she, out of her poverty, put in
everything—all she had to live on."*

—MARK 12:44

I use writing to worship and serve God, but when an acquaintance said he found no value in what I wrote, I became discouraged. I doubted the significance of my small offerings to God.

Through prayer, study of Scripture, and encouragement from my husband, the Lord affirmed that only He—not the opinions of other people—could determine our motives as a worshiper and the worth of our offerings to Him. I asked God to continue helping me develop skills and provide opportunities to share the resources He gives me.

Jesus contradicted our standards of merit regarding our giving (Mark 12:41–44). While the rich tossed large amounts of money into the temple treasury, a poor widow put in coins "worth only a few cents" (v. 42). The Lord declared her gift to be greater than the rest (v. 43).

Every act of giving—not just financial—can be an expression of worship and loving obedience. When we present God the best of our time, talents, or treasure with hearts motivated by love, we are lavishing Him with offerings of priceless worship.

—*Xochitl Dixon*

The Cure for Anxiety

PHILIPPIANS 4:1–9

*Do not be anxious about anything,
but in every situation, by prayer and
petition, with thanksgiving present your
requests to God.* —PHILIPPIANS 4:6

We were excited about moving for my husband's job. But the challenges left me feeling anxious. Thoughts of sorting and packing. Looking for a new house. My finding a new job. So unsettling! As I thought about my "to-do" list, words written by Paul echoed in my mind: Don't worry, but pray (Philippians 4:6–7).

If anyone could have been anxious about unknowns and challenges, it would have been Paul. He was shipwrecked, beaten, and jailed. In Philippians, he encouraged his friends, who also were facing unknowns, telling them, "Do not be anxious about anything, but in every situation, by prayer and petition, with thanksgiving, present your requests to God" (v. 6).

Paul's words encourage me. Life is not without uncertainties—life transitions, family issues, health scares, or financial trouble. I continue to learn that God cares. He invites us to let go of our fears of the unknown by giving them to Him. When we do, He, who knows all things, promises that His peace, "which transcends all understanding, will guard" our heart and mind in Christ Jesus (v. 7).

—*Karen Wolfe*

Breath of Life

PSALM 139:13–18

The Spirit of God has made me; the
breath of the Almighty gives me life.
—JOB 33:4

In his book *Life After Heart Surgery*, David Burke recalls his brush with death. Lying in his hospital bed after a second open-heart surgery, he was unable to draw a full breath. Feeling that he was slipping toward eternity, he prayed one last time, trusting God and thanking Him for forgiveness of his sin.

When his nurse asked how he was feeling, he replied, "I'm okay now," explaining he was ready to go to heaven and meet God. "Not on my shift, buddy!" she said. The doctors opened his chest again and removed two liters of fluid. That done, David began to recover.

It's not unusual to ponder what it will be like to face death. But those who "die in the Lord" have the certainty that they are "blessed" (Revelation 14:13) and that their death is "precious in the sight of the Lord" (Psalm 116:15).

God fashioned our days even before we existed (Psalm 139:16), and we exist now only because "the breath of the Almighty gives [us] life" (Job 33:4). Though we don't know how many breaths we have left—we rest in the knowledge that He does.

—*Cindy Hess Kasper*

What Is God Like?

HEBREWS 1:1–12

*The Son is . . . the exact representation
of [God's] being.*
—HEBREWS 1:3

To celebrate a special occasion, my husband took me
to an art gallery and said I could choose a painting as
a gift. I picked out a small picture of a brook flowing through a forest. The streambed took up most of
the canvas, and because of this much of the sky was
excluded from the picture. However, the stream's reflection revealed the location of the sun, the treetops,
and the hazy atmosphere. The only way to "see" the
sky was to look at the surface of the water.

Jesus is like the stream, in a spiritual sense. When
we want to see what God is like, we look at Jesus.
He is "the exact representation of [God's] being"
(Hebrews 1:3). We deepen our understanding of Him
by seeing how Jesus faced the same problems we have
on Earth.

In temptation, Jesus revealed God's holiness.
Wrestling with people problems, He showed God's
wisdom. In His death, He illustrated God's love.

Although we can't grasp everything about God—
we are limited in our thinking—we can be certain of
His character when we look at Christ.

—*Jennifer Benson Schuldt*

Great Love

1 JOHN 3:1–8

*See what great love the Father has lavished
on us, that we should be called children
of God! And that is what we are!*

—1 JOHN 3:1

I remember when we took our granddaughter, Moriah, overnight for the first time without her older brothers. We lavished lots of loving, undivided attention on her, and we had fun doing the things she likes to do. The next day as we were dropping her off, we said our goodbyes and headed out the door. As we did, Moriah grabbed her overnight bag and began following us.

The picture is etched in my memory: Moriah in her diaper and mismatched sandals ready to depart with Grandma and Grandpa again. She was eager to go with us.

Although she was as unable to vocalize it, our granddaughter felt loved and valued. In a small way, our love for Moriah is a picture of the love God has for us, His children. "See what great love the Father has lavished on us!" (1 John 3:1).

When we trust Jesus as our Savior, we begin to understand the lavish love He bestowed on us by dying for us (v. 16). Our desire becomes to please Him (v. 6) and to love Him—eager to spend time with Him.

—*Alyson Kieda*

Carried Through

PSALM 30:1–12

*For his anger lasts only a moment, but his favor
lasts a lifetime; weeping may stay for the night,
but rejoicing comes in the morning.*

—PSALM 30:5

I recently stumbled across some of my college journals and couldn't resist rereading them. As I did, I realized I didn't feel about myself then as I do today. My struggles with loneliness and doubts about my faith felt overwhelming then, but now I clearly see how God has carried me to a better place. Seeing how God gently brought me through those days reminded me that what feels overwhelming today will one day be part of a greater story of His healing love.

Psalm 30 is a celebration psalm that similarly looks back with gratitude on God's powerful restoration: from sickness to healing, from threat of death to life, from feeling God's judgment to enjoying His favor, from mourning to joy (vv. 2–3, 11).

David experienced restoration so incredible he could confess, "Weeping may stay for the night, but rejoicing comes in the morning" (v. 5). Despite the pain he had endured, David discovered God's powerful hand of healing.

If you're hurting today and need encouragement, recall those times when God carried you through to a place of healing. Trust Him to do so again.

—*Monica Brands*

Strangers Welcoming Strangers

LEVITICUS 19:1–9, 33–34

*When a foreigner resides among you in your land,
do not mistreat them. . . . Love them as yourself,
for you were foreigners in Egypt.*

—LEVITICUS 19:33–34

When my husband and I moved to Seattle to be near his sister, we didn't know where we would live or work. A church helped us find a rental house with many bedrooms. We lived in one bedroom and rented the others to international students. For three years, we were strangers welcoming strangers—sharing our home and meals and even a Bible study with people from all over the world.

God's people know what it means to be far from home. For several hundred years, the Israelites were foreigners—and slaves—in Egypt. In Leviticus 19, God reminded His people to empathetically care for foreigners, because they knew what it was like to be foreigners and afraid (vv. 33–34).

Not all of us as followers of God have experienced literal exile, but we all know how it feels to be "foreigners" on earth (1 Peter 2:11)—people who feel like outsiders because our ultimate allegiance is to a heavenly kingdom. We are called to create a community of hospitality—strangers welcoming strangers into God's family. This is at the heart of being the family of God (Romans 12:13).

—*Amy Peterson*

Nursing a Grudge

2 SAMUEL 14:25–15:21

*"I wish I were the judge. Then everyone could
bring their cases to me for judgment,
and I would give them justice!"*
—2 SAMUEL 15:4 (NLT)

Author Marilynne Robinson wrote, "I have always
liked the phrase, 'nursing a grudge,' because many
people are tender of their resentments, as of the
things nearest their hearts."

King David's son Absalom began *nursing* bitterness in his heart long before he rallied the people in
an attempt to usurp the throne. Hurt and frustrated,
he had watched as his sister was victimized and left
without vindication (2 Samuel 13:1–22). The family
was rife with discord and David, his father, seemed
woefully inept at working through conflict. Determined to right the wrongs, he became judge and vin-
dicator in his own right (2 Samuel 15:1–3).

The bitter heart is difficult to penetrate (Proverbs
18:19). Our mouths are the gateway through which the
enemy perverts not only our vision but also our love
(Romans 3:14). The more we rehearse the offense, the
stronger the bitterness grows. Eventually, the burden
of bitterness becomes our bondage. Letting go of our
bitterness doesn't mean we find immunity from pain.
Freedom comes, however, as we draw close to God and
learn from His forgiving ways (Ephesians 4:31–32).
—*Regina Franklin*

The House on the Rock

LUKE 6:46–49

*When a flood came, the torrent struck that house
but could not shake it, because it was well built.*
—LUKE 6:48

After living in their house for several years, my
friends realized that their living room was sinking—
cracks appeared on the walls and a window would
no longer open. They learned that this room had been
added without a foundation. Rectifying the shoddy
workmanship would mean months of work as a new
foundation was laid.

They had the work done, and when I visited them
afterwards, I couldn't detect much difference. But I
understood that a solid foundation matters.

This is true in our lives as well.

Jesus shared a parable about wise builders to illustrate the wisdom of listening to Him (Luke 6:46–49).
Those who hear and obey His words are like the person who builds a house on a firm foundation. Jesus
assured His listeners that when the storms come, their
house would stand. Their faith would not be shaken.

We can find peace knowing that as we obey Jesus,
He forms a strong foundation for our lives. Then
when we face the torrents of rain lashing against us,
we can trust that our foundation is solid. Our Savior
will provide the support we need.

—*Amy Boucher Pye*

Make a Joyful Noise

PSALM 98

Shout for joy to the LORD, all the earth,
burst into jubilant song with music.
—PSALM 98:4

Back when I was searching for a church to attend, a friend invited me to her church. The worship leaders led the congregation in a song I loved, so I sang with gusto—remembering my college choir director's advice to "Project!"

After the song, my friend's husband said to me, "You really sang loud." This was not intended as a compliment! After that, I self-consciously monitored my singing—always wondering if the people around me judged my singing.

One Sunday, I noticed the singing of a woman next to me. She seemed to sing with adoration, without a trace of self-consciousness. Her worship reminded me of the enthusiastic, spontaneous worship David demonstrated in his life. In Psalm 98, in fact, David suggests that "all the earth" should "burst into jubilant song" in worship (v. 4).

We should worship joyfully because "[God] has done marvelous things" (v. 1). Dwelling on who God is (faithful, merciful, and one who saves) can fill our hearts with praise.

What "marvelous things" has God done in your life? Recall His wondrous works and give God thanks. Lift your voice and sing!

—*Linda Washington*

Mistakes Were Made

EXODUS 32:1–5, 19–26

*"So I told them, 'Whoever has any gold jewelry,
take it off.' Then they gave me the gold, and I
threw it into the fire, and out came this calf!"*

—EXODUS 32:24

"Mistakes were made," said the CEO as he discussed his company's illegal activity. He looked regretful, yet he couldn't admit he had personally done anything wrong.

Some "mistakes" are just mistakes: taking the wrong exit, burning the toast, or forgetting a password. But then there are the deliberate deeds that we know miss the mark—God calls those sin. When God questioned Adam and Eve about disobeying Him, they tried to shift the blame (Genesis 3:8–13). And during Israel's wilderness wanderings, Aaron took no personal responsibility when the people built a golden calf to worship. He explained, "[The people] gave me the gold, and I threw it into the fire, and out came this calf!" (Exodus 32:24).

In other words: "Mistakes were made."

Minimizing our sin by calling it a "mistake" instead of acknowledging its true nature is a big problem.

However, when we take responsibility—acknowledging our sin and confessing it—the One who "is faithful and just . . . will forgive us our sins and purify us from all unrighteousness" (1 John 1:9). Our God offers forgiveness and restoration.

—*Cindy Hess Kasper*

Watch Out!

1 PETER 5:6–11

Be alert and of sober mind. Your enemy
the devil prowls around like a roaring lion
looking for someone to devour.
—1 PETER 5:8

I grew up in warm southern cities, so when I moved north, it took me a while to learn how to drive safely during the long, snowy months. During my first hard winter, I ended up stranded in a snowdrift three times! But after several years of practice, I began to feel comfortable driving in wintry conditions. In fact, I felt a little too comfortable. I stopped being as vigilant. And that's when I hit a patch of black ice and skidded into a telephone pole on the side of the road!

Thankfully, no one was hurt, but I learned something important that day. I realized how dangerous it can be to feel comfortable. Instead of being watchful, I had gone on "autopilot."

We need to practice that same kind of vigilance in our spiritual lives. Peter warns believers not to glide thoughtlessly through life, but to "be alert" (1 Peter 5:8). That's not something we have to do on our own though. God promises to be with us (v. 10). By His power, we learn to remain watchful and alert in resisting evil and following Him.

—*Amy Peterson*

What Simon Said

LUKE 5:1–11

Simon answered, "Master, we've worked hard all night and haven't caught anything. But because you say so, I will let down the nets."

—LUKE 5:5

A man named Refuge Rabindranath has been a youth worker in Sri Lanka for more than ten years. He often interacts with the youth late into the night. He enjoys working with the young people, but it can be disheartening when promising students sometimes walk away from the faith. Some days he feels a bit like Simon Peter in Luke 5.

Simon had been working hard all night but caught no fish (v. 5). He was discouraged. Yet when Jesus told him to "put out into deep water, and let down the nets for a catch" (v. 4), Simon replied, "Because you say so, I will let down the nets" (v. 5).

His willingness to trust Jesus was rewarded. Not only did Simon catch a large number of fish but he also gained a deeper understanding of who Jesus is. He moved from calling Jesus "Master" (v. 5) to calling Him "Lord" (v. 8).

Perhaps God is calling you to "let down your nets again." May we reply to the Lord as Simon did: "Because you say so, I will."

—*Poh Fang Chia*

Creation's Song

PSALM 19:1–6

The heavens declare the glory of God;
the skies proclaim the work of his hands.
—PSALM 19:1

Using acoustic astronomy, scientists can observe and listen to the sounds and pulses of space. They've found that stars don't orbit in silence but rather generate music. Like humpback whale sounds, the resonance of stars exists at wavelengths or frequencies that can't be heard by the human ear. Yet, the music of stars creates a symphony that proclaims the greatness of God.

Psalm 19:1–4 says, "The heavens declare the glory of God; the skies proclaim the work of his hands. Day after day they pour forth speech; night after night they reveal knowledge. . . . Their voice goes out into all the earth, their words to the ends of the world."

In Colossians, Paul reveals that in Jesus "all things were created: things in heaven and on earth, visible and invisible . . . all things have been created through him and for him" (1:16). In response, the natural world's heights and depths sing to its Maker. May we join creation and sing out the greatness of the One who "with the breadth of his hand marked off the [vast] heavens" (Isaiah 40:12).

—*Remi Oyedele*

A Change in Perspective

PSALM 73:12–28

*It troubled me deeply till I
entered the sanctuary of God.*
—PSALM 73:16–17

My hometown had experienced its heaviest winter in thirty years. My muscles ached from hours of shoveling the unrelenting snow. When I stepped inside, weary as I kicked off my boots, I was greeted by the warmth of a fire and my children gathered around it. As I gazed out the window, my perspective of the weather shifted. I savored the beauty of frosted tree branches and the way the snow blanketed the colorless landscape of winter.

I see a similar but more poignant shift when I read Asaph's words in Psalm 73. He laments the way the world seems to work, how wrongs seem to be rewarded. He doubts the value of being different from the crowd (v. 13). But when he enters God's sanctuary, his outlook changes (vv. 16–17): he remembers that God will deal with the world and its troubles perfectly. And it is good to be with God (v. 28).

When we're chilled by problems, we can enter God's sanctuary in prayer and be warmed by the truth that His judgment is better than ours. Our circumstances may not change, but our perspective can.
—*Kirsten Holmberg*

Why Forgive?

LUKE 23:32–34

Jesus said, "Father, forgive them, for they
do not know what they are doing."
—LUKE 23:34

When a friend betrayed me, I knew I would need to forgive her, but I wasn't sure I could. Her words left me feeling stunned with pain and anger. Although I told her I forgave her, for a long time whenever I'd see her I felt tinges of hurt. I knew I still clung to some resentment. One day, however, God answered my prayers and allowed me to let go completely. I was finally free.

Forgiveness lies at the heart of the Christian faith, with our Savior extending forgiveness as He was dying on the cross. Jesus loved those who had nailed Him there, asking His Father to forgive them. He didn't hang on to bitterness, but He showed grace to those who had wronged Him.

Let's consider before the Lord any people we might need to forgive. When we ask God through His Spirit to help us forgive, He will come to our aid—even if we take what we think is a long time to forgive. When we do, we are freed from the prison of unforgiveness.

—*Amy Boucher Pye*

Blink and Think of God

DEUTERONOMY 32:1–12

In a desert land he found him, in a barren and howling waste. He shielded him and cared for him; he guarded him as the apple of his eye.
—DEUTERONOMY 32:10

"God is like an eyelid," my friend Ryley said, and I blinked in surprise. What could she mean by that?

"Tell me more," I replied. Together, we had been studying surprising pictures of God in the Bible, things like God as a laboring mother (Isaiah 42:14) or as a beekeeper (7:18), but this one was new to me. Ryley pointed me to Deuteronomy 32, where Moses praises God's care for His people. Verse 10 says God shields and protects His people, guarding them "as the apple of his eye."

The word we translate *apple*, Ryley told me, literally means "pupil." What encircles and guards the pupil? The eyelid, of course! God is like the eyelid, which instinctively protects the tender eye. The eyelid guards the eye from danger, keeps sweat out of the eye, and lubricates the eyeball, keeping it healthy. It closes, allowing rest.

I thanked God for the metaphors He's given us to help us understand His love for us. When we close our eyes at night and open them in the morning, we can think of God and praise Him for His protection and care.

—*Amy Peterson*

Through the Cross

2 CORINTHIANS 4:8–18

*[Nothing] will be able to separate us from the
love of God that is in Christ Jesus our Lord.*
—ROMANS 8:39

My coworker Tom keeps an 8" by 12" glass cross
on his desk. His friend Phil, who like Tom is a cancer
survivor, gave it to him to help him look at everything "through the cross." It's a constant reminder
of God's love.

Paul's life was an example of having a cross-shaped
perspective. He described his times of suffering as being "persecuted, but not abandoned; struck down,
but not destroyed" (2 Corinthians 4:9). He believed
that in the hard times God is at work, "achieving for
us an eternal glory . . . So we fix our eyes not on what
is seen, but on what is unseen" (vv. 17–18).

To "fix our eyes . . . on what is unseen" doesn't
mean we minimize problems. Paul Barnett explains,
"There is to be confidence, based on the certainty of
God's purposes for [us]. . . . There is the sober recognition that we groan with hope mingled with pain."

With deep, sacrificial love, Jesus gave His life for
us. As we look at life "through the cross," we see His
love and faithfulness. And our trust grows.

—*Anne Cetas*

Free from Frostbite

PSALM 119:33–48

Direct me in the path of your commands,
for there I find delight.

—PSALM 119:35

The temperature outside hovered near zero, but my children begged to go sledding. I thought it over and said yes, but I asked them to bundle up, stay together, and come inside after fifteen minutes.

I lovingly created those rules so my children could play freely without suffering frostbite. I think the author of Psalm 119 recognized the same good intent in God as he penned two verses that might seem contradictory: "I will always obey your law" and "I will walk about in freedom, for I have sought out your precepts" (vv. 44–45). The psalmist associated freedom with a spiritually law-abiding life.

Following God's wise, loving instruction allows us to escape the consequences of bad choices. Without the weight of guilt or pain, we are freer to enjoy our lives.

While my kids were sledding, I watched them blast down the hill—smiling at the sound of their laughter. They were free within the boundaries I'd given them. This compelling paradox is present in our relationship with God—and we say, "Direct me in the path of your commands, for there I find delight" (v. 35).

—*Jennifer Benson Schuldt*

Sweet and Sour

JOB 2:1–10

*[Job] replied, "You are talking like
a foolish woman. Shall we accept
good from God, and not trouble?"*
—JOB 2:10

When our toddler first bit into a lemon wedge, he wrinkled his nose, stuck out his tongue, and squeezed his eyes shut. "Sow-wah," he said (sour).

I chuckled as I reached for the piece of fruit, intending to toss it into the trash.

"No!" Xavier scampered across the kitchen to get away from me. "Moe-wah!" (more). His lips puckered in delight with every juice-squirting bite.

My taste buds accurately reflect my partiality to the sweet moments in life. My preference for avoiding all things bitter reminds me of Job's wife, who seems to have shared my aversion to the sourness of suffering.

Job surely didn't delight in hardship or trouble, yet he honored God through heart-wrenching circumstances (Job 1:1–22). When painful sores afflicted Job's body, he endured the agony (2:7–8). His wife told him to give up on God (v. 9), but Job responded by trusting the Lord through suffering and afflictions (v. 10).

Like Job, we don't have to enjoy suffering to learn to savor the unexpected sweetness of sour moments—the divine strengthening of our faith.

—*Xochitl Dixon*

Acts of Kindness

ACTS 9:32–42

*[Tabitha] was always doing good
and helping the poor.*
—ACTS 9:36

"Estera, you got a present from our friend Helen!"
my mom told me. Growing up we didn't have much,
so receiving a present in the mail was like a second
Christmas. I felt loved and valued by God through
this wonderful woman.

The poor widows Tabitha made clothes for must
have felt similarly. A disciple of Jesus living in Joppa,
Tabitha was known for "always doing good and
helping the poor" (Acts 9:36). Then she got sick and
died. At the time, Peter was visiting a nearby city,
so two believers went after him and begged him to
come to Joppa.

When Peter arrived, the widows Tabitha had helped
showed him the evidence of her kindness—"the . . .
clothing that [she] had made" (v. 39). Led by the
Holy Spirit, Peter prayed and God brought her back
to life! The result of God's kindness was that "this
became known all over Joppa, and many people believed in the Lord" (v. 42).

As we're kind to those around us, may they turn
their thoughts to God and feel valued by Him.

—*Estera Pirosca Escobar*

Walking on Water

MATTHEW 14:25–33

Jesus immediately said to them:
"Take courage! It is I. Don't be afraid."
—MATTHEW 14:27

During an especially cold winter, I ventured out to Lake Michigan, the fifth largest lake in the world, to see it frozen over. Bundled up on the beach, I noticed that the water was frozen in waves, creating an icy masterpiece.

Because the water was frozen solid, I had the opportunity to "walk on water." I took the first few steps tentatively, fearful the ice wouldn't hold me. As I cautiously explored this unfamiliar terrain, I couldn't help but think of Jesus calling Peter out of the boat onto the Sea of Galilee.

When the disciples saw Jesus walking on the water, their response was fear. But Jesus responded, "Take courage! It is I. Don't be afraid" (Matthew 14:26–27). Peter overcame his fear and stepped out onto the water because he knew Jesus was present. When his courageous steps faltered, Peter cried out to Jesus. Jesus was still there, near enough to reach out His hand to rescue him.

If Jesus is calling you to do something that may seem as impossible as walking on water, take courage. The one who calls you will be present with you.

—*Lisa Samra*

Shelve Them and Move On

PROVERBS 15:30–33

Whoever heeds life-giving correction
will be at home among the wise.
—PROVERBS 15:31

I'm reminded of some wise advice a radio broad-caster friend once gave me. Early on in his career, as my friend struggled to deal with both criticism and praise, he felt that God was encouraging him to shelve both: Learn what you can from criticism, and accept praise. Then shelve both and humbly move on in God's grace and power.

Criticism and praise stir in us powerful emotions that, if left unchecked, can lead to either self-loathing or an overinflated ego. In Proverbs we read of the benefits of encouragement and wise counsel: "Good news gives health to the bones. Whoever heeds life-giving correction will be at home among the wise. Those who disregard discipline despise themselves, but the one who heeds correction gains understanding" (15:30–32).

If we're on the receiving end of a rebuke, may we choose to be sharpened by it. And if we're blessed with words of praise, may we be refreshed and filled with gratitude. As we walk humbly with God, He can help us learn from both criticism and praise, shelve them, and then move on in Him.

—*Ruth O'Reilly-Smith*

All I Can See

JOHN 3:25–30

He must become greater;
I must become less.
—JOHN 3:30

Krista stood in the freezing cold, looking at the beautiful snow-encased lighthouse on the lake. As she pulled out her phone to take pictures, her glasses fogged over. She couldn't see a thing, so she pointed her camera toward the lighthouse and snapped three pictures. Looking at them later, she realized the camera had been set to take "selfies." She laughed as she said, "My focus was me, me, and me. All I saw was me." This got me thinking of a similar mistake—becoming so self-focused we lose sight of the bigger picture of God's plan.

Jesus's cousin John clearly knew his focus wasn't himself. From the start, he recognized that his calling was to point others to Jesus. "Look, the Lamb of God!" he said when he saw Jesus coming toward him (John 1:29). Later, John said, "'I am not the Messiah but am sent ahead of him.' . . . He must become greater; I must become less" (3:28–30).

May the central focus of our lives be Jesus and loving Him with our whole heart.

—*Anne Cetas*

His Wonderful Face

1 CHRONICLES 16:8–27

Look to the LORD and his strength;
seek his face always.
—1 CHRONICLES 16:11

When my son was four, he was full of questions and chattered constantly. I loved talking with him, but he developed the habit of talking to me even when his back was turned. I found myself saying, "I can't hear you—please look at me when you're talking."

Sometimes I think God wants to say the same thing to us—not because He can't hear us, but because we can tend to talk to Him without really "looking" at Him. We pray, but we remain caught up in ourselves, forgetting who we're praying to.

Many of our concerns are best addressed by reminding ourselves of who God is and what He has done. We find comfort that He is loving, forgiving, sovereign, graceful.

The psalmist said to seek God's face continually (Psalm 105:4). And David encouraged worship leaders to praise God's character and tell stories of His past faithfulness (1 Chronicles 16:8–27).

When we turn our eyes toward the beautiful face of God, we can find strength and comfort that sustain us even in the midst of unanswered questions.

—*Amy Peterson*

Serve Continually

DANIEL 6:10–22

Has your God, whom you serve continually,
been able to rescue you?
—DANIEL 6:20

When educational psychologist Benjamin Bloom, researching how to develop talent in young people, examined the childhoods of 120 elite performers—athletes, artists, scholars—he found that all of them had one thing in common: they had practiced intensively for long periods of time.

Bloom's research suggests that growing in any area of our lives requires discipline. In our walk with God, too, cultivating the spiritual discipline of regularly spending time with Him is one way we can grow in our trust in Him.

Daniel is a good example of someone who prioritized a disciplined walk with God. As a young person, Daniel started making careful and wise decisions (1:8). He also was committed to praying regularly, "giving thanks to God" (6:10). His frequent seeking of God resulted in a life in which his faith was easily recognized by those around him (vv. 16, 20).

Let's come every day before God, trusting that our time with Him will result in a growing love, knowledge, and understanding of our Savior.

—*Keila Ochoa*

Jesus Loves Maysel

1 JOHN 4:7–16

This is love: not that we loved God,
but that he loved us and sent his Son
as an atoning sacrifice for our sins.
—1 JOHN 4:10

When my sister Maysel was little, she would sing a familiar song in her own way: "Jesus loves me, this I know, for the Bible tells Maysel." This irritated me to no end! As one of her older, "wiser" sisters, I knew the words were "me so," not "Maysel." Yet she persisted in singing it her way.

Now I think my sister had it right all along. The Bible does indeed tell Maysel, and all of us, that Jesus loves us. Take, for example, the writings of the apostle John, "the disciple whom Jesus loved" (John 21:7, 20). He tells us about God's love in one of the best-known verses of the Bible: John 3:16.

John reinforces that message of love in 1 John 4:10: "This is love: not that we loved God, but that he loved us and sent his Son as an atoning sacrifice for our sins." We too can have that same assurance: Jesus does love us. The Bible tells us so.

—*Alyson Kieda*

Light of the World

REVELATION 3:14–22

*"Here I am! I stand at the door and knock.
If anyone hears my voice and opens
the door, I will come in."*
—REVELATION 3:20

One of my favorite pieces of art hangs in the Keble College chapel in Oxford, England. The painting, *The Light of the World* by English artist William Holman Hunt, shows Jesus holding a lantern and knocking on a door to a home. One of the intriguing aspects of the painting is that the door doesn't have a handle. When asked about this, Hunt explained that he wanted to represent the imagery of Revelation 3:20, "Here I am! I stand at the door and knock. If anyone hears my voice and opens the door, I will come in."

The apostle John's words and the painting illustrate the kindness of Jesus. He gently knocks on the door of our souls with His offer of peace—patiently waiting for us to respond. He does not impose His will on ours. Instead, He offers to all people the gift of salvation and light to guide us.

If you hear the voice of Jesus and His gentle knock on the door of your soul, be encouraged that He patiently waits for you and will enter if you welcome Him in.

—*Lisa Samra*

Not the One

1 CHRONICLES 17:1–4, 16–25

*Do as you promised, so that it will be established
and that your name will be great forever.*
—1 CHRONICLES 17:23–24

David had drawn up the plans. He designed the furniture. He collected the materials. He made all the arrangements (see 1 Chronicles 28:11–19). But the first temple built in Jerusalem is known as Solomon's Temple, not David's.

God had said, "You are not the one" (1 Chronicles 17:4). God had chosen David's son Solomon to build the temple. David's response to this denial was exemplary. He focused on what God would do instead of what he himself could not do (vv. 16–25). He maintained a thankful spirit. He did everything he could and rallied capable men to assist Solomon.

Bible commentator J. G. McConville wrote: "Often we may have to accept that the work which we would dearly like to perform in terms of Christian service is not that for which we are best equipped. . . . It may be, like David's, a preparatory work, leading to something more gloriously grand."

David sought God's glory, not his own. May we, likewise, accept the tasks God has chosen for us and serve Him with a thankful heart! Our loving God is doing something "more obviously grand."

—*Poh Fang Chia*

Living Sacrifice

ROMANS 12:1–8

*I urge you . . . in view of God's mercy,
to offer your bodies as a living sacrifice.*
—ROMANS 12:1

My great aunt had an exciting job in advertising and traveled between Chicago and New York City. But she chose to give up that career out of love for her parents. They lived in Minnesota and needed her care. Both of her brothers had tragically died young, and she was her mom and dad's only remaining child. For her, serving her parents was an expression of her faith.

The apostle Paul's letter to the church at Rome urged Christian believers to be "a living sacrifice, holy and pleasing to God" (Romans 12:1). He hoped they would extend Christ's sacrificial love to each other. And he asked them not to think of themselves more highly than they should (v. 3). He yearned that they would show each other sacrificial love.

Each day we have the opportunity to serve others. For instance, we might let someone go ahead of us in a line or we might, like my great aunt, care for someone who is ill. Or maybe we share from our experience as we give another advice and direction. When we offer ourselves as living sacrifices, we honor God.

—*Amy Boucher Pye*

Vanity on Fire

MATTHEW 5:21–30

Create in me a pure heart, O God.
—PSALM 51:10

In February 1497, a monk named Girolama Savonarola started a fire. He and his followers had spent several months collecting items they thought might entice people to sin or neglect their religious duties—including artwork, cosmetics, instruments, and dresses. On the appointed day, thousands of vanity items were gathered in Florence, Italy, and set on fire. The event is known as the Bonfire of the Vanities.

Savonarola might have found inspiration for his extreme actions in a shocking statement from the Sermon on the Mount. "If your right eye causes you to stumble, gouge it out and throw it away," said Jesus (Matthew 5:29). This sermon is a lesson on going deeper than the surface, to focus on the state of our hearts rather than blaming our behavior on external distractions and temptations.

The Bonfire of the Vanities made a great show of destroying belongings and works of art, but it is unlikely that the hearts of those involved were changed. Only God can change a heart. That's why the psalmist prayed, "Create in me a pure heart, O God" (Psalm 51:10). It's our heart that counts.

—*Remi Oyedele*

Fearless Giving

MALACHI 3:8–12

*"Bring the whole tithe into the storehouse,
that there may be food in my house."*
—MALACHI 3:10

When my son Xavier was six, he decided he wanted to give a few of his toys to a boy who was visiting us. I delighted in his generosity—until Xavier offered a stuffed animal his daddy had searched high and low to find. When the little boy's mom tried to decline, Xavier placed the gift into his hands and said, "My daddy gives me lots of toys to share."

Though I'd like to say Xavier learned his confident giving from me, I've often withheld my resources from God and others. But when I remember that my heavenly Father gives me everything I have and need, it's easier to share.

In the Old Testament, God commanded the Israelites to trust Him by giving a portion of all He had supplied to the Levite priests, who would in turn help others. When the people refused, Malachi said they were robbing the Lord (Malachi 3:8–9).

Giving can be an act of worship. Giving freely and fearlessly can show our confidence in the care of our loving Father—the ultimate generous Giver.

—*Xochitl Dixon*

Swept Away

ISAIAH 44:6–23

*I have swept away your offenses like a cloud,
your sins like the morning mist.*

—ISAIAH 44:22

When he invented the pencil eraser in 1770, British engineer Edward Nairne was reaching instead for a piece of bread. Crusts of bread were used then to erase marks on paper. Picking up a piece of latex rubber by mistake, Nairne found it erased his error, leaving rubberized "crumbs" easily swept away by hand.

Our sins—our worst errors—can be swept away. It's the Lord—the Bread of Life—who cleans them with His own life, promising never to remember our sins.

This can seem to be a remarkable fix—and not deserved. For many, it's hard to believe our past sins can be swept away by God "like the morning mist" (Isaiah 44:22). Does God, who knows everything, forget them so easily?

That's exactly what God does when we accept Jesus as our Savior. Choosing to forgive our sins and to "remember their sins no more" (Jeremiah 31:34), our heavenly Father frees us to move forward.

Yes, consequences may remain. But God sweeps sin itself away, inviting us to return to Him for our clean new life. There's no better way to be swept away.

—*Patricia Raybon*

Postures of the Heart

2 CHRONICLES 6:7–9, 12–15

*[Solomon] knelt in front of the entire
community of Israel and lifted his hands
toward heaven [and] he prayed.*
—2 CHRONICLES 6:13–14 (NLT)

When my husband plays the harmonica for our
church praise team, he sometimes closes his eyes
when he plays a song. He says this helps him focus
and block out distractions so he can play his best—
just his harmonica, the music, and him—all praising
God.

Some people wonder if our eyes must be closed
when we pray. Since we can pray at any time in any
place, however, it might prove difficult to always
close our eyes—especially if we are taking a walk,
pulling weeds, or driving a vehicle!

The Bible gives no definitive guidelines about
prayer posture, but it gives us some examples. When
King Solomon prayed to dedicate the temple he had
built, he knelt down and "spread out his hands toward heaven" (2 Chronicles 6:13–14). Kneeling
(Ephesians 3:14), standing (Luke 18:10–13), and
even lying face down (Matthew 26:39) are all mentioned in the Bible.

It is not prayer posture that is most important—
but the attitude of our heart (Proverbs 4:23). When
we pray, may our hearts always be bowed in adoration, gratitude, and humility to our loving God.
—*Cindy Hess Kasper*

Everyday Moments

PROVERBS 15:13–15

A happy heart makes the face cheerful,
but heartache crushes the spirit.
—PROVERBS 15:13

I piled groceries in my car and carefully exited my parking spot. Suddenly a man darted across the pavement in front of me, not noticing my approach. I slammed on my brakes, just missing him. Startled, he looked up and met my gaze. I knew I had a choice: respond with rolled-eye frustration or offer a smiling forgiveness. I smiled.

Relief flickered across his face, raising the edges of his own lips in gratefulness.

Proverbs 15:13 says, "A happy heart makes the face cheerful, but heartache crushes the spirit." Is the writer directing us to cheery grins in the face of every interruption, disappointment, and inconvenience life brings? Surely not! There are times for genuine mourning, despair, and even anger at injustice. But in our everyday moments, a smile can offer relief, hope, and the grace needed to continue.

A "happy heart" is at peace, content, and yielded to God's best. With such a heart, happy from the inside out, we can respond to surprising circumstances with a genuine smile, inviting others to embrace the hope and peace they too can experience with God.

—*Elisa Morgan*

Give It to God

2 KINGS 19:9–19

Hezekiah received the letter from the messengers and read it. Then he went up to the temple of the LORD and spread it out before the LORD.
—2 KINGS 19:14

As a teenager, when I became overwhelmed by enormous challenges or high-stakes decisions, my mother taught me the merits of putting pen to paper to gain perspective. She taught me to write out the basic facts and possible actions with their likely outcomes. Then I could step back from the problem and view it more objectively.

Similarly, pouring our hearts out to God in prayer helps us gain His perspective and reminds us of His power. King Hezekiah did just that after receiving a daunting letter from an ominous adversary. The Assyrians threatened to destroy Jerusalem as they had many other nations. Hezekiah spread out the letter before the Lord, prayerfully calling on Him to deliver the people so that the world would recognize He "alone . . . [is] God" (2 Kings 19:19).

When we're faced with a situation that brings anxiety, fear, or an awareness that it's more than we can handle, like Hezekiah let's run straight to the Lord. We too can lay our problem before God and trust Him to guide our steps and calm our uneasy hearts.
—*Kirsten Holmberg*

Learning to Know God

JOHN 6:16–21

But he said to them, "It is I; don't be afraid."
—JOHN 6:20

For as long as I can remember, I've wanted to be a mother. I dreamed about holding my baby in my arms for the first time. When I got married, my husband and I never even considered waiting to have children. But with each negative pregnancy test, we were buried deeper into infertility. Months of doctors' visits, tests, and tears followed. Infertility was a bitter reality, and it left me wondering about God's goodness and faithfulness.

When I reflect on our journey, I think about the story of the disciples caught in the storm on the sea in John 6. As they struggled against the waves in the dark of the storm, Jesus unexpectedly came to them walking on the stormy waves. He calmed them with His presence, saying, "It is I; don't be afraid" (v. 20).

My husband and I had no idea what was coming in our storm; but we found comfort in knowing our faithful and true God more deeply. Although we would not have the child we had dreamed of, we learned that we can experience the power of His calming presence. He is there—powerfully working in our lives.

—*Karen Wolfe*

Love Won't Stop

LUKE 15:1–7

Rejoice with me; I have found my lost sheep.
—LUKE 15:6

After turning nineteen (pre-cellphone era), I moved more than seven hundred miles away from my mom. One morning, I left early to run errands, forgetting our scheduled call. Later that night, two policemen came to my door. Mom had been worried because I'd never missed one of our chats. After calling repeatedly and getting a busy signal, she reached out to the authorities. One of the officers said, "It's a blessing to know love won't stop looking for you."

Later, I realized I had accidentally left the receiver off its base. After I called Mom to apologize, she said she needed to spread the good news to everyone that I was okay. I think she overreacted a bit, though it felt good to be loved that much.

Scripture paints a beautiful picture of God, who is Love, relentlessly beckoning His wandering children. Like a good shepherd, He seeks out every lost sheep, affirming the priceless value of each beloved child of God (Luke 15:1–7).

Love never stops looking for us. And we can pray for others who need to know that Love. God never stops looking for them either.

—*Xochitl Dixon*

Losing to Find

MATTHEW 10:37–42

*"Whoever finds their life will lose it, and whoever
loses their life for my sake will find it."*
—MATTHEW 10:39

When I married my English fiancé and moved to London, I thought it would be a five-year adventure in a foreign land. I never dreamed I'd still be living here twenty years later, or that at times I'd feel like I was losing my old way of life. But in losing one way of life, I've found a better one.

The upside-down gift of finding life when we lose it is what Jesus promised His apostles. When He sent out the disciples to share His good news, He asked them to love Him more than their families (Matthew 10:37)—and this was in a culture where families were the cornerstone of the society. But He promised that if they would lose their life for His sake, they would find it (v. 39).

We don't have to move abroad to find ourselves in Christ. Through service and commitment—similar to the disciples going out to share the gospel—we find ourselves receiving more than we give. Of course, God loves us no matter how much we serve, but we find contentment and fulfillment when we pour ourselves out for others.

—*Amy Boucher Pye*

Taking the First Step

2 CORINTHIANS 5:11–21

*God was reconciling the world to himself
in Christ, not counting people's sins against
them. And he has committed to us the message
of reconciliation.*   —2 CORINTHIANS 5:19

Tham Dashu sensed that something was missing. So he started going to church—the one his daughter attended. But they never went together. Earlier, he had offended her, which drove a wedge between them. So Tham would slip in when the singing started and leave promptly after the service ended.

Church members shared the gospel story with him, but Tham always politely rejected their invitation to trust Jesus. Still, he kept coming to church.

One day Tham fell gravely ill. His daughter plucked up the courage to write him a letter seeking reconciliation. After reading it, Tham put his faith in Jesus and the family was reconciled. A few days later, Tham died and entered heaven—at peace with God and his loved ones.

Paul wrote that we are to "try to persuade others" about the truth of God's love and forgiveness (2 Corinthians 5:11). He said "Christ's love compels us" to carry out His work of reconciliation (v. 14).

Our willingness to forgive may help others realize that God desires to reconcile us to himself (v. 19). Would you lean on God's strength to show someone His love today?

—*Poh Fang Chia*

Good News to Tell

ACTS 8:26–35

*Philip began with that very passage of Scripture
and told him the good news about Jesus.*
—ACTS 8:35

"What's your name?" asked Arman, an Iranian student. After I said my name is Estera, his face lit up. He exclaimed, "We have a similar name in Farsi, it's Setare!" That small connection opened up an amazing conversation. I told him I was named after a Bible character, Esther, a Jewish queen in Persia (present-day Iran). Starting with her story, I shared the good news of Jesus. As a result, Arman started attending a Bible study to learn more about Christ.

One of Jesus's followers, Philip, guided by the Holy Spirit, asked a question that ignited a conversation with an Ethiopian official traveling in his chariot: "Do you understand what you are reading?" (Acts 8:30). The Ethiopian man was reading a passage from the book of Isaiah and seeking spiritual insight. Philip, realizing what an amazing opportunity this was, "began with that very passage of Scripture and told him the good news about Jesus" (v. 35).

Like Philip, we too have good news. Let's seize the daily occasions we encounter. May we allow the Holy Spirit to guide our steps and give us the words to use to share Jesus.

—*Estera Pirosca Escobar*

Unfinished Work

ROMANS 7:14–25

Who will rescue me from this body that is subject to death? Thanks be to God, who delivers me through Jesus Christ our Lord.

—ROMANS 7:24–25

At his death, the great artist Michelangelo left many unfinished projects. But four of his sculptures were never meant to be completed. With *The Bearded Slave*, *The Atlas Slave*, *The Awakening Slave*, and *The Young Slave*, Michelangelo wanted to show what it might feel like to be forever enslaved.

Rather than sculpting figures in chains, Michelangelo made figures stuck in the very marble out of which they are carved. Bodies emerge from the stone, but not completely. Muscles flex, but the figures are never able to free themselves.

The plight of the slave sculptures is not unlike my struggle with sin. I am unable to free myself. Like the sculptures, I am stuck, "a prisoner of the law of sin at work within me" (Romans 7:23). No matter how hard I try, I cannot change myself. But thanks be to God, we will not remain unfinished works.

We won't be complete until heaven, but in the meantime as we welcome the transforming work of the Holy Spirit, He changes us. God promises to finish the good work He has begun in us (Philippians 1:6).

—*Amy Peterson*

We Won't Break

MATTHEW 6:25–34

*"Can any one of you by worrying
add a single hour to your life?"*
—MATTHEW 6:27

As a native Californian I shy away from all things cold. I do, however, enjoy beautiful photos of snow. So I couldn't help but smile when my friend from Illinois shared a winter picture of a sapling outside her window. Admiration turned to sadness when I noticed its bare, knotted branches bowing under the heavy fringe of sparkling icicles.

How long could those bending boughs endure before breaking under their icy burdens? The heaviness threatening to crack the tree's limbs reminded me of my shoulders, hunched beneath the weight of worries.

Jesus encourages us to release our anxious thoughts. The Creator and Sustainer of the universe loves and provides for His children, so we don't have to worry. God knows our needs and will care for us (Matthew 6:25–32).

To help us avoid our tendency to worry, He tells us to come to Him first, trust His presence and provision in the present, and live by faith (vv. 33–34).

We face overwhelming troubles and uncertainties that can make our shoulders droop. We may temporarily bend under the weight of worrying. But when we trust God, we won't break.

—*Xochitl Dixon*

The Gift of Welcome

HEBREWS 13:1-2

*Do not forget to show hospitality to strangers,
for by so doing some people have shown
hospitality to angels without knowing it.*
—HEBREWS 13:2

The dinner where we hosted families from five nations remains a wonderful memory. Somehow the conversation didn't splinter into twos, but we all contributed to a discussion of life in London from the viewpoints of different parts of the world. Later, my husband and I reflected that we had received more than we gave, including the warm feelings we experienced in fostering new friendships and learning about different cultures.

The author of Hebrews concluded his thoughts with exhortations for community life, including that his readers should continue to welcome strangers. For in doing so, "some people have shown hospitality to angels without knowing it" (13:2). He may have been referring to Abraham and Sarah, who welcomed three strangers, reaching out to them and treating them to a feast, as was the custom of the day (Genesis 18:1–12). They didn't know they were entertaining angels who brought them a message of blessing.

We don't ask people into our homes in the hope of gaining from them, but often we receive more than we give. May the Lord spread His love through us as we reach out with His welcome.

—*Amy Boucher Pye*

Understanding Life's Trials

JOB 12:13–25

To God belong wisdom and power;
counsel and understanding are his.

—JOB 12:13

My friend's father received the dreaded diagnosis: cancer. Yet, during the chemo treatment process, he became a believer in Jesus, and his disease eventually went into remission. He was cancer free for a wonderful eighteen months, but it returned—worse than before. He and his wife faced the returned cancer with deep concern but also with a newfound, faithful trust in God.

We won't always understand why we're going through trials. This was certainly the case for Job who faced horrendous suffering and loss. Yet despite his many questions, in Job 12 he declares that God is mighty: "What he tears down cannot be rebuilt" (v. 14) and "to him belong strength and insight" (v. 16). Throughout his suffering, Job doesn't mention God's motives or why He allows pain. Job doesn't have the answers. But despite everything, he confidently says, "to God belong wisdom and power; counsel and understanding are his" (v. 13).

We may not understand why God allows certain struggles in our lives, but we can put our trust in Him. The Lord loves us and has us in His hands (v. 10; 1 Peter 5:7).

—*Julie Schwab*

Didn't Get Credit?

COLOSSIANS 4:7–18

"Let your light shine before others,
that they may see your good deeds
and glorify your Father in heaven."

—MATTHEW 5:16

Hollywood musicals were wildly popular during the 1950s and 1960s, and three actresses in particular—Audrey Hepburn, Natalie Wood, and Deborah Kerr—thrilled viewers with their compelling performances. A huge part of the appeal of these actresses was the breathtaking singing of their characters. But they weren't singing. Marni Nixon was. She dubbed the voices for those leading ladies and for a long time went uncredited for her vital contribution.

In the body of Christ, many people faithfully support others who have a more public role. Paul depended on exactly that kind of person in his ministry. Epaphras's consistent behind-the-scene prayers were an essential foundation for Paul and the early church (Colossians 4:12–13). Lydia generously opened her home when the weary apostle needed restoration (Acts 16:15). Paul's work depended on the support of these fellow servants in Christ (Colossians 4:7–18).

We may not have highly visible roles, yet when we "give [ourselves] fully to the work of the Lord" (1 Corinthians 15:58), we find value and meaning in our service as it brings glory to God and draws others to Him (Matthew 5:16).

—*Cindy Hess Kasper*

Faith, Hope, and Love

1 THESSALONIANS 1:1–3

We always thank God for all of you.
—1 THESSALONIANS 1:2

For ten years, my Aunt Kathy cared for her father (my grandfather) in her home. She cooked and cleaned for him when he was independent, and then she took on the role of nurse when his health declined.

Her service exemplifies the kind of effort for which Paul commended the Thessalonians: "work produced by faith, [their] labor prompted by love, and [their] endurance inspired by hope in our Lord Jesus Christ" (1 Thessalonians 1:3).

My aunt served in faith and love. Her daily, consistent care was the result of her belief that God called her to this important work. Her labor was borne out of love for God and her father.

She also endured in hope. It was difficult to watch my grandfather decline. She gave up time with family and friends to care for him. She could endure because of the hope that God would strengthen her each day, along with the knowledge that heaven awaited my grandfather.

However you are helping others, be encouraged as you do the work God has called you to do. Your labor can be a powerful testimony of faith, hope, and love.

—Lisa Samra

Whispering Words

EPHESIANS 4:22–32

[Build] others up according to their needs.
—EPHESIANS 4:29

The young man fidgeted as he sat down for his flight. His eyes darted back and forth to the airplane windows. Then he closed his eyes and breathed deeply, trying to calm himself—but it didn't work. An older woman across the aisle from him put her hand on his arm and gently talked to him to divert his attention. "What's your name?" "Where are you from?" and "You're doing well," she whispered. She chose a gentle touch and a few reassuring words. Little things. When they landed three hours later, he said, "Thank you so much for helping me."

Kindness doesn't always come naturally; our primary concern is often ourselves. But when Paul urged, "Be kind and compassionate to one another" (Ephesians 4:32), he was not saying it all depends on us. After we've been given a new life by faith in Jesus, the Spirit begins a transformation. Kindness is the ongoing work of the Spirit renewing our thoughts and attitudes (Galatians 5:22–23).

The God of compassion is at work in our hearts, allowing us to touch others' lives by reaching out and whispering words of encouragement.

—*Anne Cetas*

Anger Management

EPHESIANS 4:14, 26–32

"In your anger do not sin": Do not let the sun go down while you are still angry.
—EPHESIANS 4:26

A friend told me how fed up she was with a family member. But she was reluctant to say anything to him about his annoying habit of ignoring or mocking her. But when she did try to confront him about the problem, he responded sarcastically. She exploded in anger. Both parties dug in their heels, and the family rift widened.

I can relate, because I sometimes handle anger the same way. I also have a hard time confronting people. If a friend or family member says something mean, I usually suppress how I feel until that person or someone else comes along and says or does something else mean. After a while, I explode.

Paul has some inspired advice for us: "Do not let the sun go down while you are still angry" (Ephesians 4:26). Setting a time limit on unresolved issues keeps anger in check. Meanwhile, we can ask God for help to "[speak] the truth in love" (Ephesians 4:15).

Got a problem with someone? Rather than hold it in, hold it up to God. He can fight the fire of anger with the power of His forgiveness and love.

—*Linda Washington*

Three-Lettered Faith

HABAKKUK 3:17–19

Yet I will rejoice in the LORD;
I will be joyful in God my Savior.
—HABAKKUK 3:18

With a tendency toward pessimism, I quickly jump to negative conclusions. If I'm thwarted in my efforts on a work project, I'm easily convinced that none of my other projects will be successful either, and—even though utterly unrelated—I will probably never be able to touch my toes comfortably. And, woe is me, I'm an awful mother who can't do anything right. Defeat in one area affects my feelings in many.

I can imagine how Habakkuk might have reacted to what God showed him. He had cause for despair after seeing the coming troubles for God's people. His words lure me into a pessimistic bed of hopelessness until he jars me awake again with the three-letter word *yet*. "Yet I will rejoice in the LORD" (3:18). Despite all the hardships ahead, Habakkuk found cause for rejoicing simply because of who God is.

While we might exaggerate our problems, Habakkuk faced truly extreme hardships. If he could summon praise for God in those moments, perhaps we can too. When we're bogged down in despair, we can look to God who lifts us up.

—*Kirsten Holmberg*

Held by God

PSALM 131

I have calmed and quieted myself,
I am like a weaned child with its mother.
—PSALM 131:2

As I was nearing the end of lunch with my sister and her children, she told my three-year-old niece, Annica, it was naptime. Her face filled with alarm. "But Aunt Monica did not hold me yet!" she objected. My sister smiled. "Okay, she may hold you first—how long do you need?" "Five minutes," she replied.

As I held my niece, I was grateful for how she constantly reminds me what it looks like to love and be loved. Sometimes we forget that our faith journey is one of learning to experience love—God's love—more fully than we can imagine (Ephesians 3:18). When we lose that focus, we can find ourselves, like the older brother in Jesus's parable of the prodigal son, trying desperately to win God's approval while missing out on all He has already given us (Luke 15:25–32).

Psalm 131 can help us "become like little children" (Matthew 18:3) and let go of the inner battle over what we don't understand (Psalm 131:1). Through time with Him we can return to a place of peace (v. 2), finding hope (v. 3) in His love.

—*Monica Brands*

Only a Gypsy Boy

1 PETER 2:4–10

You are a chosen people, a royal priesthood,
a holy nation, God's special possession.
—1 PETER 2:9

"Oh, it's only a gypsy boy," someone whispered in disgust when Rodney Smith walked to the front of the chapel to trust Christ during a service in 1877. Nobody thought much of this teenager, the son of uneducated parents. Yet, Rodney didn't listen to others. Certain that God had a purpose for his life, he bought himself a Bible and an English dictionary and taught himself how to read and write. He once said, "The way to Jesus is not by Cambridge, Harvard, Yale, or the poets. It is . . . an old-fashioned hill called Calvary." Rodney became an evangelist God used to bring many to Jesus.

Peter too was just a simple, religiously untrained man (Acts 4:13)—a fisherman from Galilee—when Jesus called him with two simple words: "Follow me" (Matthew 4:19). Yet the same Peter later affirmed that those who follow Jesus are "a chosen people, . . . God's special possession" (1 Peter 2:9).

Through Jesus Christ all people—whatever their background—can be a part of God's family and be used by Him. All who believe in Jesus become God's "special possession."

—*Estera Pirosca Escobar*

I Will

LEVITICUS 19:9–18

"Love your neighbor as yourself."
—LEVITICUS 19:18

Shirley settled into her recliner after a long day. She looked out the window and noticed an older couple struggling to move a section of old fence left in a yard and labeled "free." Shirley grabbed her husband, and they headed out the door to help. The four of them wrestled the fence onto a dolly and pushed it up the city street and around the corner to the couple's home—laughing all the way at the spectacle they must be. As they returned to get a second section of fence, the woman asked Shirley, "You be my friend?" "Yes, I will," she replied. Shirley later learned that her new Vietnamese friend knew little English and was lonely because her grown children had moved hours away.

In Leviticus, God reminded the Israelites that they knew how it felt to be strangers (19:34) and how to treat others (vv. 9–18). God had set them apart to be His own nation, and in return they were to bless their "neighbors" by loving them as themselves. Jesus, the greatest blessing from God to the nations, later restated His Father's words and extended them to us all: "Love the Lord your God. . . . Love your neighbor as yourself" (Matthew 22:37–39).

Through Christ's Spirit living in us, we can love God and others because He loved us first (Galatians 5:22–23; 1 John 4:19). Can we say with Shirley, "Yes, I will"?
—*Anne Cetas*

Unlikely Friends

ISAIAH 11:1–10

*The wolf will live with the lamb, the leopard
will lie down with the goat, the calf and
the lion and the yearling together.*

—ISAIAH 11:6

My Facebook friends often post endearing videos of unlikely animal friendships, such as a video I watched of an inseparable deer and cat, and another of an orangutan mothering several tiger cubs.

These heartwarmingly unusual friendships remind me of the garden of Eden. In this setting, Adam and Eve lived in harmony with God, with each other, and with the animals. This idyllic scene was disrupted when Adam and Eve sinned (Genesis 3:21–23). Now in both human relationships and the creation, we see constant struggle and conflict.

Yet the prophet Isaiah reassures us that one day, "The wolf will live with the lamb" (Isaiah 11:6). Many interpret that future day as when Jesus comes again to reign. When He returns, there will be no more divisions and "no more death . . . or pain, for the old order of things has passed away" (Revelation 21:4). On that renewed earth, creation will be restored to its former harmony and people of every kind will join together to worship God (7:9–10; 22:1–5).

Until then, God can help us to restore broken relationships and to develop new, unlikely friendships.

—*Alyson Kieda*

Passing on the Legacy

PSALM 79:8–13

Then we your people, the sheep of your pasture, will praise you forever; from generation to generation we will proclaim your praise. —PSALM 79:13

My phone beeped, indicating an incoming text. My daughter wanted my grandmother's recipe for Peppermint Ice Cream Pie. As I thumbed through my aged recipe box, I found it—recorded in my grandmother's unique handwriting with notes by my mother. This recipe was making its entrance into a fourth generation within my family.

I wondered what other family heirlooms might be handed down. What about choices regarding faith? Besides the pie, would the faith of my grandmother—and my own—play out in the lives of my daughter and her offspring?

In Psalm 79, the psalmist bemoans a wayward Israel, which has lost its faith moorings. He begs God to rescue His people from the ungodly and to restore Jerusalem to safety. This done, he promises a restored commitment to God's ways. "Then we your people, the sheep of your pasture, will praise you forever; from generation to generation we will proclaim your praise" (v. 13).

As I eagerly shared the recipe with my daughter, I prayed for the most lasting hand-me-down of all: the influence of our family's faith from one generation to the next.

—*Elisa Morgan*

We Would See Jesus

JOHN 12:20-26

They came to Philip . . . with a request. "Sir,"
they said, "we would like to see Jesus."
—JOHN 12:21

As I looked down at the pulpit where I was sharing prayers at a funeral, I glimpsed a brass plaque quoting John 12:21: "We would see Jesus" (KJV). How fitting to consider how we saw Jesus in the woman we were celebrating that day. Although she had faced challenges and disappointments, she never gave up her faith in Christ. And because God's Spirit lived in her, we could see Jesus.

After Jesus rode into Jerusalem (see John 12:12–16), some Greeks approached Philip, saying, "Sir, . . . we would like to see Jesus" (v. 21). When their request was passed along to Jesus, He announced that His hour had come to be glorified (v. 23) meaning He would die for the sins of the people. He would fulfill His mission to reach not only the Jews but also the Gentiles ("Greeks," v. 20). Now they would see Jesus.

After Jesus died, He sent the Holy Spirit to dwell in His followers (14:16–17). Thus as we love and serve Jesus, those around us can see Him in us!

—*Amy Boucher Pye*

Searching for Treasure

PROVERBS 4:5–19

*[Wisdom] is more profitable than silver
and yields better returns than gold.*

—PROVERBS 3:14

Buried treasure. It's like something out of a children's storybook. But millionaire Forrest Fenn claims to have left a box of jewels and gold worth up to $2 million in the Rocky Mountains. Many people have searched for it. In fact, four people have died looking for the hidden riches.

The author of Proverbs gives us reason to stop and think: *Does any kind of treasure merit such a quest?* In Proverbs 4, a father writing to his sons about how to live well suggests that wisdom is worth seeking at any cost (v. 7). Wisdom, he says, will lead us through life, keep us from stumbling, and crown us with honor (vv. 8–12). Writing hundreds of years later, James also emphasized the importance of wisdom. "The wisdom that comes from heaven," he writes, "is first of all pure; then peace-loving, considerate, submissive, full of mercy and good fruit, impartial and sincere" (James 3:17). When we seek wisdom, we find all kinds of good things.

To seek wisdom is to seek God, the source of all wisdom. His wisdom is worth more than any buried treasure imaginable.

—*Amy Peterson*

Look What Jesus Has Done

LUKE 8:1–8

Excel in this grace of giving.
—2 CORINTHIANS 8:7

The boy was only eight when he announced to his parents' friend Wally, "I love Jesus and want to serve God overseas." During the next ten years or so, Wally prayed for him. When this young man later announced his intentions to go to Mali, West Africa, Wally told him, "It's about time! I invested some money and have been saving it for you, waiting for this exciting news." Wally had a heart for spreading God's good news.

When Jesus and His disciples needed financial support as they traveled from village to village telling the good news (Luke 8:1–3), a group of women Jesus had healed helped to support them "out of their own means" (v. 3). One was Mary Magdalene, who had been freed from demons. Another was Joanna, the wife of an official in Herod's court. There were "many others" (v. 3) whose spiritual needs Jesus had met. Now they were helping Him and His disciples through their financial resources.

When we consider what Jesus has done for us, His heart for others becomes our own. Let's ask God how He wants to use us.

—Anne Cetas

Surrounded by God

PSALM 125:1–5

As the mountains surround Jerusalem,
so the LORD surrounds his people
both now and for evermore.
—PSALM 125:2

In a busy airport, a young mother struggled alone. Her toddler was in full tantrum mode—screaming, kicking, and refusing to board their plane. Overwhelmed and heavily pregnant, the burdened young mother finally gave up, sinking to the floor in frustration, covering her face, and starting to sob.

Suddenly six or seven women travelers, all strangers, formed a circle around the young mother and her child—sharing snacks, water, gentle hugs, and even a nursery song. Their loving circle calmed the mother and child, who then boarded their plane. The other women returned to their seats, not needing to discuss what they had done, but knowing their support had strengthened a young mother exactly when she needed it.

This illustrates a beautiful truth from Psalm 125. "As the mountains surround Jerusalem," says verse 2, "so the LORD surrounds his people." He supports and stands guard over our souls "both now and for evermore." Thus, on tough days, look up, "unto the hills," as the psalmist puts it (Psalm 121:1 KJV). God awaits with strong help, steady hope, and everlasting love.
—*Patricia Raybon*

Ham and Eggs

2 CHRONICLES 16:1–9

*For the eyes of the LORD range throughout
the earth to strengthen those whose
hearts are fully committed to him.*
—2 CHRONICLES 16:9

In the fable of the chicken and the pig, the animals discuss opening a restaurant together. As they plan their menu, the chicken suggests they serve ham and eggs. The pig objects saying, "No thanks. I'd be committed, but you would only be involved."

Although the pig didn't care to put himself on the platter, his understanding of commitment is instructive to me as I learn to follow God wholeheartedly.

To protect his kingdom, Asa, king of Judah, sought to break up a treaty between Israel and Aram. He sent personal treasure along with "silver and gold out of the treasuries of the LORD's temple" to secure favor with Ben-Hadad, the king of Aram (2 Chronicles 16:2). Ben-Hadad agreed, and their joint forces repelled Israel.

But God's prophet Hanani called Asa foolish for relying on human help instead of God. Hanani asserted, "The eyes of the LORD range throughout the earth to strengthen those whose hearts are fully committed to him" (v. 9).

As we face our own battles, let's remember that God is our best ally. He strengthens us when we're willing to "serve up" total commitment to Him.

—*Kirsten Holmberg*

Change Is Possible

PHILIPPIANS 2:1–4

*It is God who works in you to will and
to act in order to fulfill his good purpose.*
—PHILIPPIANS 2:13

One Saturday afternoon, some young people from my church gathered to ask one another hard questions based on Philippians 2:3–4: "Do nothing out of selfish ambition or vain conceit. Rather, in humility value others above yourselves, not looking to your own interests but each of you to the interests of the others." Their queries included: How often do you take an interest in others? Would someone describe you as humble or proud? Why?

I was encouraged by their honest answers. They agreed that it's easy to acknowledge our shortcomings, but it's hard to change. As one teen lamented, "Selfishness is in my blood."

The desire to drop our self-focus and serve others is possible only through Jesus's Spirit living in us. That's why Paul reminded the people that God had graciously adopted them, comforted them with His love, and given His Spirit to help them (Philippians 2:1–2). How could they—and we—respond to such grace with anything less than humility?

Because God gives us "the desire and power to do what pleases him" (v. 13 NLT), we can focus less on ourselves and humbly serve others.

—*Poh Fang Chia*

Hiding Our Hurts

HEBREWS 4:12–13

*The word of God . . . judges the thoughts
and attitudes of the heart.*
—HEBREWS 4:12

I was guest-speaking in a church, and my topic was an honest story about presenting our brokenness before God and receiving the healing He wants to give. Before closing in prayer, the pastor stood and spoke passionately to his gathered congregants: "As your pastor I have the privilege of seeing you midweek and hearing your heart-breaking stories of brokenness. Then in our weekend worship services, I have the pain of watching you hide your hurt."

My heart ached at the hidden hurts God came to heal. The writer of Hebrews describes the Word of God as alive and active. Jesus is the *living* Word of God, and He died to give us access to God's presence.

While we all know it's not wise to share *everything* with *everyone*, we also know that God intends His church to be a place where we can live unapologetically as broken and forgiven believers—where we "carry each other's burdens" (Galatians 6:2).

What are you hiding from others today? And how are you trying to hide from God as well? God sees us and loves us. Will we let Him?

—*Elisa Morgan*

Open Arms

PSALM 139:17-24

*Search me, God, and know my heart; test me
and know my anxious thoughts.*
—PSALM 139:23

The day my husband, Dan, and I began our care-giving journey with our aging parents, we felt as if we were plunging off a cliff. We didn't know that in the process of caregiving, the hardest task we would face would be to allow God to use this special time to make us like Him in new ways.

On days when I felt I was plunging toward earth in an out-of-control free-fall, God showed me my agendas, my reservations, my fears, my pride, and my selfishness. He used my broken places to show me His love and forgiveness.

My pastor has said, "The best day is the day you see yourself for who you are—desperate without Christ. Then see yourself as He sees you—complete in Him." This was the blessing of caregiving in my life. As I saw who God had created me to be, I cried out with the psalmist: "Search me, God, and know my heart" (Psalm 139:23).

As we see ourselves in the midst of our own circumstances, let's turn and run into the open, loving, and forgiving arms of God.

—*Shelly Beach*

God of All the People

ACTS 2:1–11

Now there were staying in Jerusalem God-fearing
Jews from every nation under heaven.

—ACTS 2:5

Former Newsboys lead vocalist Peter Furler describes the performance of the band's praise song "He Reigns." The song paints a vivid picture of believers from every tribe and nation coming together to worship God in unity. Furler observed that whenever the Newsboys sang it he could sense the moving of the Holy Spirit.

Furler's description of his experiences with "He Reigns" would likely have resonated with the crowds who converged on Jerusalem at Pentecost. When the disciples were filled with the Holy Spirit (Acts 2:4), things began to happen! As a result, Jews representing every nation came together, because each one heard their own language being spoken to make God's wonders known (vv. 5–6, 11).

This all-inclusive display of God's awesome power made the crowd receptive to Peter's declaration of the gospel, leading to three thousand converts that day alone (v. 41). These new believers then returned to their corner of the world, taking the good news with them.

The good news still resounds today—God's message of hope for all people. His Spirit still moves among us, bringing people of every nation together in wonderful unity. He reigns!

—*Remi Oyedele*

With God's Help

JOSHUA 14:7–15

"Now then, just as the LORD promised,
he has kept me alive for forty-five years
since the time he said this to Moses."
—JOSHUA 14:10

As I've grown older, I feel less like a conqueror and more like someone conquered by the challenges of becoming a senior citizen.

That's why my hero is an older man named Caleb—the former spy sent by Moses to scout out Canaan, the promised land (Numbers 13–14). In Joshua 14, the time had come for Caleb to receive his portion of land. But there were enemies still to drive out. Not content to retire and leave the battle to the younger generation, Caleb declared, "The Anakites were there and their cities were large and fortified, but, the LORD helping me, I will drive them out just as he said" (Joshua 14:12).

"The LORD helping me." That's the kind of mindset that kept Caleb battle-ready. He focused on God's power, not his own, nor on his advanced age.

Most of us don't think of taking on anything monumental when we reach a certain age. But we can still do great things for God, no matter our age. When Caleb-sized opportunities come our way, let's not shy away from them. With the Lord helping us, we can conquer!

—*Linda Washington*

Enjoying Beauty

ECCLESIASTES 3:9–13

He has made everything beautiful in its time.
—ECCLESIASTES 3:11

The painting caught my eye like a beacon. Displayed on the wall of a long hospital hallway, its deep pastel hues and Navajo Native American figures were so arresting I stopped to marvel and stare.

"Beautiful," I whispered.

Many things in life are beautiful indeed. Master paintings. Scenic vistas. Inspired crafts. But so is a child's smile. A friend's hello. A robin's blue egg. A seashell's strong ridges. "[God] has made everything beautiful in its time" (Ecclesiastes 3:11). In such beauty, Bible scholars explain, we get a glimpse of the perfection of God's creation—including the glory of His perfect rule to come.

Some days life looks drab and futile. But God mercifully provides moments of beauty to ponder.

The artist of the painting I admired, Gerard Curtis Delano, understood that. "God [gave] me a talent to create beauty," he once said, "and this is what He wanted me to do."

Seeing such beauty, how can we respond? We can thank God for eternity to come while pausing to enjoy the glory we already see.

—*Patricia Raybon*

We Have a King!

JUDGES 2:11–23

In those days Israel had no king; all the people did whatever seemed right in their own eyes.

—JUDGES 21:25 (NLT)

After attacking my husband with hurtful words when a situation didn't go my way, I snubbed the Holy Spirit's authority as He reminded me of Bible verses that revealed my sinful attitudes. But was nursing my stubborn pride worth the collateral damage in my marriage or being disobedient to God? Absolutely not. By the time I asked for forgiveness from the Lord and my spouse, I'd left a wake of wounds behind me—the result of ignoring wise counsel and living as if I didn't have to answer to anyone but myself.

Many times the Israelites had a rebellious attitude. For instance, after Joshua and the generation that outlived him died, the Israelites forgot God and what He had done (Judges 2:10). They rejected godly leadership and embraced sin (vv. 11–15).

Things improved when the Lord raised up judges (vv. 16–18). But when each judge died, the Israelites returned to defying God. Living as if they didn't have anyone to answer to but themselves, they suffered devastating consequences (vv. 19–22).

Let's not repeat their mistakes. Let's submit to the sovereign authority of our loving Lord.

—*Xochitl Dixon*

Hands-On Learning

TITUS 2:1–8

*Follow my example, as I follow
the example of Christ.*
—1 CORINTHIANS 11:1

My six-year-old son, Owen, received a new board game, but he was frustrated. He couldn't figure out how it worked. Later, when a friend came over who already knew how to play, Owen finally got to enjoy his present. Watching them play, I was reminded of how much easier it is to learn something new if you have an experienced teacher.

Paul understood this too. Writing to Titus about how he could help his church grow in faith, Paul emphasized the value of experienced believers who could model Christian faith. Of course, teaching "sound doctrine" was important, but it didn't just need to be talked about—it needed to be lived. Paul wrote that older people ought to be self-controlled, kind, and loving (Titus 2:2–5). "In everything," he said, "set them an example by doing what is good" (v. 7).

I'm thankful for the many people in my life who have been hands-on teachers. They have shown me by their lives what it looks like to follow Christ and have made it easier for me to see how I can walk that path too.

—*Amy Peterson*

Serve and Be Served

PHILIPPIANS 4:10–19

I rejoiced greatly in the Lord that at last you renewed your concern for me. Indeed, you were concerned, but you had no opportunity to show it.
—PHILIPPIANS 4:10

Marilyn had been ill for weeks, and many people had encouraged her through this difficult time. *How will I ever repay all their kindnesses?* she worried. Then one day she read the words of a prayer: "Pray that [others] will develop humility, allowing them not only to serve, but also to be served." Marilyn realized there was no need to balance any scale but just be thankful and allow others to experience the joy of serving.

In Philippians 4, Paul expressed his gratitude for all who shared "in [his] troubles" (v. 14). He depended on others to support him as he preached. He understood that the gifts provided for him were simply extensions of people's love for God: "[Your gifts] are a fragrant offering, an acceptable sacrifice, pleasing to God" (v. 18).

With humility we can allow God to care for us through their goodness.

Paul wrote, "My God will meet all your needs" (v. 19). It was something he had learned during a life of trials. God is faithful, and His provision for us has no limits.

—*Cindy Hess Kasper*

"God Saved My Life"

JOHN 8:42–47

When he lies, he speaks his native language,
for he is a liar and the father of lies.
—JOHN 8:44

When Aaron (not his real name) was fifteen, he began praying to Satan: "I felt like he and I had a partnership." Aaron started to lie, steal, and manipulate his family and friends. He also experienced nightmares: "I woke up and saw the devil at the end of the bed. He told me I was going to pass my exams and then die." Yet when he finished his exams, he lived. Aaron reflected, "It was clear that he was a liar."

Hoping to meet girls, Aaron went to a Christian festival, where a man offered to pray for him. "While he was praying," Aaron felt something "more powerful, and more liberating," than what he felt from Satan. The man told Aaron that God had a plan and Satan is a liar, echoing Jesus's words: "He is . . . the father of lies" (John 8:44).

Aaron turned to Christ. Now a minister, he's a living testament of God's saving power: "I can say with confidence that God saved my life."

God is the source of all that is good, holy, and true. We can turn to Him to find truth.

—*Amy Boucher Pye*

Trusting God Even If

DANIEL 3:13–25

The God we serve is able to deliver us.
—DANIEL 3:17

Due to an injury in 1992, I suffer from chronic back, shoulder, and neck pain. During the most excruciating and disheartening moments, it's not always easy to trust or praise the Lord. But when my situation feels unbearable, God's constant presence comforts me. He strengthens me and reassures me of His unchanging goodness and sustaining grace. And when I'm tempted to doubt Him, I'm encouraged by the determined faith of Shadrach, Meshach, and Abednego. They worshiped God and trusted Him even when their situation seemed hopeless.

When King Nebuchadnezzar threatened to throw them into a blazing furnace if they didn't turn away from the true God to worship his golden statue (Daniel 3:13–15), they displayed courageous and confident faith. They never doubted that the Lord was worthy of their worship (v. 17), "even if" He didn't rescue them (v. 18). God didn't leave them alone in their time of need; He joined them in the furnace (vv. 24–25).

God doesn't leave us alone either. He remains with us through our trials. Even if our suffering doesn't end in this life, we can rely on His constant and loving presence.

—*Xochitl Dixon*

Every Story Whispers His Name

LUKE 24:17–27

*Beginning with Moses and all the Prophets, he
explained to them what was said in all
the Scriptures concerning himself.*

—LUKE 24:27

I opened the whimsically illustrated children's Bible
and began to read to my grandson. Immediately we
were enthralled as the story of God's love and provision unfurled in prose. Marking our place, I read the
title once again: *The Jesus Storybook Bible: Every
Story Whispers His Name*. Every story whispers His
name. Every story.

Sometimes the Bible, especially the Old Testament,
is hard to understand. Why do those who don't know
God seem to triumph over God's own? How can God
permit such cruelty when we know that His character
is pure and that His purposes are for our good?

After His resurrection, Jesus met two followers on
the road to Emmaus. They didn't recognize Him and
were struggling with disappointment over the death
of their hoped-for Messiah (Luke 24:19–24). They
had "hoped that he was the one who was going to
redeem Israel" (v. 21). Then Jesus reassured them:
"Beginning with Moses and all the Prophets, [Jesus]
explained to them what was said in all the Scriptures
concerning himself" (v. 27).

Every story whispers His name—pointing to the
redemption God designed for us.

—*Elisa Morgan*

What's Your Father's Name?

JOHN 8:39–47

*To all who did receive him, to those
who believed in his name, he gave the
right to become children of God.*
—JOHN 1:12

When I went to buy a cell phone in the Middle East, I was asked the typical questions: name, nationality, address. But then as the clerk was filling out the form, he asked, "What's your father's name?" That question surprised me, and I wondered why it was important. I was told it was necessary in order to establish my identity. In some cultures, ancestry is important.

The Israelites believed in the importance of ancestry too. They were proud of their patriarch Abraham, and they thought being part of Abraham's clan made them God's children. Their human ancestry was connected, in their opinion, to their spiritual family.

Hundreds of years later when Jesus was talking with the Jews, He pointed out that this was not so. They could say Abraham was their earthly ancestor, but if they didn't love Him—the One sent by the Father—they weren't part of God's family.

That's still true. If we believe in Jesus, God gives us the right to become His children (John 1:12). By trusting in Jesus for the forgiveness of sins, you become part of God's family. And He becomes your spiritual Father.

—*Keila Ochoa*

No Cosigner Required

HEBREWS 6:13–20

*People swear by someone greater than themselves,
and the oath confirms what is said.*

—HEBREWS 6:16

Sometimes, would-be borrowers have to use a cosigner to get a loan. The borrower may not have established good credit, so the cosigner agrees to take on the responsibility if the loan is not paid. It's a promise to the lender that the loan will be repaid.

When someone makes a promise to us—whether for financial, marital, or other reasons—we expect that person to keep it. We want to know that God will keep His promises too. When He promised Abraham that He would bless him and give him "many descendants" (Hebrews 6:14; see Genesis 22:17), Abraham took God at His word. As the Creator of all that exists, there is no one greater than He; only God could guarantee His own promise.

Abraham had to wait for the birth of his son (Hebrews 6:15) and never saw how innumerable his offspring would grow to be, but God proved faithful to His promise. When He promises to be with us always (13:5), to hold us securely (John 10:29), and to comfort us (2 Corinthians 1:3–4), we too can trust Him to be true to His word.

—*Kirsten Holmberg*

Two-Winged Son

ISAIAH 38:1–8

*"[The Lord says]: 'I have heard your
prayer and seen your tears.'"*
—ISAIAH 38:5

A few years ago, an ancient clay seal was dug up near the southern part of Jerusalem's old city wall. After much study, a researcher who carefully scrutinized the letters on the three-thousand-year-old object discovered that the inscription, written in ancient Hebrew, reads: "Belonging to Hezekiah [son of] Ahaz king of Judah."

At the center of the seal is a two-winged sun surrounded by two images symbolizing life. Archaeologists believe that King Hezekiah began using this seal as a symbol of God's protection after the Lord healed him from a life-threatening illness (Isaiah 38:1–8). Hezekiah had been pleading with the Lord to heal him, and God heard his prayer. He also gave Hezekiah a sign that He would indeed do what He had promised, saying, "I will cause the sun's shadow to move ten steps backward" (v. 8 NLT).

The people in the Bible were learning, as we are, to call on the Lord. And even when His answers are not what we want or expect, we can rest assured that He is compassionate and powerful. The One who orders the movement of the sun can certainly move in our hearts.

—*Poh Fang Chia*

From Trash to Treasure

2 CORINTHIANS 4:5-7

*We have this treasure in jars of clay
to show that this all-surpassing power
is from God and not from us.*
—2 CORINTHIANS 4:7

The trash man's house in a poor Bogota neighborhood doesn't look special. Yet the unassuming abode in Colombia's capital is home to a free library of 25,000 books—discarded literature that José Alberto Gutiérrez collected to share with poor children in his community.

Local kids crowd into the house during weekend "library hours." Prowling through rooms full of books, the children recognize the humble home as more than Señor Jose's house—it's a priceless treasury.

The same is true for followers of Christ. We're made of humble clay—marred by cracks and easily broken. But we're entrusted by God as a home for His empowering Spirit, who enables us to carry the good news of Christ into a hurting, broken world. It's a big job for ordinary, fragile people.

"We have this treasure in jars of clay to show that this all-surpassing power is from God and not from us" (2 Corinthians 4:7), the apostle Paul told his congregation in the ancient city of Corinth.

Paul also said we are to tell others about the priceless One living inside of us. Jesus alone turns our ordinary lives into a priceless treasury.

—*Patricia Raybon*

Outside In?

GALATIANS 3:23–29

For all of you who were baptized into Christ
have clothed yourselves with Christ.
—GALATIANS 3:27

"Change: From the Inside Out or the Outside In?"
the headline read, reflecting a popular trend today—
the idea that outward changes like a makeover or
better posture can be an easy way to change how
we feel on the inside—and even change our lives.
Focusing on simple external changes offers hope that
there is a quicker path toward improving our lives.

But although such changes can improve our lives,
Scripture invites us to seek a deeper transformation—
one that is impossible on our own. In fact, in Galatians 3 Paul argued that even God's law—a priceless
gift that revealed His will—couldn't heal the brokenness of God's people (vv. 19–22). True healing and
freedom required them to, through faith, be "clothed"
in Christ (v. 27) through His Spirit (5:5). They would
find their true identity and worth—every believer
equally an heir to all of God's promises (3:28–29).

We could easily devote much energy to self-
improvement techniques. But the deepest and most
satisfying changes in our hearts come in knowing
the love that surpasses knowledge (Ephesians 3:17–
19)—the love that changes everything.

—*Monica Brands*

Eyes in the Back of My Head

PSALM 33:6–19

From his dwelling place [God]
watches all who live on earth.
—PSALM 33:14

I was mischievous in my early years and tried to hide my bad behavior to avoid getting into trouble. Yet my mother usually found out what I had done. I recall being amazed at how accurately she knew about my antics. When I asked how she knew, she replied, "I have eyes in the back of my head." This, of course, led me to study her head whenever she'd turn her back—were the eyes invisible or merely cloaked by her red hair? Eventually, I gave up looking for her extra pair of eyes and realized I just wasn't as sneaky as I thought. Her watchful gaze was evidence of her loving concern for us.

As grateful as I am for my mother's attentive care, I'm even more grateful that God "sees all mankind" (Psalm 33:13). He sees so much more than what we do; He sees our sadness, our delights, and our love for one another.

God sees our true character and always knows what we need. With perfect vision, He watches over those who love Him and put their hope in Him (v. 18). He's our attentive, loving Father.

—*Kirsten Holmberg*

Jesus in Disguise

MATTHEW 25:31–40

"The King will reply, 'Truly I tell you, whatever you did for one of the least of these brothers and sisters of mine, you did for me.'"

—MATTHEW 25:40

When a friend cared for her housebound mother-in-law, she asked her what she longed for the most. "For my feet to be washed," she replied. My friend told me, "How I hated that job! Each time she asked me to do it I was resentful and would ask God to hide my feelings from her."

But one day her grumbling attitude changed in a flash. As she got out the bowl and towel and knelt at her mother-in-law's feet, she said, "I looked up, and for a moment I felt like I was washing the feet of Jesus himself. She was Jesus in disguise!" After that, she felt honored to do it.

When I heard this moving account, I thought of Jesus's story about the end of time, which He taught on the Mount of Olives. The King welcomes into His kingdom His sons and daughters, saying that when they visited the sick or fed the hungry, they did it for Him (Matthew 25:40). We too serve Jesus himself when we visit those in prison or give clothes to the needy.

Today, might you echo my friend, who now wonders when she meets someone new, "Are you Jesus in disguise?"

—*Amy Boucher Pye*

Let Your Hair Down

JOHN 12:1–8

Then Mary took about a pint of pure nard,
an expensive perfume; she poured it on Jesus'
feet and wiped his feet with her hair.

—JOHN 12:3

Shortly before Jesus was crucified, a woman named Mary poured a bottle of expensive perfume on His feet. Then, in what may have been an even more daring act, she wiped His feet with her hair (John 12:3). Not only did Mary sacrifice what may have been her life's savings but she also sacrificed her reputation. In first-century Middle Eastern culture, respectable women never let down their hair in public. But true worship is not concerned about what others think of us (2 Samuel 6:21–22). To worship Jesus, Mary was willing to be thought of as immodest, perhaps even immoral.

We may feel pressured to be perfect when we go to church. Metaphorically speaking, we work hard to ensure that every hair is in place. But a healthy church is where we can let down our hair and not hide our flaws behind a façade of perfection.

Worship doesn't involve behaving as if nothing is wrong; it's making sure everything is right—right with God and with one another. When our greatest fear is letting down our hair, perhaps our greatest sin is keeping it up.

—*Julie Ackerman Link*

Who Is This?

LUKE 19:28–40

*"Blessed is the king who comes
in the name of the Lord!"*
—LUKE 19:38

Imagine standing shoulder to shoulder with on-lookers by a dirt road. The woman behind you is on her tiptoes, trying to see who is coming. In the distance, you glimpse a man riding a donkey. As He approaches, people toss their coats onto the road. Suddenly, you hear a tree crack behind you. A man is cutting down palm branches, and people are spreading them out ahead of the donkey.

Jesus's followers zealously honored Him as He entered Jerusalem a few days before His crucifixion. The multitude rejoiced and praised God for "all the miracles they had seen" (Luke 19:37). Jesus's devotees surrounded Him, calling out, "Blessed is the king!" (v. 38). Their enthusiastic honor affected the people of Jerusalem. When Jesus arrived, "the whole city was stirred and asked, 'Who is this?'" (Matthew 21:10).

Today, people are still curious about Jesus. Although we can't pave His way with palm branches or shout praises to Him in person, we can still honor Him. We can discuss His remarkable works, assist people in need, and love each other deeply. Then we must be ready to answer the onlookers who ask, "Who is Jesus?"

—*Jennifer Benson Schuldt*

Escaping the Noise

1 KINGS 19:9–13

After the fire came a gentle whisper.
—1 KINGS 19:12

Several years ago, the president of a college suggested that students join her in "powering down" for an evening. Although the students agreed, it was with great reluctance that they laid aside their cell phones and entered the chapel. For the next hour, they sat quietly in a service of music and prayer. Afterward, one participant described the experience as "a wonderful opportunity to calm down . . . a place to just tune out all of the extra noise."

Sometimes, it's difficult to escape "extra noise." But when we're willing to "power down," we begin to understand the psalmist's reminder to be still so we can know God (Psalm 46:10). In 1 Kings 19, we discover as well that when the prophet Elijah looked for the Lord, he didn't find Him in the pandemonium of the wind or the earthquake or the fire (vv. 9–13). Instead, Elijah heard God's gentle whisper (v. 12).

When we quietly open our hearts, we find that time with God is even sweeter. Like Elijah, we're more likely to encounter God in the stillness. And sometimes, if we listen, we too will hear that gentle whisper.

—*Cindy Hess Kasper*

At Home with Jesus

JOHN 14:1–4

*"If I go and prepare a place for you, I will
come back and take you to be with me
that you also may be where I am."*
—JOHN 14:3

"There's no place like home." The phrase reflects a
deeply rooted yearning within us to have a place to
rest and to belong. Jesus addressed this desire for
rootedness when, after He and His friends had their
last supper together, He promised that although He
would go away, He would come back for them. And
He would prepare a place for them. A home.

He made this place for them—and us—through
fulfilling the requirements of God's law when He died
on the cross. He assured His disciples that if He went
to the trouble of creating this home, He would come
back for them and not leave them alone. They didn't
need to fear or be worried about their lives, whether
on earth or in heaven.

We believe and trust that He makes a home for us,
that He makes His home within us (see John 14:23),
and that He has gone ahead to prepare our heavenly home. Whatever sort of physical place we live
in, we belong with Jesus, upheld by His love and
surrounded in His peace. With Him, there's no place
like home.

—*Amy Boucher Pye*

The Via Dolorosa

HEBREWS 10:1–10

*We have been made holy through the sacrifice
of the body of Jesus Christ once for all.*
—HEBREWS 10:10

During Holy Week, we remember the final days before Jesus's crucifixion. The road Jesus traveled to the cross through the streets of Jerusalem is known as the Via Dolorosa, the way of sorrows.

But the writer of Hebrews viewed the path Jesus took as more than just a path of sorrows. The way of suffering that Jesus willingly walked to Golgotha made a "new and living way" into the presence of God for us (Hebrews 10:20).

For centuries the Jewish people had sought to come into God's presence through animal sacrifices and by seeking to keep the law. But the law was "only a shadow of the good things that are coming," for "it is impossible for the blood of bulls and goats to take away sins" (vv. 1, 4).

Jesus's journey down the Via Dolorosa led to His death and resurrection. Because of His sacrifice, we can be made holy when we trust in Him for forgiveness. We can draw near to God without fear, fully confident that we are welcomed and loved (vv. 10, 22).

Christ's way of sorrow opened for us a new and living way to God.

—*Amy Peterson*

Look and Be Quiet

LUKE 23:44–49

*Look around and see. Is any
suffering like my suffering?*
—LAMENTATIONS 1:12

In the song "Look at Him," Mexican composer Rubén Sotelo describes Jesus at the cross. He invites us to look at Jesus and be quiet, because there is really nothing to say before the type of love Jesus demonstrated at the cross.

When Jesus breathed His last, those who "had gathered to witness this sight . . . beat their breasts and went away" (Luke 23:48). Others "stood at a distance, watching these things" (v. 49). They looked and were quiet. Only one spoke, a centurion, who said, "Surely this was a righteous man" (v. 47).

Many years before, Jeremiah wrote about Jerusalem's pain after its devastation. "Is it nothing to you, all you who pass by?" (Lamentations 1:12). He was asking people to look and see; he thought there was no greater suffering than Jerusalem's. However, has there been any suffering like Jesus's suffering?

All of us are passing by the road of the cross. Will we look and see His love? Let us take a moment to ponder Jesus's death. In the quietness of our hearts, may we whisper to Him our deepest devotion.

—*Keila Ochoa*

Refreshing Spring Rains

HOSEA 6:1–4

*"He will come to us . . . like the spring rains
that water the earth."*

—HOSEA 6:3

While I was taking a walk in the nearby park, a burst of green caught my attention. Out of the mud appeared shoots of life that in a few weeks would be cheerful daffodils, heralding spring and the warmth to come. We had made it through another winter!

As we read through the book of Hosea, it can feel like an unrelenting winter. The Lord gave this prophet the unenviable task of marrying an unfaithful woman as a picture of the Creator's love for His people Israel (1:2–3). Hosea's wife, Gomer, broke their wedding vows, but Hosea welcomed her back, yearning that she would love him devotedly (3:1–3). So too the Lord desires that we love Him with a strength and commitment that won't evaporate like the morning mist.

How do we relate to God? Do we seek Him in times of trouble while ignoring Him during our seasons of celebration? Are we like the Israelites, easily swayed by the idols of our age—such things as busyness, success, and influence?

May we recommit ourselves to the Lord, who loves us as surely as the flowers bud in the spring.

—*Amy Boucher Pye*

The Advance Team

JOHN 14:1–14

"In My Father's house are many dwelling places; if not, I would have told you. I am going to prepare a place for you."
—JOHN 14:2 (HCSB)

A friend recently prepared to relocate to a city more than 1,000 miles from her current hometown. She and her husband divided the labor of moving to accommodate a short timeline. He secured new living arrangements, while she packed their belongings. I was astounded by her ability to move without participating in the house hunt. She said she knew she could trust her husband because of his attention to her preferences and needs.

In the upper room, Jesus spoke with His disciples of His coming betrayal and death. The darkest hours of Jesus's earthly life, and that of the disciples, lay ahead. He comforted them with the assurance that He would prepare a place for them in heaven. When the disciples questioned Jesus, He pointed them to their mutual history and the miracles they had witnessed. Though they would grieve Jesus's death and absence, He reminded them He could be counted on to do as He'd said.

Even in the midst of our own dark hours, we can trust Him to lead us forward to a place of goodness. As we walk with Him, we too will learn to trust in His faithfulness.

—*Kirsten Holmberg*

The Point of Being Alive

LUKE 12:22-34

*Watch out! Be on your guard against
all kinds of greed; life does not consist
in an abundance of possessions.*

—LUKE 12:15

While almost all financial advice books I've read imply that the primary reason to cut costs is to live like millionaires later, one book offered a refreshingly different perspective. It said living *simply* is essential for a rich life. If you need more stuff to feel joy, the book suggested, "You're missing the point of being alive."

That idea brought to mind Jesus's response when a man asked Him to urge his brother to divide an inheritance with him. Instead of sympathizing, Jesus warned him sternly about "all kinds of greed"— because "life does not consist in an abundance of possessions" (Luke 12:14–15). He then came to a blistering conclusion about this wealthy person's plans to store his crops and enjoy a luxurious lifestyle. His wealth did him no good, since he died that night (vv. 16–20).

Jesus's words remind us to check our motivation. Our hearts should be focused on pursuing God's kingdom—not just on securing our own futures (vv. 29–31). As we live for Him and freely share with others, we can fully enjoy a rich life with Him *now* (vv. 32–34).

—*Monica Brands*

Full of Joy

JOHN 15:9–16

"I have told you this so that my joy may be in you and that your joy may be complete."
—JOHN 15:11

Our God certainly appears to treasure ordinary, yet beautiful things. But in His creativity, the ordinary is extraordinary. God continues to delight each of us in the panorama of His creation. Moreover, God the Father, Son, and Holy Spirit share love and joy together.

In Romans 14:17, Paul wrote, "The Kingdom of God is not a matter of what we eat or drink, but of living a life of goodness and peace and joy in the Holy Spirit" (NLT). And in Romans 15:13, he declared, "I pray that God, the source of hope, will fill you completely with joy and peace because you trust in him" (NLT). Joy is a hallmark of kingdom life made possible by the Spirit as we place our trust in Jesus.

Jesus says, "When you obey my commandments, you remain in my love. . . . I have told you these things so that you will be filled with my joy. Yes, your joy will overflow!" (John 15:10–11 NLT). Even in the ordinary and what some might think of as monotonous, we can experience the joy He exudes!

—*Marlena Graves*

Perfect Peace

JOHN 14:25–31

"Peace I leave with you; my peace I give you. I do not give to you as the world gives. Do not let your hearts be troubled and do not be afraid."

—JOHN 14:27

A friend shared with me that for years she searched for peace and contentment. She and her husband built up a successful business, so she was able to buy a big house, fancy clothes, and expensive jewelry. But neither these possessions nor her friendships with influential people could satisfy her inner longings for peace. One day, when she was feeling low and desperate, a friend told her about the good news of Jesus. There she found the Prince of Peace, and her understanding of true peace and contentment was forever changed.

Jesus spoke words of peace to His friends after their last supper together (John 14) when He prepared them for the events that would soon follow: His death, resurrection, and the coming of the Holy Spirit. Describing a remarkable peace, He wanted them to learn how to find a sense of well-being even in the midst of hardship.

Later, when the resurrected Jesus appeared to the frightened disciples after His death, He greeted them, saying, "Peace be with you!" (John 20:19). He gave them, and us, a new understanding of what true peace is all about.

—*Amy Boucher Pye*

Up a Tree

JONAH 2:1–10

"In my distress I called to the LORD,
and he answered me."

—JONAH 2:2

When my mother discovered my kitten Velvet devouring her homemade bread, she scooted the feline out the door. Later, as we searched for the missing cat, a faint meow whistled on the wind. I looked up to the peak of a poplar tree where a black smudge tilted a branch.

In her haste to flee my mother's frustration, Velvet chose a more precarious predicament. Is it possible that we sometimes do something similar—running from our errors and putting ourselves in danger? Even then, God comes to our rescue.

The prophet Jonah fled in disobedience from God's call to preach to Nineveh, and he was swallowed up by a great fish. "From inside the fish Jonah prayed to the LORD his God" (Jonah 2:1–2). God heard Jonah's plea, and the fish expelled the prophet (v. 10). Then God gave Jonah another chance (3:1).

After we failed to woo Velvet down, we summoned the fire department. A kind man climbed a ladder, plucked my kitten from her perch, and returned her safely to my arms.

Oh the heights—and the depths—God goes to in rescuing us from our disobedience with His redeeming love!

—*Elisa Morgan*

The King's Crown

MATTHEW 27:27–31

They . . . twisted together a crown
of thorns and set it on his head.
—MATTHEW 27:28–29

We sat around the table, each person adding a toothpick to the foam disc before us. At our evening meal in the weeks leading up to Easter, we created a crown of thorns—with each toothpick signifying something we had done that day for which we were sorry and for which Christ had paid the penalty.

The crown of thorns that Jesus was made to wear was part of a cruel game the Roman soldiers played before He was crucified. They also dressed Him in a royal robe and gave Him a staff as a king's scepter, which they then used to beat Him. They mocked Him, calling Him "king of the Jews" (Matthew 27:29), not knowing that their actions would be remembered thousands of years later. This was no ordinary king. He was the King of Kings whose death, followed by His resurrection, gives us eternal life.

On Easter morning, we celebrated the gift of forgiveness and new life by replacing the toothpicks with flowers. What joy we felt, knowing that God had erased our sins and had given us freedom and life forever!

—*Amy Boucher Pye*

Fitting In

MALACHI 3:13–18

Then those who feared the LORD talked with each other, and the LORD listened and heard.

—MALACHI 3:16

Lee is a diligent and reliable bank employee. Yet he often finds himself sticking out like a sore thumb for living out his faith—for instance when he leaves the break room during an inappropriate conversation. At a Bible study, he shared with his friends, "I fear that I'm losing promotion opportunities for not fitting in."

Believers during the prophet Malachi's time faced a similar challenge. They had returned from exile and the temple had been rebuilt, but there was skepticism about God's plan for their future. Some of the Israelites were saying, "It is futile to serve God. . . . Certainly evildoers prosper, and even when they put God to the test, they get away with it" (Malachi 3:14–15).

How can we stand firm for God in a culture that wants us to blend in? The faithful in Malachi's time responded to a similar challenge by meeting with like-minded believers to encourage each other. Then "the LORD listened and heard" (v. 16).

God cares for all who fear and honor Him. He doesn't call us to "fit in" but to draw closer to Him each day as we encourage each other. Let's stay faithful!

—*Poh Fang Chia*

Called by Name

JOHN 20:11–18

Jesus said to her, "Mary." She turned toward him and cried out in Aramaic, "Rabboni!"
—JOHN 20:16

Advertisers have concluded that the most attention-grabbing word that viewers react to is their own name. Thus a television channel in the UK introduced personalized advertisements with their online streaming services.

Even more than that, there's a closeness that comes when someone who loves us says our name. Mary Magdalene's attention was arrested when, at the tomb where Jesus's body had been laid after He was crucified on the cross, He spoke her name (John 20:16). With that single word, she turned in recognition to the Teacher she loved, and she followed Him. The familiarity with which He spoke her name confirmed for her that the One who'd known her perfectly was alive.

Like Mary, we too are personally loved by God. Jesus told Mary that He would ascend to His Father (v. 17), but He had also told His disciples that He would not leave them alone (John 14:15–18). God would send the Holy Spirit to live and dwell in His children (see Acts 2:1–13).

God's story doesn't change. Whether then or now, He knows those He loves (see John 10:14–15). He calls us by name.

—*Amy Boucher Pye*

We've Got the Power

ROMANS 7:14–25

*Since we live by the Spirit, let us
keep in step with the Spirit.*
—GALATIANS 5:25

When I realized I had accidently tapped the start button on the empty coffee maker, I ran back to the kitchen. Unplugging the appliance, I grabbed the handle of the carafe and touched the bottom of it to see if it was still hot. It was! It burned my fingertips.

As my husband nursed my wound, I shook my head. "I honestly do not know why I touched it," I told him.

My response reminded me of Paul's reaction to a more serious issue in Scripture—the nature of sin.

The apostle admits to not knowing why he does things he knows he shouldn't do and doesn't want to do (Romans 7:15). He acknowledges the real, complex war constantly being waged in our heart in the struggle against sin (vv. 15–23). Confessing his weaknesses, he offers hope for victory now and forever (vv. 24–25).

When we surrender to Christ, He gives us His Holy Spirit, who empowers us to choose to do right (8:8–10). When we do, we can avoid the searing sin that separates us from the abundant life God promises those who love Him.

—*Xochitl Dixon*

Ending Envy

ROMANS 6:11–14

*Let each one examine his own work,
and then he will have rejoicing in
himself alone, and not in another.*
—GALATIANS 6:4 (NKJV)

The famous French artist Edgar Degas is remembered worldwide for his paintings of ballerinas. Less known is the envy he expressed of his friend and artistic rival Édouard Manet, another master painter. Said Degas of Manet, "Everything he does he always hits off straightaway, while I take endless pains and never get it right."

It's a curious emotion, envy—listed by the apostle Paul among the worst traits, as bad as "every kind of wickedness, sin, greed, hate, envy, murder, quarreling, deception, malicious behavior, and gossip" (Romans 1:29 NLT). It results from foolish thinking, Paul writes—the result of worshiping idols instead of worshiping God (v. 28).

Yet there's a remedy for envy. Turn back to God. "Offer every part of yourself to him," Paul wrote (Romans 6:13)—your work and life especially. In another of his letters Paul wrote, "Let each one examine his own work, and then he will have rejoicing in himself alone, and not in another" (Galatians 6:4 NKJV).

Thank God for His blessings—not just things, but for the freedom of His grace. Seeing our own God-given gifts, we find contentment again.

—*Patricia Raybon*

A Song in the Night

PSALM 42:1–11

If we hope for what we do not yet have,
we wait for it patiently.
—ROMANS 8:25

My father's life was one of longing. He longed for wholeness, even as Parkinson's disease gradually crippled his mind and body. He longed for peace but was tormented by the deep pain of depression. He longed to feel loved and cherished but often felt utterly alone.

He found himself less alone when he read Psalm 42, his favorite psalm. Like him, the psalmist knew a desperate longing for healing (vv. 1–2). And the psalmist knew a sadness that seemed never to go away (v. 3), robbing him of times of pure joy (v. 6). Like my dad, the psalmist felt abandoned by God and asked, "Why?" (v. 9).

As the words of the psalm washed over him, assuring him he was not alone, Dad sensed the beginnings of a quiet peace. A tender voice surrounded him—assuring him that although the waves still crashed over him, he was dearly loved (v. 8).

Hearing that quiet song of love was enough. Enough for my dad to quietly cling to glimmers of hope, love, and joy. And enough for him to wait patiently for the day his longings would finally be satisfied (vv. 5, 11).

—*Monica Brands*

An Angry God?

EXODUS 33:18-19, 34:1-7

*The LORD, the LORD, the compassionate
and gracious God, slow to anger,
abounding in love and faithfulness.*
—EXODUS 34:6

When I studied Greek and Roman mythology in college, I was struck by how easily angered the mythological gods were in the stories. The people on the receiving end of their anger found their lives destroyed, sometimes on a whim.

I was quick to scoff, wondering how anyone could believe in gods like that. But then I asked myself, *Is my view of the God who actually exists much different? Don't I view Him as easily angered whenever I doubt Him?* Sadly, yes.

That's why I appreciate Moses's request of God to "show me your glory" (Exodus 33:18). Having been chosen to lead people who often grumbled against him, Moses wanted to know that God would indeed help him. Moses's request was rewarded by a demonstration of God's glory. God announced to Moses His name and characteristics. He is "the compassionate and gracious God, slow to anger, abounding in love and faithfulness" (34:6).

We can see God and His glory in His patience with us, the encouraging word of a friend, a beautiful sunset, or—best of all—the whisper of God's grace inside of us.

—*Linda Washington*

Something's Wrong

PSALM 34:11–18

*The LORD is close to the brokenhearted and
saves those who are crushed in spirit.*
—PSALM 34:18

The morning after our son, Allen, was born, the doctor sat down next to me and said, "Something's wrong." Our son, so perfect on the outside, had a life-threatening birth defect and needed to be flown to a hospital 700 miles away for immediate surgery.

When the doctor tells you something is wrong with your child, your life changes. Fear of what lies ahead can crush your spirit, and you stumble along, desperate for God to strengthen you.

Then my husband, Hiram, arrived and heard the news. After the doctor left, Hiram said, "Jolene, let's pray." He took my hand. "Thank you, Father, for giving Allen to us. He's yours, God, not ours. You loved him before we knew him, and he belongs to you. Be with him when we can't. Amen."

Hiram is often a man of few words. But on a day when my heart was broken, my spirit crushed, and my faith gone, God gave Hiram strength to pray the words I couldn't pray. Clinging to my husband's hand, in deep silence and through many tears, I sensed that God was very near.

—*Jolene Philo*

Keep On Going

EXODUS 10:21–29

*By faith [Moses] left Egypt, not fearing
the king's anger.* —HEBREWS 11:27

Working in the corporate world allowed me to inter-
act with many talented and levelheaded people.
However, one project led by an out-of-town supervi-
sor was an exception. Regardless of our team's progress, this manager harshly criticized our work and
demanded more effort during each weekly status call.

These run-ins left me discouraged and fearful. At
times, I wanted to quit.

Moses may have felt that way when he encoun-
tered Pharaoh during the plague of darkness. God
had hurled eight other epic disasters at Egypt, and
Pharaoh finally exploded, "[Moses,] get out of my
sight! . . . The day you see my face you will die"
(Exodus 10:28).

Despite this threat, Moses was used by God to
free the Israelites from Pharaoh's control. "[By faith]
Moses left the land of Egypt, not fearing the king's anger. He kept right on going because he kept his eyes on
the one who is invisible" (Hebrews 11:27 NLT). Moses
overcame Pharaoh by believing that God would keep
His promise of deliverance (Exodus 3:17).

Today, we can rely on the promise that God is
with us in every situation, supporting us through His
Holy Spirit. The Spirit provides the courage we need
to keep going.

—*Jennifer Benson Schuldt*

A Good Ending

REVELATION 22:1–5

*The throne of God and of the Lamb will be
in the city, and his servants will serve him.
They will see his face.*
—REVELATION 22:3–4

As the lights dimmed and we prepared to watch
Apollo 13, my friend said under his breath, "Shame
they all died." I watched the movie about the 1970
spaceflight with apprehension, waiting for tragedy
to strike. Only near the closing credits did I realize
I'd been duped. Although the astronauts faced many
hardships, they made it home alive.

In Christ, we can know the end of the story—that
we too will make it home alive. By that I mean we
will live forever with our heavenly Father. The book
of Revelation tells us the Lord will create a "new
heaven and a new earth" (21:1, 5). In the new city,
the Lord God will welcome His people to live with
Him, without fear and without the night. Knowing
the end of the story gives us hope.

This can transform times of extreme difficulty,
such as when people face the loss of a loved one.
Although we recoil at the thought of dying, we can
embrace the promise of eternity. We long for the city
where we'll live forever by God's light (22:5).

—*Amy Boucher Pye*

Goodbye for Now

1 THESSALONIANS 4:13–18

You do not grieve like the rest of mankind,
who have no hope.
—1 THESSALONIANS 4:13

My granddaughter Allyssa and I have a regular "good-bye" routine. We wrap our arms around each other and loudly wail with dramatic sobs for about twenty seconds. Then we step back and casually say, "See ya," and turn away. Despite our silly practice, we always expect that we will see each other again—soon.

Sometimes the pain of separation from those we care about can be difficult. When Paul said farewell to the elders from Ephesus, "They all wept. . . . What grieved them most was [Paul's] statement that they would never see his face again" (Acts 20:37–38).

The deepest sorrow, however, comes when death means we say goodbye for the last time in this life. That separation seems unthinkable. How can we face the heartbreak?

Still . . . we don't grieve like those who have no hope. Paul writes of a future reunion for those who "believe that Jesus died and rose again" (1 Thessalonians 4:13–18). He declares: "The Lord himself will come down from heaven," and a great reunion will take place.

And best of all, we'll be forever with Jesus.

—*Cindy Hess Kasper*

Glory to the Grower

MARK 4:26–29

So neither the one who plants nor the one
who waters is anything, but only God,
who makes things grow.
—1 CORINTHIANS 3:7

One day, I noticed an unexpected splash of yellow to the right of our driveway. Six stalks of daffodils, sandwiched between two large stones, bloomed bright and tall. Because I hadn't planted the bulbs, I couldn't figure out how or why the flowers had sprouted in our yard.

Jesus illustrated a mystery of spiritual growth in the parable of the growing seed. He compares the kingdom of God to a farmer scattering seed on the ground (Mark 4:26). The one who scattered the seed may have done what he could to care for the soil. But Jesus said the seed sprouted whether or not that man did anything (vv. 27–29).

The maturing of the seeds in Jesus's parable, like the blooming of my daffodils, occurred in God's time and because of God's growing power. Whether we're considering personal spiritual growth or God's plan to expand the church until Jesus returns, the Lord's mysterious ways aren't dependent on our abilities or understanding of His works. Still, God invites us to know, serve, and praise the Grower, reaping the benefits of the spiritual maturity He cultivates in and through us.

—*Xochitl Dixon*

Removing Barriers

PHILEMON 1:8–16

*He is very dear to me but even dearer to you, both
as a fellow man and as a brother in the Lord.*
—PHILEMON 1:16

I saw Mary every Tuesday when I visited a home that helps former prisoners reintegrate into society. My life looked different from hers: fresh out of jail, fighting addictions, separated from her son. She lived on the edge of society.

Like Mary, Onesimus knew what it meant to live on the edge of society. As a slave, Onesimus had apparently wronged his Christian master, Philemon, and was now in prison. While there, he met Paul and came to faith in Christ (v. 10). Though now a changed man, Onesimus was still a slave. Paul sent him back to Philemon with a letter urging him to receive Onesimus "no longer as a slave, but . . . as a dear brother" (Philemon 1:16).

Philemon had a choice: He could treat Onesimus as his slave or welcome him as a brother in Christ. I also had a choice with Mary. As she was my sister in the Lord, we were privileged to walk together in our faith journey.

The walls of socioeconomic status, class, or cultural differences can separate us. The gospel removes those barriers, changing our lives and our relationships forever.

—*Karen Wolfe*

Love and Peace

PSALM 16

You will not abandon me to the realm of the dead.
. . . You make known to me the path of life;
you will fill me with joy in your presence.
—PSALM 16:10–11

It always amazes me the way peace—powerful, un-explainable peace (Philippians 4:7)—can somehow fill our hearts even in our deepest grief. I experienced this at my father's memorial service. As a long line of sympathetic acquaintances passed by offering their condolences, I was relieved to see a good high school friend. Without a word, he simply wrapped me in a long bear hug. His quiet understanding flooded me with the first feelings of peace within grief that difficult day, a powerful reminder that I wasn't as alone as I felt.

The kind of peace and joy God brings into our lives isn't caused by a choice to stoically stomp down the pain during hard times. David implies that it's more like a gift we can't help but experience when we take refuge in our good God (Psalm 16:1–2).

The life God has given us—even in its pain—is still beautiful and good (vv. 6–8). And we can surrender to His loving arms that tenderly carry us through our pain into a peace and joy that even death can never quench (v. 11).

—*Monica Brands*

Beyond the Stars

PSALM 8:1–9

You have set your glory in the heavens.
—PSALM 8:1

In 2011, the National Aeronautics and Space Administration celebrated thirty years of space research. In those three decades, shuttles carried more than 355 people into space and helped construct the International Space Station. After retiring five shuttles, NASA has now shifted its focus to deep-space exploration.

The human race has invested massive amounts of time and money, with some astronauts even sacrificing their lives, to study the immensity of the universe. Yet the evidence of God's majesty stretches far beyond what we can measure.

When we consider the Sculptor and Sustainer of the universe, who knows each star by name (Isaiah 40:26), we can understand why the psalmist David praises His greatness (Psalm 8:1). The Lord's fingerprints are on "the moon and the stars, which [He] set in place" (v. 3). The Maker of the heavens and the earth reigns above all, yet He remains near all His beloved children, caring for each intimately and personally (v. 4).

As we study our star-spattered night skies, our Creator invites us to seek Him with passion and persistence. He hears every prayer and song of praise flowing from our lips.

—*Xochitl Dixon*

A Friend's Comfort

JOB 2:7–13

*No one said a word to him, because they
saw how great his suffering was.*
—JOB 2:13

A mom was surprised to see her daughter muddy
from the waist down when she walked in the door
after school. Her daughter explained that a friend
had fallen into a mud puddle. While a classmate ran
to get help, the little girl felt sorry for her friend. So,
she went over and sat in the mud puddle with her
friend until a teacher arrived.

When Job experienced the devastating loss of
his children and became afflicted with painful sores
on his entire body, his suffering was overwhelming.
Three of his friends wanted to comfort him. "They
began to weep aloud, and they tore their robes and
sprinkled dust on their heads. Then they sat on the
ground with him for seven days and seven nights. No
one said a word to him, because they saw how great
his suffering was" (Job 2:12–13).

Job's friends initially showed remarkable understanding. Although they later gave Job some poor
advice, their first response was good by showing true
empathy.

Often the best thing we can do when comforting
a hurting friend is to sit with them in their suffering.
—*Lisa Samra*

Like a Little Child

MARK 10:13–16

*"Let the little children come to me,
and do not hinder them."*
—MARK 10:14

The little girl moved joyfully and gracefully to the music of praise. She was the only one in the aisle, but that didn't keep her from spinning and waving her arms to the music. Her mother, a smile on her lips, didn't try to stop her.

My heart lifted as I watched, and I longed to join her—but didn't. I'd long ago lost the unselfconscious expression of joy and wonder of my childhood. Even though we are meant to grow and mature and put childish ways behind us, we were never meant to lose the joy and wonder, especially in our relationship with God.

When Jesus lived on Earth, He welcomed little children to Him and often referred to them in His teaching (Matthew 11:25; 18:3; 21:16). On one occasion, He rebuked His disciples for attempting to keep parents from bringing their children to Him for a blessing, saying, "Let the little children come to me, . . . for the kingdom of God belongs to such as these" (Mark 10:14).

Childlike wonder and joy open our hearts to be more receptive to Him. He is waiting for us to run into His arms.

—*Alyson Kieda*

Will You Come Back?

HOSEA 3:1–5

*Love [your wife] as the LORD loves the Israelites,
though they turn to other gods.*
—HOSEA 3:1

Ron and Nancy's marriage was deteriorating rapidly.
She had an affair, but after some time she admitted
her sin to God. She knew what He wanted her to
do, but it was difficult. She shared the truth with
Ron. Instead of asking for a divorce, Ron chose to
give Nancy a chance to win his trust back, and God
restored their marriage.

Ron's actions are a picture of God's love and forgiveness. The prophet Hosea understood this well.
God commanded him to marry an unfaithful woman
to show Israel their status of unfaithfulness before
Him (Hosea 1). If that wasn't heartbreaking enough,
when Hosea's wife left him, God told him to ask her
to come back. He said, "Show your love to your wife
again, though she is loved by another man and is an
adulteress" (3:1).

Just as Hosea loved his unfaithful wife, pursued
her, and sacrificed for her, so God loved His people.
His righteous anger and jealousy were motivated by
His great love.

God longs for us today to be near Him. As we
come to Him in faith, we can trust that in Him we
will find complete fulfillment.

—*Estera Pirosca Escobar*

From Empty to Full

2 KINGS 4:1–7

*When all the jars were full, she said to
her son, "Bring me another one."*
—2 KINGS 4:6

A children's book tells the story of a poor country boy who took off his cap to honor King Derwin. An identical hat appeared on his head, inciting the king's anger for apparent disrespect. Bartholomew removed hat after hat, but each time, a new one appeared. The hats grew increasingly fancy. The 500th hat was the envy of King Derwin, who pardoned Bartholomew and purchased the hat for 500 pieces of gold. Bareheaded now, he walked home with freedom and money to support his family.

A widow came to Elisha in financial distress, fearing her children would be sold into slavery to pay her debts (2 Kings 4). She had no assets other than a jar of oil. God multiplied that oil to fill enough borrowed jars to settle the debts plus care for their daily needs (v. 7).

God provided financially for the widow in much the same way He provides salvation. I am bankrupted by sin, but Jesus paid my debt—and offers me eternal life as well! Without Jesus, we have no means to pay our King for our offenses against Him. With Jesus, we have life abundant forever.

—*Kirsten Holmberg*

Created for Relationship

GENESIS 2:15–25

The LORD God said, "It is not good for the man to be alone. I will make a helper suitable for him."

—GENESIS 2:18

There's a growing "rent-a-family" industry in many countries to meet the needs of lonely people. Some use the service to maintain appearances, so that at a social event they can appear to have a happy family. Some hire actors to impersonate estranged relatives, so they can feel, if briefly, a familial connection they long for.

Humans are created for relationship. In the creation story found in Genesis, God looks at each thing He has made and sees that it's "very good" (1:31). But when God considers Adam, He says, "It is not good for the man to be alone" (2:18). The human needed another human.

The Bible tells us where to find relationships: among Jesus's followers. Jesus, at His death, told His friend John to consider Christ's mother as his own. They would be family to each other even after Jesus was gone (John 19:26–27). And Paul instructed believers to treat others like parents and siblings (1 Timothy 5:1–2). God designed the church as one of the best places to find community.

Thanks be to God, who has made us for relationship and given us His people to be our family!

—*Amy Peterson*

Spiritually Exhausted?

1 KINGS 19:1–9

An angel touched him and said,
"Get up and eat."
—1 KINGS 19:5

"Emotionally, we've sometimes worked a full day in one hour," Zack Eswine writes in his book *The Imperfect Pastor*. He was referring to the burdens pastors frequently carry, but it's true for any of us. Weighty emotions and responsibilities can leave us exhausted.

In 1 Kings 19, Elijah was depleted. Queen Jezebel threatened to put him to death (vv. 1–2) after she discovered he had the prophets of Baal killed (see 18:16–40). Elijah was so afraid he ran away and prayed he would die (19:3–4).

In his distress, he lay down. An angel touched him twice and told him to "get up and eat" (vv. 5, 7). After the second time, Elijah was strengthened by the food God provided, and he traveled forty days until he came to a cave (vv. 8–9). There, the Lord appeared (vv. 9–18), and he was refreshed and able to continue God's work.

Sometimes we too need to be encouraged in the Lord—by talking with another believer, through a worship song, or time in prayer and God's Word.

Feeling exhausted? Give your burdens to God today and be refreshed!

—*Julie Schwab*

Second Chances

RUTH 4:12–17

"The LORD bless him!" Naomi said to her
daughter-in-law. "He has not stopped showing
his kindness to the living and the dead."
—RUTH 2:20

By making wrong decisions, Linda had ended up in prison in a country not her own. When she was set free after six years, she had nowhere to go. She thought her life was over! But her family gathered money to buy her ticket home, and a kind couple offered her lodging, food, and a helping hand. Linda was so touched by their kindness that she listened as they told her the good news of a loving God who wants to give her a second chance.

Linda reminds me of Naomi, a widow who lost her husband and two sons in a foreign land and thought her life was over (See Ruth 1). However, the Lord hadn't forgotten Naomi, and through the love of her daughter-in-law Ruth and the compassion of godly Boaz, Naomi saw God's love and was given a second chance (4:13–17).

God still cares, and He wants to give us a fresh start. We need to see God's hand in our everyday lives and realize He never stops showing us His kindness.
—*Keila Ochoa*

Love Changes Us

ACTS 9:1–22

*At once he began to preach in the synagogues
that Jesus is the Son of God.*
—ACTS 9:20

Before I met Jesus, I'd been wounded so deeply that I avoided close relationships in fear of being hurt more. My mom remained my closest friend, until I married Alan. Seven years later and on the verge of divorce, I toted our kindergartener, Xavier, into church. I sat near the exit door—afraid to trust but desperate for help.

Thankfully, believers reached out, prayed for our family, and taught me how to nurture a relationship with God. Over time, the love of Christ and His followers changed me.

Two years later, Alan, Xavier, and I were baptized. Sometime later, my mom said, "You're different. Tell me more about Jesus." Soon she too trusted Christ as her Savior.

Jesus transforms lives . . . lives like Saul's, one of the most feared persecutors of the church (Acts 9:1–5). Others helped Saul learn more about Jesus (vv. 17–19). His transformation added to the credibility of his Spirit-empowered teaching (vv. 20–22).

As people notice how Christ's love changes us, we'll have opportunities to tell them what He did for us.

—*Xochitl Dixon*

Waiting in Anticipation

PSALM 130:1–6

*I wait for the Lord more than
watchmen wait for the morning, more
than watchmen wait for the morning.*

—PSALM 130:6

Every May Day in Oxford, England, an early morning crowd gathers to welcome spring. At 6:00, the Magdalen College Choir sings from the top of Magdalen Tower. Thousands wait in anticipation for the dark night to be broken by song and the ringing of bells.

Like those revelers, I often wait. I wait for answers to prayers or guidance from the Lord. I'm learning to wait expectantly. In Psalm 130 the psalmist writes of being in deep distress as he faces a situation that feels like the blackest of nights. He chooses to trust God and stay alert like a guard on duty charged with announcing daybreak: "I wait for the Lord more than watchmen wait for the morning" (v. 6).

The anticipation of God's faithfulness breaking through the darkness gives the psalmist hope. Based on the promises of God, that hope allows him to keep waiting although he has yet to see the first rays of light.

Be encouraged if you're enduring a dark night. Dawn is coming! In the meantime, don't give up hope. Keep watching for the deliverance of the Lord. He will be faithful.

—*Lisa Samra*

Anonymous Kindness

MATTHEW 6:1–4

"When you give to the needy, do not let your left hand know what your right hand is doing."
—MATTHEW 6:3

When I first graduated from college, I adopted a strict grocery budget—twenty-five dollars a week. One day at the grocery store, I suspected my items cost slightly more than my remaining money. "Stop when we reach twenty dollars," I told the cashier, and I was able to purchase everything I'd selected but a bag of peppers.

As I was about to drive home, a man stopped by my car. "Here's your peppers, ma'am," he said, handing the bag to me. Before I had time to thank him, he was already walking away.

The simple goodness of this kind act brings to mind Jesus's words in Matthew 6. Criticizing those who made a show of giving to the needy (v. 2), Jesus taught His disciples a different way. He urged that giving should be done so secretly it's like the left hand isn't even aware the right is giving (v. 3)!

Giving should never be about us. We give because of what our generous God has so lavishly given us (2 Corinthians 9:6–11). As we give quietly and generously, we reflect who He is—and God receives the thanksgiving (v. 11).

—*Monica Brands*

Basin of Love

JOHN 13:1–7

After that, he poured water into a basin
and began to wash his disciples' feet.
—JOHN 13:5

Sometimes we miss or overlook the "stuff" of life simply because we can't take it all in. And sometimes we don't see what's been there all along.

It was like that for me as I recently read again the account of Jesus washing His disciples' feet. The story is a familiar one, for it is often read during Passion Week. That our Savior and King would stoop to cleanse the feet of His disciples awes us. In Jesus's day, even Jewish servants were spared this task because it was seen as beneath them. But what I hadn't noticed before was that Jesus, who was both man and God, washed the feet of Judas. Even though He knew Judas would betray Him, as we see in John 13:11, Jesus still humbled himself and washed Judas's feet.

Love poured out in a basin of water—love that He shared even with the one who would betray Him. As we ponder the events of this week leading up to the celebration of Jesus's resurrection, may we too be given the gift of humility so we can extend Jesus's love to our friends and any enemies.

—*Amy Boucher Pye*

The Greatest Gift

JOHN 1:43–51

We found . . . Jesus of Nazareth,
the son of Joseph.
—JOHN 1:45

Over the years, my friend Barbara has given me countless encouraging cards and thoughtful presents. After I told her I'd received Jesus as my Savior, she handed me a great gift—my first Bible. She said, "You can grow closer to God . . . by meeting with Him daily, reading Scripture, praying, and trusting and obeying Him." My life changed when Barbara invited me to get to know God better.

Barbara reminds me of the apostle Philip. After Jesus invited Philip to follow Him (John 1:43), the apostle immediately told his friend Nathanael that Jesus was "the one Moses wrote about in the Law" (v. 45). When Nathanael doubted, Philip didn't argue, criticize, or give up on his friend. He simply invited him to meet Jesus face to face. "Come and see," he said (v. 46).

The Holy Spirit initiates our intimate relationship with God and then lives in all who respond in faith. He enables us to know Him personally and to invite others to encounter Him daily through His Spirit and the Scriptures. An invitation to know Jesus better is a great gift to receive and give.

—*Xochitl Dixon*

Another View

JOB 36:1–25

Everyone has seen these things,
though only from a distance.
—JOB 36:25 (NLT)

Facing unexpected circumstances with loved ones is difficult, and sometimes we feel powerless in not being able to answer their question "Why?" In our desperation, we rifle through our thoughts in an attempt to at least ease their pain. But those who've been through deep waters of trial can attest that the silence of a friend is more golden than misspoken words, especially when the attempt to form answers only produces more pain.

The story of Job serves to prove this eternal truth: *We can't answer for God.* The working of His hands is simply beyond our finite understanding (Romans 11:33–34)—something we find difficult to accept.

Job's friends spoke a measure of truth, but their understanding was limited.

Job's friend Elihu, for example, though he did more than just try to get Job to repent of some unconfessed sin as others had done, still didn't get the full picture. Job's suffering wasn't simply about his relationship with God.

Times of suffering do reveal our level of dependency on God. But the journey through deep waters also becomes an opportunity for revelation and growth—for ourselves and others.

—*Regina Franklin*

What God Sees

2 CHRONICLES 16:7–9

*The eyes of the L*ORD *range throughout the
earth to strengthen those whose hearts
are fully committed to him.*
—2 CHRONICLES 16:9

One morning I was surprised to find a bald eagle boldly balanced on a high branch in the wilderness area behind our house, surveying the terrain as if the entire expanse belonged to him. Likely he was looking for "breakfast." His all-inclusive gaze seemed regal.

In 2 Chronicles 16, Hanani (God's prophet) informed a king that his actions were under a royal gaze. He told Asa, king of Judah, "You relied on the king of Aram and not on the LORD your God" (v. 7). Then Hanani explained, "The eyes of the LORD range throughout the earth to strengthen those whose hearts are fully committed to him" (v. 9). Because of Asa's misplaced dependence, he would always be at war.

We might get the false idea that God watches our every move so He can pounce on us. But Hanani's words focus on the positive: Our God continually watches and waits for us to call on Him when we're in need.

Like my backyard eagle, how might God's eyes be roaming our world—even now—looking to find faithfulness? How might He provide the hope and help we need?

—*Elisa Morgan*

What Remains in the Eye

PSALM 104:24–35

How many are your works, Lord!
—PSALM 104:24

The hummingbird gets its name from the hum made by its rapidly beating wings. It is known as the "flower-kisser" in Portuguese and "flying jewels" in Spanish. One of my favorite names for this bird is *biulu*, "what remains in the eye" (Mexican Zapotec). Once you see a hummingbird, you'll never forget it.

G. K. Chesterton wrote, "The world will never starve for want of wonders, but only for want of wonder." The hummingbird is one of those wonders. What is so fascinating about these tiny creatures? Maybe it is their small size (averaging two to three inches) or the speed of their wings, which can flap from 50 to 200 times per second.

The writer of Psalm 104 was captivated by nature's beauty. After describing creation's wonders like the cedars of Lebanon and wild donkeys, he sings, "May the Lord rejoice in his works" (v. 31). He prays, "May my meditation be pleasing to him" (v. 34).

Nature has plenty of things that "remain in the eye" because of their beauty. We can observe, rejoice, and thank God as we contemplate His works and recapture the wonder.

—*Keila Ochoa*

We Need Each Other

COLOSSIANS 3:12–17

*Let the peace of Christ rule in your hearts, since as
members of one body you were called to peace.*
—COLOSSIANS 3:15

While on a hike with my kids, we discovered a light,
springy green plant growing in small clumps on the
trail. The plant is commonly called deer moss, but it's
not actually a moss. It's a lichen. A lichen is a fungus
and an alga growing together in a mutualistic relationship in which both organisms benefit from each
other. Neither the fungus nor the alga can survive on
its own, but together they form a hardy plant that
can live for up to 4,500 years.

The relationship between the fungus and the alga
reminds me of our human relationships. We rely on
each other. To grow and flourish, we need to be in
relationship with each other.

Paul describes how our relationships should look.
We are to clothe ourselves with "compassion, kindness, humility, gentleness and patience" (Colossians
3:12). We ought to forgive each other and live in
peace "as members of one body" (v. 15).

It's not always easy to live in peace with others.
But when the Spirit empowers us in our relationships,
our love for each other points to Christ (John 13:35)
and brings glory to God.

—*Amy Peterson*

Son Followers

LUKE 8:11–15

The seed on good soil stands for those with
a noble and good heart, who hear the word,
retain it, and by persevering produce a crop.
—LUKE 8:15

Sunflowers sprout in a carefree manner all over the world. Pollinated by bees, the plants spring up in so many places. To produce a harvest, however, sunflowers need good soil to produce tasty sunflower seeds, pure oil, and also a livelihood for hard-working sunflower growers.

We also need "good soil" for spiritual growth (Luke 8:15). As Jesus taught in His parable of the farmer scattering seed, God's Word can sprout even in rocky or thorny soil (see vv. 6–7). It only thrives, however, in the soil of "honest, good-hearted people who hear God's word, cling to it, and patiently produce a huge harvest" (v. 15 NLT).

Young sunflowers are patient in their growth. Following the sun's movement, they turn sunward daily in a process called heliotropism. Mature sunflowers turn eastward permanently, warming the face of the flower and increasing visits from pollinator bees. This in turn produces a greater harvest.

As with those who care for sunflowers, we can provide a rich medium for God's Word to grow by clinging to His Word and following after His Son. It's a daily process. May we follow the Son and grow.
—*Patricia Raybon*

Of Saints and Sinners

LUKE 22:54–62

The third time [Jesus] said to him, "Simon son of John, do you love me?" . . . [Peter] said, "Lord, you know all things; you know that I love you."
—JOHN 21:17

Before she followed in John the Baptist's footsteps by living in the desert, Mary of Egypt (c. AD 344–421) spent her youth pursuing illicit pleasures. At the height of her sordid career, she journeyed to Jerusalem in an attempt to corrupt pilgrims. Instead, she experienced deep conviction of her sins and thereafter lived a life of repentance and wilderness solitude. Mary's radical transformation illustrates the magnitude of God's grace and the restoring power of the cross.

Peter denied Jesus three times. Only hours before, Peter had declared his willingness to die for Jesus (Luke 22:33), so the realization of his failure was a crushing blow (vv. 61–62). After Jesus's death and resurrection, Peter was fishing when Jesus appeared. Jesus allowed Peter to declare his love for Him three times—one for each denial (John 21:1–3). With each declaration, Jesus charged Peter to care for His people (vv. 15–17). Because of this stunning display of grace, Peter played a key role in building the church.

Each of our stories could begin with a litany of our failures. But God's grace always allows for redemption and a far different ending.

—*Remi Oyedele*

Rooted in God

JEREMIAH 17:5–8

*They will be like a tree planted by the water
that sends out its roots by the stream.*
—JEREMIAH 17:8

When friends planted wisteria near their fence, they looked forward to the lavender blossoms it would produce. For two decades the wisteria flourished. But suddenly it died. Their neighbors had used some weed killer on the other side of the fence. The poison seeped into the wisteria's roots and the tree perished—or so my friends thought. To their surprise, the following year some new shoots came through the ground.

The prophet Jeremiah gives us the image of trees flourishing and perishing as he describes God's people who either trust in the Lord or ignore His ways. Those who follow God will send their roots into soil near water and bear fruit (Jeremiah 17:8), but those who follow their own hearts will be like a bush in the desert (vv. 5–6). The prophet says that those who rely on the true and living God would be "a tree planted by the water" (v. 8).

We know that the "Father is the gardener" (John 15:1) and that in Him we can trust and have confidence (Jeremiah 17:7). May we follow Him with our whole heart as we bear fruit that lasts.

—*Amy Boucher Pye*

Celebrating Creativity

GENESIS 1:1–21

*God said, "Let the water teem
with living creatures."*
—GENESIS 1:20

A rarely seen jellyfish waltzed with the currents, four thousand feet deep in the ocean near Baja, California. Its body shone with fluorescent shades of blue, purple, and pink, bright against the backdrop of black water. Elegant tentacles waved gracefully with each pulsing of its bell-shaped hood. As I watched the amazing footage of the Halitrephes maasi jellyfish on a *National Geographic* video, I reflected on how God chose the specific design of this beautiful, gelatinous creature—and the other 2,000 types of jellyfish that scientists have identified.

It should make us contemplate the profound truth revealed in Genesis 1. Our amazing God brought forth light and life into the creatively diverse world He crafted with the power of His word. He designed "the great creatures of the sea and every living thing with which the water teems" (Genesis 1:21).

God also intentionally sculpted each person in the world, giving purpose to every day of our lives before we drew our first breaths (Psalm 139:13–16). As we celebrate the Lord's creativity, we can also rejoice over the many ways He helps us imagine and create with Him and for His glory.

—Xochitl Dixon

A Hopeful Lament

LAMENTATIONS 3:49–68

I called on your name, LORD,
from the depths of the pit.
—LAMENTATIONS 3:55

To visit Clifton Heritage National Park in Nassau, Bahamas, is to revisit a tragic era in history. Near the water's edge, stone steps lead up a cliff. Slaves brought to the Bahamas by ship in the eighteenth century would ascend these steps, often leaving family behind and entering a life of inhumane treatment. At the top, there's a memorial to those slaves. Cedar trees have been carved into the shapes of women looking out to sea toward the homeland and family members they've lost. Each sculpture is scarred with marks of the slave captain's whip.

They are reminders of the injustices of our world, and they call on us to lament those cruelties. Lamenting, being honest with God about trouble, should be familiar to Christians. Forty percent of the Psalms are laments, and in Lamentations, God's people cry out to Him after their city has been destroyed by invaders (3:55).

Ultimately, lament is hopeful: when we lament what is not right, we call ourselves to be active in seeking change.

The sculpture garden in Nassau has been named "Genesis." The place of lament is recognized as the place of new beginnings.

—*Amy Peterson*

What Lasts Forever?

PSALM 102:25–28

"You remain the same, and your years will never end."
—PSALM 102:27

My friend, who had endured many difficulties, wrote, "As I reflect on the past four semesters of student life, so many things have changed. . . . It is really scary. Nothing stays forever."

Indeed, many things can happen in two years. Good or bad, a life-altering experience may be lurking just around the corner, waiting to pounce! What a comfort to know that our loving heavenly Father does not change.

The psalmist says, "You remain the same, and your years will never end" (Psalm 102:27). God is forever loving, just, and wise. As Bible teacher Arthur W. Pink states: "Whatever the attributes of God were before the universe was called into existence, they are precisely the same now, and will remain so forever."

In our changing circumstances, we can always be assured that our good God will always be consistent to His character.

It may seem that nothing lasts forever, but our God will remain consistently good to those who are His own.

—*Poh Fang Chia*

The Best Gift

LUKE 11:9–13

"Seek and you will find."
—LUKE 11:9

When I was packing up to go home to London, my mother offered me a gift—one of her rings I had long admired. Surprised, I asked, "What's this for?" She replied, "I think you should enjoy it now. Why wait until I die?" With a smile I received her unexpected gift, an early inheritance that brings me joy.

Mom gave me a material gift, but Jesus promises that His Father gives us a gift of utmost importance: the Holy Spirit (Luke 11:13). Through the gift of the Holy Spirit (John 16:13), we can experience hope, love, joy, and peace even in times of trouble—and we can share these gifts with others.

Growing up, we may have had parents who were unable to love and care for us fully. Or we may have had mothers and fathers who were shining examples of sacrificial love. Or our experience may have been somewhere in between. Whatever we've known with our earthly parents, we can hold onto the promise that our heavenly Father loves us unceasingly. He gave His children the gift of the Holy Spirit.

—*Amy Boucher Pye*

Washed Clean

JEREMIAH 2:13, 20–22

The blood of Jesus, [God's] Son,
purifies us from all sin.
—1 JOHN 1:7

I couldn't believe it. A blue gel pen had hidden itself among my white towels and survived the washing machine, only to explode in the dryer. Ugly dark stains ruined my towels.

As I reluctantly consigned the towels to the rag pile, I was reminded of Jeremiah's lament describing the damaging effects of sin. By rejecting God and turning to idols (Jeremiah 2:13), Jeremiah declared that the people of Israel had caused a permanent stain in their relationship with God: " 'Although you wash yourself . . . , the stain of your guilt is still before me,' declares the Sovereign LORD" (v. 22). They were powerless to undo the damage.

On our own, it is impossible to remove the stain of our sin. But Jesus has done what we could not. Through the power of His death and resurrection, He "purifies [believers] from all sin" (1 John 1:7).

There's no damage from sin that Jesus can't totally remove. God can wash away the effects of sin for anyone willing to return to Him (v. 9). Through Christ, we can live each day in freedom and hope.

—*Lisa Samra*

Wisdom's Source

1 KINGS 3:16–28

Give your servant a discerning heart.
—1 KINGS 3:9

A man filed a lawsuit against a woman, claiming she had his dog. In court, the woman insisted it was her dog. The real owner's identity was revealed when the judge released the animal in the courtroom. Tail wagging, it ran to the man!

Solomon needed to settle a tough question of true ownership. Two women each claimed to be the mother of the same baby boy. After considering both arguments, he requested a sword to divide the infant in half. The real mother begged Solomon to give the baby to the other woman, choosing to save her son's life even if she could not have him (1 Kings 3:26). Solomon had his answer.

If we value wisdom, we can ask God for it, as Solomon did (v. 9). God may answer our request by helping us balance our needs and desires with the interests of others. He may also help us weigh short-term benefits against long-term (sometimes eternal) gains so we can honor Him.

Our God is not only a perfectly wise judge but He is also a personal counselor who is willing to give us godly wisdom (James 1:5).

—*Jennifer Benson Schuldt*

Promise of a Peaceful Home

PSALM 91

He will cover you with his feathers. And under his wings you will find refuge.
—PSALM 91:4

When I think of protection, I don't automatically think of a bird's feathers. Though a bird's feathers might seem like a flimsy form of protection, there is more to them than meets the eye.

Bird feathers are an amazing example of God's design. Feathers have a smooth part and a fluffy part. The smooth part has stiff barbs with tiny hooks that lock together like zipper prongs. The fluffy part keeps a bird warm. Together both parts of the feather protect the bird from wind and rain.

The image of God "[covering] us with his feathers" in Psalm 91:4 and in other Bible passages (see Psalm 17:8) is one of comfort and protection. Like a parent whose arms are a safe place to retreat from a scary storm or a hurt, God's comforting presence provides safety and protection from life's emotional storms.

We can face trouble and heartache without fear as long as our faces are turned toward God. He is our "refuge" (91:2, 4, 9).

—*Linda Washington*

Tested

LUKE 22:15–34

*"I have prayed for you, Simon, that your faith
may not fail. And when you have turned back,
strengthen your brothers."*
—LUKE 22:32

As a kid, when I helped my mom in the kitchen, one
tool that fascinated me was the sifter. As I turned the
handle, I'd watch as the heavy clump of flour met
with the metal pieces and screening to become a soft,
light product.

Luke 22:15–34 records one of Jesus's final interactions
with His disciples before His crucifixion. While
He had already addressed Peter's need to trust God's
will above his own (Matthew 16:23), Jesus knew Peter's
confidence in his own abilities remained an issue.

The disciples began the dangerous game of comparison
(Luke 22:23–34). *Who would ever choose
self-protection over the call of Christ?*

You and I would.

God would not allow spiritual sifting if it were
not transformational. Always, though, we have a
choice as to how we respond to the process. Will we
remain the heavy clump of spiritual knowledge with
a tendency toward pride, or will we be sifted into
the impassioned yet humble messenger of His truth?

As Peter learned, we overcome our spiritual challenges
when we allow God to test and change us—
making us into something He can truly use.

—*Regina Franklin*

The Debt Eraser

PSALM 103:1–12

*As far as the east is from the west, so far has
he removed our transgressions from us.*
—PSALM 103:12

I blinked back tears as I reviewed my medical bill.
Considering my husband's severe cut in salary after
a lengthy unemployment, even paying half of the balance would require years. I prayed before calling the
doctor's office to explain our situation and request
a payment plan.

After leaving me on hold for a short time, the re-
ceptionist informed me the doctor had zeroed out
our account.

I sobbed a thank you as the call ended. The generous gift overwhelmed me with gratitude to God. I
considered saving the bill as a reminder of what God
had done.

My doctor's generosity brought to mind God's
choice to forgive the insurmountable debt of my sins.
Scripture assures us that God is "compassionate and
gracious" and "abounding in love" (Psalm 103:8). He
"does not treat us as our sins deserve" (v. 10). He removes our sins "as far as the east is from the west"
(v. 12) when we repent and accept Christ as our Savior.
His sacrifice erases the debt we once owed. Completely.

In response, we can offer our devoted worship and
grateful affection—living for Him and sharing Him
with others.

—*Xochitl Dixon*

The Good Shepherd

ISAIAH 40:6–11

He tends his flock like a shepherd:
He gathers the lambs in his arms and
carries them close to his heart.

—ISAIAH 40:11

I sat in the hospital room with my husband, waiting anxiously. Our young son was having corrective eye surgery, and I felt the butterflies jostle in my stomach as I fretted and worried. I tried to pray, asking God for peace. As I leafed through my Bible, I thought about Isaiah 40, so I turned to the familiar passage, wondering if anything fresh would strike me.

As I read, I caught my breath, for the words from so many years ago reminded me that the Lord "tends his flock like a shepherd" as He "gathers the lambs in his arms and carries them close to his heart" (v. 11). My anxiety left me. I realized the Lord was taking care of us. *That was just what I needed, Lord,* I breathed silently. I felt enveloped in God's peace during and after the surgery (which thankfully went well).

The Lord promised His people through the prophet Isaiah that He would be their shepherd. We too can know His gentle tending as we tell Him our anxious thoughts. He is our Good Shepherd, holding us close to His heart.

—*Amy Boucher Pye*

The Beauty of Love

PROVERBS 5

May your fountain be blessed.
—PROVERBS 5:18

The "Jarabe Tapatío," the Mexican hat dance, celebrates romance. During this upbeat dance, the man places his sombrero on the ground. At the end, the woman grabs the hat and both hide behind it to seal their romance with a kiss.

This dance reminds me of the importance of faithfulness in marriage. In Proverbs 5, after explaining the high cost of immorality, the writer mentions that marriage is exclusive: "Drink water from your own cistern" (v. 15). While dancing the Jarabe on stage, each person focuses on his or her partner. We can rejoice in undivided commitment to our spouse (v. 18).

Our romance is also being observed. The dancers, while enjoying their partner, know someone is watching. Similarly, "your ways are in full view of the LORD, and he examines all your paths" (v. 21). God wants to protect our marriages by watching over us. We please Him through the loyalty we show each other.

Just like in the Jarabe, there's a rhythm to follow in life. When we keep the beat of our Creator by being faithful to Him—whether married or unmarried—we find blessings and joy.

—*Keila Ochoa*

What's the Best Gift?

2 CHRONICLES 2:1–10

"The temple I am going to build will be great,
because our God is greater than all other gods."
—2 CHRONICLES 2:5

My husband recently celebrated a milestone birthday, one that ends in a zero. I thought hard about the best way to honor him. I discussed many ideas with our children to help me pick the best one. I wanted our gift to be in keeping with how precious he is to our family and to reflect the importance of this milestone in his life.

King Solomon wanted to give God a much greater gift than a "big birthday" would merit. He wished for the temple he was building to be worthy of God's presence. To secure raw materials, he messaged the king of Tyre. In his letter, he remarked that the temple would be great "because our God is greater than all other gods" (2 Chronicles 2:5). He acknowledged that God's goodness far exceeded what could ever be built with human hands, yet they were going about the task out of love and worship.

Our God is indeed great! He's done wondrous things, prompting our hearts to bring Him loving and precious offerings. Solomon knew his gift wouldn't match God's worth, yet he joyfully set his offering before Him. We can too.

—*Kirsten Holmberg*

They Smelled Like Christ

2 CORINTHIANS 2:14–17

*For we are to God the pleasing aroma of Christ
among those who are being saved.*
—2 CORINTHIANS 2:15

Hot and dusty, Bob got off the bus he had ridden to a city far from home. He was tired from a long day of travel and grateful he would be able to have dinner with friends of friends who lived in the area. They welcomed him, and he immediately felt comfortable, safe, and valued.

Later, wondering why he had felt such peace in an unfamiliar place, Bob found an answer in 2 Corinthians. Paul describes people who follow God as having the "pleasing aroma of Christ." "That's it!" Bob said to himself. His hosts had "smelled like" Christ.

When Paul says that God leads His people in Christ's "triumphal procession" spreading the fragrance of His truth, he's referring to an ancient practice. Victorious armies would burn incense as they marched through the streets. For their supporters, the smell brought joy. Similarly, Paul says the people of God carry a pleasing fragrance to those who believe.

Bob is my dad, and that trip took place more than forty years ago, but he's never forgotten it. He's still telling the story of the people who smelled like Christ.
—*Amy Peterson*

Servant's Heart

MARK 9:33–37

*"Anyone who wants to be first must be
the very last, and the servant of all."*

—MARK 9:35

Cook. Event Planner. Nutritionist. Nurse. These are just some of the responsibilities regularly performed by modern moms. Recent research estimates that moms likely work between fifty-nine and ninety-six hours per week doing child-related tasks.

No wonder moms are always exhausted! Being a mom means giving a lot of time and energy to care for children, who need so much help as they learn to navigate the world.

Maybe that's why I find great hope when I see Jesus affirming those who serve. In the gospel of Mark, the disciples were having an argument about which them was the greatest. Jesus quietly reminded them that "anyone who wants to be first must be the very last, and the servant of all" (9:35). Then He took a child in His arms to illustrate the importance of serving others, especially the most helpless (vv. 36–37).

Christ's standard is a heart willing to care for others. And Jesus has promised that God's empowering presence will be with those who serve (v. 37).

As you serve, be encouraged that Jesus greatly values the time and effort you give in service to others.

—*Lisa Samra*

From Worms to War

JUDGES 6:11–16, 36–40

*But the LORD said to him, "Peace! Do not
be afraid. You are not going to die."*
—JUDGES 6:23

It was ten-year-old Cleo's first time fishing, and as he
looked into the container of bait he seemed hesitant
to get started. Finally he said to my husband, "Help
me, I'm scared of worms!" His fear had made him
unable to act.

Fear can paralyze grownups too. Gideon must've
been afraid when an angel told him he had been
chosen by God to lead His people in battle (Judges
6:12–14).

Gideon's response? "Pardon me, my lord, . . . but
how can I save Israel? My clan is the weakest in
Manasseh, and I am the least in my family" (v. 15).
After being assured of the Lord's presence, Gideon
still seemed fearful and asked for signs that God
would use him to save Israel as He promised (vv. 36–
40). And God responded to Gideon's requests. The
Israelites were successful in battle and then enjoyed
peace for forty years.

We all have fears of various kinds—from worms
to wars. Gideon's story teaches us that we can be
confident of this: If God asks us to do something,
He'll give us the strength and power to do it.

—*Anne Cetas*

Fearless Love

1 JOHN 4:7–12

We love because he first loved us.
—1 JOHN 4:19

For years I wore a shield of fear to protect my heart. It became an excuse to avoid trying new things, following my dreams, and obeying God. But fear of loss, heartache, and rejection hindered me from developing loving relationships with God and others. Fear made me an insecure, anxious, jealous wife, and an overprotective, worrying mother.

As I continue learning how much God loves me, however, He's changing the way I relate to Him and to others. Because I know God will care for me, I feel more secure and willing to place others' needs before mine.

God is love (1 John 4:7–8). Christ's death on the cross—the ultimate demonstration of love—displays the depth of His passion for us (vv. 9–10). Because God loves us, we can love others based on who He is and what He's done (vv. 11–12).

Growing in trust and faith can gradually eliminate fear, because we know that God loves us deeply and completely (vv. 18–19).

As we experience God's personal and unconditional love, we can risk relating to Him and others with fearless love.

—*Xochitl Dixon*

Exceedingly Better

1 CHRONICLES 17:1–15

"He is the one who will build a house for me,
and I will establish his throne forever."
—1 CHRONICLES 17:12

My birthday is the day after my mother's. As an adolescent, I would strive to think of a gift I could afford that would delight my mom. She always received my purchases with appreciation, and on the following day, my birthday, she would present her gift to me. Because her resources far outshone mine, her gift likewise outshone mine.

My gift-giving reminds me of David's wish to build a home for God. Struck by the contrast between his palace and the tent-tabernacle, David longed to build God a temple. Instead of granting David's wish, however, God responded by giving David a much better gift. God promised that not only would his son Solomon build the temple (1 Chronicles 17:11) but that He would also build David a house, a dynasty. That promise began with Solomon but found its fulfillment in Jesus, whose throne was indeed "established forever" (see v. 12). David wanted to give from his finite resources, but God promised something infinite.

May we always be moved to give to God out of gratitude and love—always noticing how much more abundantly He has given to us in Jesus.

—*Kirsten Holmberg*

Through the Valley

PSALM 23

Even though I walk through the darkest valley,
I will fear no evil, for you are with me.
—PSALM 23:4

A woman was imprisoned in a North Korean labor camp for crossing the border into China. The days and nights were torture, she said, with brutal guards, backbreaking work, and little sleep on an ice-cold floor with rats and lice. But God helped her, including showing her which prisoners to befriend and share her faith with.

After she was released and living in South Korea, she reflected on her time of imprisonment, saying that Psalm 23 summed up her experience. Although she'd been trapped in a dark valley, Jesus her Shepherd gave her peace: "Even though it felt as if I was literally in a valley full of the shadow of death, I wasn't afraid. God comforted me every day. I knew I would experience God's goodness and love." And she knew she'd stay in the Lord's presence forever.

Despite her dire circumstances, she felt God's love and leading; and He sustained her and removed her fear. Likewise, if we follow Jesus, He will lead us through our times of trouble here, and "[we] will dwell in the house of the LORD forever" (23:6).

—*Amy Boucher Pye*

Unexplainable Love

JOHN 13:3–35

*"As I have loved you, so you must
love one another."*
—JOHN 13:34

Our small congregation decided to surprise my son on his sixth birthday. The church members decorated his Sunday school classroom with balloons and set up a small table with a cake on it. When my son opened the door, everyone shouted, "Happy birthday!"

Later on, as I was cutting the cake, my son came over and whispered in my ear, "Mom, why does everyone here love me?" I had the same question! These people had known us for only six months but were treating us as longtime friends.

Their love for my son reflected God's love for us. We can't understand why He loves us, but He does—and His love is freely given. We've done nothing to deserve His love, and yet He lavishly loves us. Scripture tells us: "God is love" (1 John 4:8). It's part of who He is.

The people in our small church community love us because God's love is in them. It shines through and identifies them as followers of Jesus. We can't comprehend God's love fully, but we can pour it out on others—being examples of His unexplainable love.

—*Keila Ochoa*

Sweet and Bitter

PSALM 119:65–72

You are good, and what you do is good.
—PSALM 119:68

Some people like bitter chocolate and some prefer sweet. Ancient Mayans in Central America enjoyed chocolate as a beverage and seasoned it with chili peppers. They liked this "bitter water," as they called it. Many years later it was introduced in Spain, but the Spaniards preferred chocolate sweet, so they added sugar and honey to counteract its natural bitterness.

Like chocolate, days can be bitter or sweet as well. A seventeenth-century French monk named Brother Lawrence wrote, "If we knew how much [God] loves us, we would always be ready to receive equally . . . from His hand the sweet and the bitter." Accept the sweet and the bitter equally? This is difficult! What is Brother Lawrence talking about? The key lies in God's character. The psalmist said of God, "You are good, and what you do is good" (Psalm 119:68).

Let us embrace life today, with its different flavors—reassured of God's goodness. Let us say, "You have done many good things for me, LORD, just as you promised" (v. 65 NLT).

—*Keila Ochoa*

Quiet Awe

PSALM 104:10–24

How many are your works, LORD! In wisdom you made them all; the earth is full of your creatures.
—PSALM 104:24

My life often feels frenzied and hectic. Out of sheer exhaustion one Sunday, I collapsed into our backyard hammock. My phone was inside, as was my family. At first I planned to sit for just a moment or two, but in the undistracted stillness, I began to notice things that invited me to linger longer. I could hear the creak of the hammock swinging gently, the buzz of a bee in the nearby lavender, and the flap of a bird's wings overhead. The sky was a brilliant blue, and the clouds moved on the wind.

I found myself moved to tears in response to all God had made. When I slowed long enough to take in the many wonderful things around me, I was stirred to worship in gratitude for God's creative power. The writer of Psalm 104 was equally humbled by the work of God's hands, noting "you fill the earth with the fruit of your labor" (v. 13 NLT).

In the midst of a harried life, a quiet moment can remind us of God's creative might!

—*Kirsten Holmberg*

Hidden Beauty

1 SAMUEL 16:1–7

People look at the outward appearance,
but the LORD looks at the heart.
—1 SAMUEL 16:7

Our children needed a little coaxing to believe that it was worth putting on snorkeling gear to peer beneath the surface of the Caribbean Sea. But after they dove in, they resurfaced ecstatic, "There are thousands of fish! It's so beautiful! I've never seen such colorful fish!"

Our children could have missed the beauty hidden just below the surface.

When the prophet Samuel went to Bethlehem to anoint one of Jesse's sons to be the next king, Samuel was impressed by the appearance of the oldest son, Eliab. He thought he had found the right man, but the Lord rejected Eliab. God reminded Samuel that "people look at the outward appearance, but the LORD looks at the heart" (1 Samuel 16:7).

As the story goes, Samuel anointed Jesse's youngest son, a shepherd boy, instead. He didn't look the part, but he was the one.

Often we look at people on a surface level and don't take the time to see their inner, sometimes hidden, beauty. We don't always value what God values. But if we peer beneath the surface, we may find great treasure.

—Lisa Samra

The Ultimate Satisfaction

ISAIAH 55:1–7

Come, all you who are thirsty, come to the waters;
and you who have no money, come, buy and eat!
—ISAIAH 55:1

As we distributed snacks for children at a Bible school program, we noticed a little boy who devoured his snack. He also ate the leftovers of other children at his table. Even an extra bag of popcorn didn't satisfy him. We wondered why this little boy was so hungry.

It occurred to me that we can be like that boy when it comes to our emotions. We look for ways to satisfy our deepest longings, but we never find what fully satisfies us.

The prophet Isaiah invites those who hunger and thirst to "come, buy and eat" (Isaiah 55:1). Isaiah is talking about more than physical hunger. God can satisfy our spiritual and emotional hunger through the promise of His presence. The "everlasting covenant" (v. 3) is a reminder of a promise God made to David in 2 Samuel 7:8–16. Through David's family line, a Savior would come to reconnect people to God. Later, in John 6:35 and 7:37, Jesus extended the same invitation Isaiah gave, thus identifying himself as the foretold Savior.

Hungry? God invites you to come and be filled in His presence.

—*Linda Washington*

Trust Tally

DEUTERONOMY 1:21–33

See, the LORD your God has given you the land.
Go up and take possession of it.
—DEUTERONOMY 1:21

Before my husband and I surrendered our lives to Christ, we contemplated divorce. But after committing to love and obey God, we recommitted to each other. We sought wise counsel and invited the Holy Spirit to transform us. Our Lord continues to help us develop healthy communication skills—teaching us to love and trust Him—and one another—no matter what.

Yet, even after celebrating twenty-five years together, I occasionally forget what God has done in and through our trials. Sometimes, I struggle with a deep-seated fear of the unknown—experiencing anxiety instead of relying on God's track record.

In Deuteronomy 1, Moses affirmed the Lord's reliability. He encouraged the Israelites to move forward in faith so they could enjoy their inheritance (v. 21). But God's people demanded details about what they'd be up against and what they'd receive before committing to trust Him with their future (vv. 22–33).

Worrying can keep us from depending on faith, and it may even damage our relationships with God and others. The Holy Spirit can help us create a trust tally of the Lord's faithfulness—giving us courageous confidence in God's trustworthiness.

—*Xochitl Dixon*

Hope in Grief

LUKE 24:13–32

Then their eyes were opened and they recognized him, and he disappeared from their sight.

—LUKE 24:31

When I was nineteen, one of my close friends was killed in a car accident. For months, I walked each day in a tunnel of grief. The pain of losing someone so young and wonderful clouded my vision. I felt so blinded by pain and grief that I simply could not see God.

In Luke 24, two disciples, confused and brokenhearted after Jesus's death, didn't realize they were walking with their resurrected Teacher himself, even as He explained from Scripture why the promised Savior had to die and rise again. Only when He broke bread did they realize this was Jesus (vv. 30–31). Through Jesus's resurrection from the dead, God showed them how to hope again.

We too might feel weighed down with confusion or grief. But we can find hope and comfort in the reality that Jesus is alive and at work in the world—and in us. Although we still face heartache and pain, we can welcome Christ to walk with us in our tunnel of grief. As the Light of the world (John 8:12), He can bring rays of hope to brighten our fog.

—*Amy Boucher Pye*

Praising through Problems

JOB 1:13–22

*Shall we accept good from God,
and not trouble?*

—JOB 2:10

"It's cancer." I wanted to be strong when Mom said those words to me. But I burst into tears. You never want to hear those words even one time. But this was Mom's third bout with cancer. This time it was a malignant tumor under her arm.

Though Mom was the one with bad news, she had to comfort me. Her response was eye-opening for me: "I know God is always good to me. He's always faithful." Even as she faced a difficult surgery, followed up by radiation treatments, Mom was assured of God's presence and faithfulness.

How like Job. Job lost his children, his wealth, and his health. But after hearing the news, "he fell to the ground in worship" (1:20). When advised to curse God, he said, "Shall we accept good from God, and not trouble?" (2:10). What a radical initial response! Ultimately, Job realized that God was still with him and that He still cared.

For most of us, praise is not our first response to difficulties. But watching Mom's response reminded me that God is still present, still good. He will help us through hard times.

—*Linda Washington*

Engraved on His Hands

ISAIAH 49:14–18

"See, I have engraved you on
the palms of my hands."
—ISAIAH 49:16

In Charles Spurgeon's decades as pastor at a London church during the 1800s, he loved to preach on the riches of Isaiah 49:16, which says that God engraves us on the palms of His hands. This thought is so precious that we can contemplate it again and again.

Spurgeon made the connection between this promise of the Lord to His people, the Israelites, and God's Son, Jesus, on the cross as He died for us. Spurgeon asked, "What are these wounds in Your hands? . . . The engraver's tool was the nail, backed by the hammer. He must be fastened to the Cross, that His people might be truly engraved on the palms of His hands." As the Lord promised to engrave His people on His palms, so Jesus stretched out His arms on the cross, receiving the nails in His hands so we could be free of our sins.

If and when we're tempted to think that God has forgotten us, we only need to look at our palms and remember God's promise. He has put indelible marks on His hands for us; He loves us that much.

—*Amy Boucher Pye*

More Than Feelings

2 KINGS 17:35–18:6

*He removed the pagan shrines, smashed the sacred
pillars, and cut down the Asherah poles. He broke
up the bronze serpent that Moses had made.*
—2 KINGS 18:4 (NLT)

I smiled at my phone as I looked at the emoji message my daughter had texted. How in the world had such a small graphic manage to perfectly capture my teenage daughter's impatient eye-roll and slightly annoyed tone while saying, "Mom"?

While my response to my daughter's text that day was lighthearted, I realized that we don't always wield our emotions well.

Often we make our emotional state the barometer of what we believe or our compass for decision-making.

Hezekiah's radical cleansing of the temple reveals how far-reaching the impact can extend when we don't resist idolatry (2 Kings 17:41). A gift to bring healing, the bronze serpent had become an object of worship because it was more tangible than an unseen God (Numbers 21:8–9; 2 Kings 18:4).

God created us to live in the fullness of His image—emotions included. But it's vital that we choose, as Hezekiah did, to trust in God's "great strength and . . . powerful arm" to lead us (2 Kings 17:36 NLT). Regardless of our emotions, we find true security through faithful obedience to the One who remains consistent and trustworthy.

—*Regina Franklin*

Lack Nothing

MARK 6:7–12

God is able to bless you abundantly, so that in all things at all times, having all that you need, you will abound in every good work.

—2 CORINTHIANS 9:8

Imagine going on a trip without luggage. No basic necessities. No change of clothing. No money. Sounds both unwise and terrifying, doesn't it? But that's what Jesus told His disciples to do when He sent them out on their first mission to preach and heal. "Take nothing for the journey except a staff," said Jesus (Mark 6:8–9).

Later, when Jesus was preparing them for their work after He was gone, He told His disciples, "If you have a purse, take it, and also a bag; and if you don't have a sword, sell your cloak and buy one" (Luke 22:36).

So, what's the point here? It's about trusting God to supply.

When Jesus referred back to that first trip, He asked the disciples, "When I sent you without purse, bag or sandals, did you lack anything?" And they answered, "Nothing" (v. 35). He was able to supply them with the power to do His work (Mark 6:7).

Do we trust God to supply our needs? Are we also taking personal responsibility and planning? Let's have faith that He will give us what we need to carry out His work.

—*Poh Fang Chia*

Where to Find Hope

ROMANS 5:1–11

And hope does not put us to shame, because God's
love has been poured out into our hearts through
the Holy Spirit, who has been given to us.
—ROMANS 5:5

Elizabeth struggled with drug addiction, and when she recovered she wanted to help others. So she wrote notes and placed them throughout her city. Elizabeth tucked these notes under car windshield wipers and tacked them on poles.

Before, she desperately sought signs of hope; now she leaves them for others. One of her notes concluded with these words: "Much love. Hope sent."

Hope with love—that's what Jesus gives. He brings us His love with each new day and strengthens us with that hope. His love flows freely out of His heart and is poured lavishly into ours: "We know how dearly God loves us, because he has given us the Holy Spirit to fill our hearts with his love" (Romans 5:5 NLT). He desires to use the hard times to develop perseverance and character and bring us a satisfying, hope-filled life (vv. 3–4). Even when we're far from Him, He still loves us (vv. 6–8).

Looking for signs of hope? The Lord offers hope with love through inviting us to grow in a relationship with Him. Our hope for a fulfilling life is anchored in His unfailing love.

—*Anne Cetas*

How Long?

HABAKKUK 1:2–11

How long, Lord, must I call for help,
but you do not listen? Or cry out to you,
"Violence!" but you do not save?
—HABAKKUK 1:2

When I married, I thought I would have children immediately. That did not happen, and the pain of infertility brought me to my knees. I often cried out to God, "How long?" I knew God could change my circumstance. Why wasn't He?

Are you waiting on God? Are you asking, *How long, Lord, before justice prevails in our world? Before there is a cure for cancer? Before I am no longer in debt?*

The prophet Habakkuk was well acquainted with that feeling. In the seventh century BC, he cried out: "How long, Lord, must I call for help, but you do not listen? . . . Why do you tolerate wrongdoing?" (Habakkuk 1:2–3). He prayed for a long time, struggling to reconcile how a just and powerful God could allow wickedness, injustice, and corruption to continue in Judah. Why was God doing nothing?

There are days when we too feel as if God is doing nothing. But as with Habakkuk, God hears our burdens. We must continue to cast them on the Lord because He cares for us. God hears us. In His time, He will give an answer.

—*Karen Wolfe*

The Perfect Father

PSALM 27

Though my father and mother forsake me,
*the L*ORD *will receive me.*
—PSALM 27:10

Standing in the crowded store aisle, I struggled to find the perfect Father's Day card. Although we had reconciled after years of a strained connection, I had never felt close to my dad.

The woman next to me groaned and shoved another card back into the display. "Why can't they make cards for people who don't have good relationships with their fathers but are trying to do the right thing?"

She stormed off before I could respond, so I prayed for her. Thanking God for affirming that only He could be a perfect Father, I asked Him to strengthen my relationship with my dad.

I long for deeper intimacy with my heavenly Father too. I want David's confidence in God's constant presence, power, and protection (Psalm 27:1–6).

When David cried out for help, he expected God's answers (vv. 7–9). David sometimes struggled, but the Holy Spirit helped him persevere in trust and dependence on the Lord (v. 14).

We will encounter difficult relationships. But even when people fall short, fail us, or hurt us, we're still completely loved and protected by the only Perfect Father.

—*Xochitl Dixon*

Common Colors

1 CORINTHIANS 9:19–23

*I try to find common ground with everyone, doing
everything I can to save some. I do everything to
spread the Good News and share in its blessings.*
—1 CORINTHIANS 9:22–23 (NLT)

In the space of two days, I saw two chameleons—one
bright green and the other dark brown. The brown
one was on a tree trunk; it took me a while to find
it—demonstrating that a chameleon changes color as
a form of camouflage.

But this camouflage thing is only partially true!
Truth is, a chameleon changes color primarily as a
visual sign of mood and aggression, territory, and
mating behavior.

The apostle Paul did some clever altering himself.

He became like others and communicated in a way
that would resonate—so that many would come to
know and believe in Jesus (1 Corinthians 9:19). When
he was with the Jews, Paul lived like a Jew—never
ignoring or violating the law of God (vv. 20–21).

He said, "When I am with those who are weak, I
share their weakness, for I want to bring the weak
to Christ" (v. 22).

May we also meet people where they are today,
sharing the good news of Jesus with respect and rele-
vancy as He leads us!

—*Ruth O'Reilly-Smith*

Radical Love

LUKE 14:7–14

*When you give a banquet, invite the poor, the
crippled, the lame, the blind.* —LUKE 14:13

Just one week before her scheduled wedding date,
Sarah's engagement ended. Despite her sadness and
disappointment, she decided not to waste the food
purchased for her reception.

She did, however, change the celebration plans.
She took down the gift table and revamped the guest
list, inviting the residents of local homeless shelters
to the feast.

Jesus upheld this sort of no-strings-attached kindness when speaking to the Pharisees, saying, "When
you give a banquet, invite the poor, the crippled,
the lame, the blind, and you will be blessed" (Luke
14:13–14). He noted that the blessing would come
from God because these guests weren't able to repay the host. Jesus approved of helping people who
couldn't supply charity donations, sparkling conversation, or social connections.

Love, I've heard, is giving to meet the needs of others without expecting anything in return. This is how
Jesus has loved each of us. He saw our inner poverty
and responded by giving His life for us.

Knowing Christ personally is a journey into His
infinite love. All of us are invited to explore "how
wide and long and high and deep is the love of
Christ" (Ephesians 3:18).

—*Jennifer Benson Schuldt*

Letting Go

GENESIS 12:1–9

The LORD had said to Abram, "Go from your
country, your people and your father's
household to the land I will show you."
—GENESIS 12:1

For our wedding anniversary, my husband borrowed a tandem bike for a romantic adventure together. As we began to pedal on our way, I quickly realized that as the rider on the back my vision of the road ahead was eclipsed by my husband's broad shoulders. Also, my handlebars were fixed; they didn't affect the steering of our bike. Only the front handlebars determined our direction; mine served merely as support for my upper body. I had a choice: either be frustrated by my lack of control or embrace the journey and trust Mike.

When God asked Abram to leave his homeland and family, He didn't offer much information concerning the destination. No geographic coordinates. No description of the new land or its natural resources. No indication of how long it would take to get there. God simply said, "Go." Abram's obedience to God's instruction, despite lacking the details most humans crave, is credited to him as faith (Hebrews 11:8).

If we find ourselves grappling with uncertainty or a lack of control in life, let's seek to adopt Abram's example of following and trusting God. The Lord will steer us well.

—*Kirsten Holmberg*

Is There Wi-Fi?

PROVERBS 15:9–21

*A wise person is hungry for knowledge,
while the fool feeds on trash.*
—PROVERBS 15:14 (NLT)

As I was preparing for a mission trip with some young people, the most frequently asked question was, "Is there Wi-Fi?" I assured them there would be. So just imagine the wails and groans one night when the Wi-Fi was down!

Many of us become anxious when we're separated from our smartphones. And when we do have them, we can be fixated on our screens.

The internet and all that it allows us to access can become either a distraction or a blessing. It depends on what we do with it. In Proverbs we read, "A wise person is hungry for knowledge, while the fool feeds on trash" (15:14 NLT).

Seeking God's wisdom, we can ask: Do we check our social networks compulsively? What does that say about the things we hunger for? And do the things we read or view online encourage sensible living (vv. 16–21), or are we feeding on trash?

As we yield to the Holy Spirit, we can fill our minds with things that are "true, honorable, right, pure, lovely, and admirable" (Philippians 4:8 NLT). By God's wisdom we can make good choices that honor Him.

—*Poh Fang Chia*

Seeing Masterpieces

PSALM 139:11–18

For you created my inmost being; you knit me together in my mother's womb. —PSALM 139:13

My father creates custom quivers designed for archers to carry their arrows. He carves elaborate wildlife pictures into pieces of genuine leather before stitching the material together.

One day I watched him construct one of his works of art. His careful hands applied just the right pressure as he pressed a sharp blade into the supple leather. Then he dipped a rag into crimson dye and covered the leather with even strokes, magnifying the beauty of his creation.

As I admired my dad's confident craftsmanship, I realized how often I fail to appreciate my heavenly Father's creativity manifested in others and even in myself. I recalled King David's affirmation that God creates our "inmost being" and that we're "fearfully and wonderfully made" (Psalm 139:13–14).

We can praise our Creator in confidence because we know His "works are wonderful" (v. 14). And we can be encouraged to respect each other more, especially when we remember that God knew us inside and out and planned our days "before one of them came to be" (vv. 15–16).

We all, intentionally designed to be unique and purposed as God's beloved masterpieces, reflect God's magnificence.

—Xochitl Dixon

Always a Child of God

ROMANS 8:9–17

*For those who are led by the Spirit of God
are the children of God.*

—ROMANS 8:14

During a church service I attended with my parents, we all held hands while saying the Lord's Prayer together. As I stood with one hand clasped to my mother's and the other to my father's, I was struck by the thought that I will always be their daughter. Although I'm firmly in my middle age, I can still be called "the child of Leo and Phyllis." I reflected that not only am I their daughter but I will also always be a child of God.

The apostle Paul wanted the people in the church at Rome to understand that their identity was based on being adopted members of God's family (Romans 8:15). Because they had been born of the Spirit (v. 14), they were "heirs of God and co-heirs with Christ" (v. 17).

What difference does this make? Quite simply, everything! Our identity as children of God provides our foundation and shapes how we see ourselves and the world. Knowing that we are part of God's family gives us confidence to speak freely about our faith in Him.

Why not ponder what else it means to you to be God's child!

—*Amy Boucher Pye*

Better Than a Piñata

EPHESIANS 2:1–10

*God, who is rich in mercy, made us alive with
Christ even when we were dead in transgressions
—it is by grace you have been saved.*
—EPHESIANS 2:4–5

There cannot be a Mexican party without a piñata—a
carton or clay container filled with candies and treats.
Children strike it with a stick and try to break it,
hoping to enjoy its contents.

Monks used piñatas in the sixteenth century to
teach lessons to the indigenous people of Mexico.
Piñatas were stars with seven points that represented
the seven deadly sins. Beating the piñata showed the
struggle against evil, and once the treats inside fell to
the ground, people could take them home in remembrance of the rewards of keeping the faith.

But we cannot fight evil on our own. God is not
waiting for our efforts so He will show His mercy.
Ephesians teaches that "by grace you have been saved
through faith, . . . it is the gift of God" (2:8). We don't
beat sin; Christ has done that.

We don't get these spiritual blessings because we
have kept the faith and are strong; we get them because we believe in Jesus. Spiritual blessings come
only through grace—undeserved grace!

—*Keila Ochoa*

Strength for Your Journey

HABAKKUK 3:16–19

The Sovereign LORD is my strength;
he makes my feet like the feet of a deer,
he enables me to tread on the heights.
—HABAKKUK 3:19

Hinds Feet on High Places, a classic allegory of the Christian life, is based on Habakkuk 3:19. The story follows the character Much-Afraid as she goes on a journey with the Shepherd. Much-Afraid is scared, so she asks the Shepherd to carry her.

He replies, "I could carry you all the way up to the High Places myself. . . . But if I did, you would never be able to develop hinds' feet, and become my companion and go where I go." Much-Afraid echoes the questions of Habakkuk (and all of us): "Why must I experience suffering?" "Why is my journey difficult?"

Habakkuk lived in Judah before the Israelites went into exile. He was in a society that overlooked social injustice and was immobilized by the fear of imminent Babylonian invasion (Habakkuk 1:2–11). He asked the Lord to intervene and remove suffering (1:13). God replied that He would act justly but in His timing (2:3). In faith, Habakkuk chose to trust the Lord.

God is our strength to help us endure suffering. We can use the most challenging of life's journeys to deepen our fellowship with Christ.

—*Lisa Samra*

When We're Weary

GALATIANS 6:1–10

Let us not become weary in doing good.
—GALATIANS 6:9

Recently I sent a prayerfully thought-out email meant to encourage a friend, only to have it met with an angry response. My immediate reaction was a mixture of hurt and anger. *How could I be so misunderstood?*

Before I responded, I remembered that we won't always see positive results when we tell someone that Jesus loves them. When we do good things for others—hoping to draw them to Him—they may spurn us. Our gentle, encouraging efforts may be ignored.

Galatians 6 is a good place to turn when we're discouraged by someone's response to our sincere efforts. Paul encourages us to consider our motives—to "test our actions"—for what we say and do (vv. 1–4). When we have done so, he encourages us to persevere: "Let us not become weary in doing good, for at the proper time we will reap a harvest if we do not give up. Therefore, as we have opportunity, let us do good to all people" (vv. 9–10).

God wants us to continue living for Him, which includes praying for and telling others about Him—"doing good." He will see to the results.

—*Alyson Kieda*

For Our Friends

JOHN 15:5–17

*"My command is this: Love each other
as I have loved you."*
—JOHN 15:12

In Emily Brontë's novel *Wuthering Heights*, a cantankerous man who often quotes the Bible to criticize others is memorably described as "the wearisomest self-righteous Pharisee that ever ransacked a Bible to [apply] the promises to himself and fling the curses to his neighbours."

It's a funny line; and it may even bring someone to mind. But aren't we *all* a bit like this—prone to condemn others' failures while excusing our own? In Scripture some people did the opposite—willing to give up God's promises for themselves and becoming cursed to save others. Consider Moses, who said he'd rather be blotted out of God's book than to see the Israelites unforgiven (Exodus 32:32). Or Paul, who said he'd choose to be "cut off from Christ" if it meant his people would find Him (Romans 9:3).

Ultimately, such love points to Jesus. "Greater love has no one than this," Jesus taught, than "to lay down one's life for one's friends" (John 15:13).

Through Christ, we are loved like this (15:9–12). And as we pour into others Christ's unimaginable love, the world will catch a glimpse of Him.

—*Monica Brands*

Lavish Expressions of Love

2 CORINTHIANS 9:6–15

You will be enriched in every way so that you can be generous on every occasion.
—2 CORINTHIANS 9:11

On our wedding anniversary, my husband, Alan, gives me a large bouquet of fresh flowers. When he lost his job during a corporate restructure, I didn't expect this extravagant display of devotion to continue. But on our nineteenth anniversary, the color-splashed blossoms greeted me from their spot on our dining room table. Alan had saved some money each month to ensure he'd have enough for this personal show of affection.

Alan's exuberant generosity is similar to what Paul encouraged in the Corinthian believers. The apostle complimented the church for their intentional and enthusiastic offerings (2 Corinthians 9:2, 5), reminding them that God delights in generous and cheerful givers (vv. 6–7). After all, no one gives more than our loving Provider, who's always ready to supply all we need (vv. 8–10).

We can be generous in all kinds of giving because the Lord meets all of our material, emotional, and spiritual needs (v. 11). As we give, we can express our gratitude for all God has given us. Openhanded giving, a lavish expression of love and gratitude, demonstrates our confidence in God's provision for all His people.

—*Xochitl Dixon*

Stones of Remembrance

JOSHUA 3:14–4:7

*Remember the wonders he has done, his miracles,
and the judgments he pronounced.*

—PSALM 105:5

Some mornings when I go online, Facebook shows me "memories"—things I've posted on that day in previous years. These memories, such as my brother's wedding or my daughter playing with my grandmother, usually make me smile. But sometimes they have a more profound effect. When I see a note about a visit to my brother-in-law during his chemotherapy or a picture of the staples across my mother's scalp after her brain surgery three years ago, I'm reminded of God's faithful presence during difficult circumstances.

All of us are prone to forget the things God has done for us. We need reminders. After Joshua led God's people across the Jordan River (Joshua 3:15–16), which God had miraculously parted (v. 17), they created a memorial of this miracle. They took twelve stones from the riverbed and stacked them on the other side (4:3, 6–7). When others would later ask what the stones meant, God's people would tell the story of what God had done that day.

Physical reminders of God's faithfulness in the past can remind us to trust Him in the present—and with the future.

—*Amy Peterson*

Advice from My Father

PROVERBS 3:1–7

*Trust in the LORD with all your heart and
lean not on your own understanding.*
—PROVERBS 3:5

After being laid off from an editorial job, I prayed, asking for God to help me find a new one. But when weeks went by and nothing came of my attempts at getting a new job, I began to pout. "Don't you know how important it is that I have a job?" I asked God.

When I talked to my father, who often reminds me about believing God's promises, about my job situation, he said, "I want you to get to the point where you trust what God says."

My father's advice reminds me of Proverbs 3, which includes wise advice from a parent to a beloved child: "Trust in the LORD . . . and lean not on your own understanding; . . . submit to him, and he will make your paths straight" (vv. 5–6). To "make . . . paths straight" means God will guide us toward His goals for our growth.

Those paths won't always be easy, but we can trust that His direction and timing are ultimately for our good.

Are you waiting on God for an answer? Draw near to Him and trust that He will guide you.

—*Linda Washington*

You Love Me?

MALACHI 1:1–5

How have you loved us?
—MALACHI 1:2

As a teenager, I went through the typical season of rebellion against my mother's authority. My father died before I entered adolescence, so my mom had to navigate these turbulent parenting waters without his help.

I recall thinking that Mom didn't want me to have any fun—and maybe didn't even love me—because she frequently said no. I see now that she said no to activities that weren't good for me precisely because she does love me.

The Israelites questioned how much God loved them because of their captivity in Babylon. But that captivity was God's correction for their continued rebellion. When God sent the prophet Malachi to them, his opening words from the Lord were, "I have loved you" (Malachi 1:2). Israel replied skeptically, as if to say, "Really? How?" But God, through Malachi, reminded them of the way He had demonstrated that love: He had chosen them over the Edomites.

When we are tempted to question God's love during difficult times, let's recall the many ways He's shown us His unfailing love. When we stop to consider His goodness, we find that He is indeed a loving Father.

—*Kirsten Holmberg*

Hard Mysteries

NAHUM 1:1–7

The LORD is slow to anger but great in power.
—NAHUM 1:3

As my friend and I went for a walk, we talked about our love for the Bible. She surprised me when she said, "I don't like the Old Testament much. All of that hard stuff and vengeance—give me Jesus!"

We might resonate with her words when we read a book like Nahum, perhaps recoiling at this statement: "The LORD takes vengeance and is filled with wrath" (Nahum 1:2). Yet the next verse fills us with hope: "The LORD is slow to anger but great in power" (v. 3).

When we examine the subject of God's anger, we understand that when He exercises it, He's most often defending His people or His name. Because of His overflowing love, He seeks justice for wrongs committed and the redemption of those who have turned from Him. We see this when He sends His Son to be the sacrifice for our sins.

We can trust that He not only exercises justice but is also the source of all love. He is "good, a refuge in times of trouble. He cares for those who trust in him" (v. 7).

—*Amy Boucher Pye*

What's Inside

2 CORINTHIANS 4:7–18

*But we have this treasure in jars of clay
to show that this all-surpassing power
is from God and not from us.*
—2 CORINTHIANS 4:7

"Do you want to see what's inside?" my friend asked. I had just complimented her on the old-fashioned rag doll her daughter held in her arms. When I said yes, she turned the doll face down and pulled open a discreet zipper sewn into its back. From within the cloth body, Emily gently removed a treasure: the rag doll she had held and loved throughout her own childhood. The "outer" doll was merely a shell without this inner core to give it strength and form.

Paul describes the truth of Jesus's life, death, and resurrection as a treasure, carried about in the frail humanity of God's people—in jars of clay (2 Corinthians 4:7). That treasure enables those who trust in Him to bear up under unthinkable adversity and continue in their service. When they do, His light—His life—shines brightly through the "cracks" of their humanness.

Like the "inner" doll, the gospel-treasure within us lends both purpose and fortitude to our lives. When God's strength shines through us, it invites others to ask, "What's inside?" Then we can reveal the life-giving promise of salvation in Christ.

—*Kirsten Holmberg*

Blooming in the Desert

ISAIAH 35:1–10

They will see the glory of the LORD,
the splendor of our God.
—ISAIAH 35:2

The Mojave Desert includes the expected sand dunes, dry canyons, mesas, and mountains of most deserts. But American biologist Edmund Jaeger observed that every few years an abundance of rain results in "such a wealth of blossoms that almost every foot of sand or gravelly soil is hidden beneath a blanket of flowers." Researchers confirm that the dry earth needs to be soaked by storms and warmed by the sun, at just the right times, before blooms will cover the desert with vibrant colors.

This image of God bringing forth life despite the arid terrain reminds me of the prophet Isaiah. He shared an encouraging vison of hope after delivering God's message of judgment on all nations (Isaiah 35). Describing a future time when God will make all things right, the prophet said, "The desert and the parched land will be glad; the wilderness will rejoice and blossom" (v. 1). God's rescued people would enter His kingdom "with singing; everlasting joy will crown their heads" (v. 10).

Deeply rooted in God's love, we can grow, blooming into His likeness until, at just the right time, Jesus returns and sets all things right.

—*Xochitl Dixon*

Take the Time

LUKE 19:1–10

*"Come down immediately. I must
stay at your house today."*
—LUKE 19:5

Rima, a Syrian woman who had recently moved
to the US, tried to explain to her tutor with limited
English why she was upset. Tears trickled down her
cheeks as she held up a beautifully arranged platter
of *fatayer* (meat, cheese, and spinach pies) she had
made. Then she said, "One man," and she made a
swishing sound as she pointed from the door to the
living room and then back to the door. Apparently,
several people from a nearby church were supposed
to visit Rima's family and bring gifts. But only one
man showed up. He had hurried in, dropped off a
box of items, and rushed out. She and her family were
lonely. They longed for community and to share their
fatayer with new friends.

Taking time for people is what Jesus was all about.
He attended dinner parties, taught crowds, and took
time for interaction with individuals. He even invited
himself to Zacchaeus's house (Luke 19:1–9). And
Zacchaeus's life was changed forever.

We don't always have the time to visit others.
But when we do, we have the wonderful privilege of
watching the Lord work through us.

—*Anne Cetas*

Stop

PSALM 46

Be still, and know that I am God.
—PSALM 46:10

My friend and I sat in the sand near the ever-rhythmic ocean. As the sun sank, wave after wave curled, paused, and then rippled toward our extended toes, stopping just short each time. "I love the ocean," she smiled. "It moves so I don't have to."

What a thought! We struggle to *stop*. We do, do, do and go, go, go—afraid that if we cease our efforts we will cease to be. Or that by stopping we will expose ourselves to the realities we work to keep at bay.

In Psalm 46:8–9, God flexes His omnipotent muscles, putting His power on display. "Come and see what the LORD has done . . . . He makes wars cease to the ends of the earth. He breaks the bow and shatters the spear." God can create calm within the chaos of our days.

And there's this: "Be still, and know that I am God" (v. 10).

The psalmist's invitation to cease striving beckons us into a different kind of knowing God. We can stop—and still be—because God never stops. It is God's power that gives us ultimate value, protection, and peace.

—*Elisa Morgan*

The Blessing of Encouragers

ACTS 9:26–31

But Barnabas took [Saul] and
brought him to the apostles.
—ACTS 9:27

The movie *The King's Speech* tells the story of England's King George VI, who unexpectedly became monarch when his brother abandoned the throne. With the country on the brink of World War II, government officials wanted a well-spoken leader. King George VI, however, struggled with a stuttering problem.

I was especially drawn to the film's portrayal of George's wife, Elizabeth. Throughout George's painful struggle to overcome his speech difficulty, she was his constant source of encouragement. Her steadfast devotion helped provide the support he needed to overcome his challenge and rule well during the war.

After his conversion, Paul needed the support of Barnabas, whose name literally means "son of encouragement." When the disciples were fearful of Paul, Barnabas, at the risk of his own reputation, vouched for him (Acts 9:27). His endorsement was essential to Paul being welcomed by the Christian community. Barnabas later served as Paul's traveling and preaching companion (Acts 14).

Believers in Jesus are still called to "encourage one another and build each other up" (1 Thessalonians 5:11). May we be eager to offer encouragement to help support others, especially as they face difficult circumstances. —*Lisa Samra*

Open My Eyes

JOHN 14:23–31

*"The Holy Spirit, whom the Father will send
in my name, will teach you all things."*
—JOHN 14:26

The first time I visited the gorgeous Chora Church in Istanbul, I was able to figure out some Bible stories from the Byzantine frescos and mosaics on the ceiling. But I missed so much. The second time, however, I had a guide. He pointed out all the details I had previously missed, and suddenly everything made perfect sense! The first aisle, for instance, depicted the life of Jesus as recorded in the gospel of Luke.

Sometimes when we read the Bible we wonder about the connections—those details that weave Scripture into the one perfect story. We have Bible commentaries and study tools, yes, but we also need a guide—someone to help us see the wonders of God's written revelation. Our guide is the Holy Spirit, who teaches us "all things" (John 14:26). Paul wrote that He explains "spiritual realities with Spirit-taught words" (1 Corinthians 2:13).

How wonderful to have the Author of the Book to show us the wonders of it! Let's pray with the psalmist, saying, "Open my eyes that I may see wonderful things in your law" (Psalm 119:18).

—*Keila Ochoa*

God's Care for Us

GENESIS 3:1–13

*The Lord God made garments of skin for
Adam and his wife and clothed them.*
—GENESIS 3:21

My young grandsons enjoy dressing themselves. Sometimes they pull their shirts on backwards, and often the younger one puts his shoes on the wrong feet. I usually don't tell them; besides, I find their innocence endearing.

I love seeing the world through their eyes. To them, everything is an adventure, whether walking the length of a fallen tree, spying a turtle sunning itself, or excitedly watching a fire truck roar by. I know that my little grandsons are not truly innocent. Yet I love them dearly.

I picture Adam and Eve, God's first people, as being in some ways like my grandchildren. Everything they saw in the garden must have been a marvel as they walked with God. But one day they willfully disobeyed. They ate of the one tree they were forbidden to eat (Genesis 2:15–17; 3:6). And that disobedience immediately led to lies and blame-shifting (3:8–13).

Still, God loved and cared for them. He sacrificed animals to clothe them (v. 21)—and later He provided a way of salvation for all sinners through the sacrifice of His Son (John 3:16). He loves us that much!

—*Alyson Kieda*

Out of the Deep

2 SAMUEL 22:17–20

"He drew me out of deep waters."
—2 SAMUEL 22:17

I scanned the water intently, on alert for signs of trouble. During my six-hour shifts as a lifeguard, I watched diligently to ensure the safety of the swimmers. Leaving my post or even becoming lax in my attentiveness could have grave consequences. If a swimmer was in danger of drowning due to injury or lack of skill, it was my responsibility to pluck them from the water and return them to safety.

After experiencing God's aid in battle against the Philistines (2 Samuel 21:15–22), David likens his rescue to being drawn out of "deep waters" (22:17). David's life—and that of his men—was in serious danger from his enemies. God buoyed David as he was drowning in disaster. While lifeguards are paid to assure the safety of swimmers, God saved David because of His delight in him (v. 20). How comforting to know that God doesn't watch over and protect me because He's obliged to but because He wants to.

When we feel overcome by the troubles of life, we can rest in the knowledge that God, our Lifeguard, watches over us and protects us.

—*Kirsten Holmberg*

Being Real with God

1 PETER 5:6–10

Cast all your anxiety on him
because he cares for you.
—1 PETER 5:7

I bow my head, close my eyes, lace my fingers together and begin to pray. "Dear Lord, I'm coming to you today as your child. I recognize your power and goodness. . ."

Suddenly, my eyes snap open. I remember that my son hasn't finished his history project—due the next day. I recall that he has an after-school basketball game, and I imagine him awake until midnight finishing his schoolwork. This leads me to worry that his fatigue will put him at risk for the flu!

Writing about prayer distractions in his book *The Screwtape Letters*, C. S. Lewis concluded that it was better to accept "the distraction as [our] present problem and [lay] that before [God] and make it the main theme of [our] prayers."

A persistent worry or even a sinful thought that disrupts a prayer may become the centerpiece of our discussion with God. God wants us to be real as we talk with Him. His interest in us is like the attention we would receive from a close friend. We're encouraged to give all of our worries and cares to God—because He cares for us (1 Peter 5:7).

—*Jennifer Benson Schuldt*

Able and Available

PSALM 46

God is our refuge and strength,
an ever-present help in trouble.

—PSALM 46:1

My husband was at work when I received news about my mom's cancer diagnosis. I left him a message and reached out to friends and family. None were available. Covering my face with trembling hands, I sobbed, "Help me, Lord." A resulting assurance that God was with me comforted me when I felt alone.

I thanked the Lord when my husband came home and support from friends and family trickled in. Still, the calming awareness of God's presence I sensed in those first few hours of lonely grieving affirmed that God is readily and faithfully available wherever and whenever I need help.

In Psalm 46, the psalmist proclaims God is our sanctuary, strength, and steadfast supporter (v. 1). When it feels as if we're surrounded by chaos or when everything we thought was stable crashes down around us, we don't have to fear (vv. 2–3). God doesn't falter (vv. 4–7). His power is evident and effective (vv. 8–9).

When we call on God, we can trust Him to keep His promises to provide for us. He will comfort us through His people as well as through His personal presence.

—*Xochitl Dixon*

Asking for Help

MARK 10:46–52

"What do you want me to do for you?"
Jesus asked him.
—MARK 10:51

Her email arrived late in a long day. Working overtime to help a family member manage his serious illness, I didn't have time for social distractions. So I didn't open it.

The next morning when I opened my friend's message, I saw this: "Can I help you in any way?" Feeling embarrassed, I started to answer no. Then I noticed that her question sounded familiar—if not divine.

That's because Jesus asked it. Hearing a blind beggar call out to Him on the Jericho Road, Jesus stopped to ask Bartimaeus, a similar question. *Can I help?* Or as Jesus said: "What do you want me to do for you?" (Mark 10:51).

The question is stunning. It shows that the Healer, Jesus, longs to help us. But first, we're invited to admit needing Him—a humbling step. The "professional" beggar Bartimaeus simply told Jesus his most basic need: "I want to see."

It was an honest plea. Jesus healed him immediately of his basic need. Do you know your basic need today? When a friend asks, tell it. Then take your plea even higher. Tell God.

—*Patricia Raybon*

The Lighthouse

ISAIAH 61:1–6

*[The Lord bestows] on them a crown
of beauty instead of ashes, the oil
of joy instead of mourning.*

—ISAIAH 61:3

By its existence, a ministry center in Rwanda called the Lighthouse symbolizes redemption. This structure, constructed on the grounds of a former burned out home, was built by Christians as a beacon of light as the nation continues to recover from the genocide of 1994. Housed there is a Bible institute and other services for the community. Out of the ashes has come new life. Those who built the Lighthouse look to Jesus as their source of hope and redemption.

When Jesus went to the synagogue in Nazareth on the Sabbath, He read from the book of Isaiah and announced that He was the Anointed One who came to bind up the brokenhearted and offer redemption and forgiveness (Luke 4:14–21). In Jesus we see beauty coming from the ashes (Isaiah 61:3).

The atrocities of the Rwandan genocide, when intertribal fighting cost more than a half-million lives, were harrowing, and we hardly know what to say about them. Yet we know that the Lord can redeem the atrocities—either here on earth or in heaven. He who bestows the oil of joy gives us hope even in the midst of the darkest of situations.

—*Amy Boucher Pye*

The Mood Mender

PSALM 94:2, 16–23

When anxiety was great within me,
your consolation brought me joy.
—PSALM 94:19

As I waited at the train station for my weekly commute, negative thoughts crowded my mind—stress over debt, unkind remarks, helplessness in the face of a recent injustice done to a family member. By the time the train arrived, I was in a terrible mood.

On the train, another thought came to mind: write a note to God, giving Him my lament. Soon after I finished pouring out my complaints, I pulled out my phone and listened to the praise songs on my playlist. Soon my bad mood had completely changed.

Without knowing it, I was following a pattern set by the writer of Psalm 94. The psalmist first poured out his complaints: "Rise up, Judge of the earth; pay back to the proud what they deserve. . . . Who will rise up for me against the wicked?" (Psalm 94:2, 16). He spoke passionately to God about injustice done to widows and orphans. Following the lament, the psalmist transitioned into praise: "But the LORD has become my fortress" (v. 22).

God invites us to take our laments to Him. He can turn our difficulties into praise.

—*Linda Washington*

Twinkle

PHILIPPIANS 2:14–16

Shine among them like stars in the sky as
you hold firmly to the word of life.
—PHILIPPIANS 2:15–16

"Twinkle, Twinkle, Little Star" is an English lullaby. Its lyrics, originally a poem by Jane Taylor, capture the wonder of God's universe where stars hang "up above the world so high." In the rarely published later stanzas, the star acts as a guide: "As your bright and tiny spark lights the traveler in the dark."

In Philippians, Paul challenges believers in Philippi to be blameless and pure as they "shine . . . like stars in the sky" while offering the good news of the gospel to all around them (2:15–16). We often feel inadequate and struggle to think our "light" is bright enough to make a difference. But stars don't *try* to be stars. They just are. God brought physical light into our world (Genesis 1:3); and through Jesus, God brings spiritual light into our lives (John 1:1–4).

We are to shine in such a way that those around us see God's light and are drawn Him. When we shine, we follow Paul's directive to "hold firmly to the word of life" in a world in deep darkness, and we draw others to the source of our hope: Jesus.

—*Elisa Morgan*

From Fear to Faith

HABAKKUK 3:16–19

The Sovereign Lord is my strength;
he makes my feet like the feet of a deer,
he enables me to tread on the heights.
—HABAKKUK 3:19

The doctor's words landed in her heart with a thud. It was cancer. Her world stopped as she thought of her husband and children. They had prayed diligently, hoping for a different outcome. What would they do? With tears streaming down her face, she said softly, "God, this is beyond our control. Please be our strength."

What do we do when the prognosis is devastating? Where do we turn when the outlook seems hopeless?

The prophet Habakkuk's situation was out of his control, and the fear that he felt terrified him. The coming judgment would be catastrophic (Habakkuk 3:16–17). Yet, in the midst of the impending chaos, Habakkuk made a choice to live by his faith (2:4) and rejoice in God (3:18). He placed his confidence and faith in the goodness and greatness of God. His trust in God compelled him to proclaim: "The Sovereign Lord is my strength" (v. 19).

When we are faced with difficult circumstances—sickness, family crisis, financial trouble—we too have only to place our faith and trust in God. He is with us in everything we face.

—*Karen Wolfe*

Ask the Animals

JOB 12:7–10

Ask the animals, and they will teach you, or the birds in the sky, and they will tell you.

—JOB 12:7

Our grandkids, enraptured, got a close-up look at a rescued bald eagle. The zoo volunteer told us that this powerful bird, which had a wingspan of six and one-half feet, weighed just eight pounds.

This reminded me of the majestic eagle I had seen soaring above a lake. And I thought of another big bird—the spindly legged blue heron I had spied standing motionless on the edge of a pond. They're just two among the nearly 10,000 species of birds that can direct our thoughts to our Creator.

In the book of Job, his friends, debating the reasons for his suffering, "Can you fathom the mysteries of God?" (see 11:5–9). Job responds, "Ask the animals, and they will teach you, or the birds in the sky, and they will tell you" (Job 12:7). Animals testify to the truth that God designed, cares for, and controls His creation: "In his hand is the life of every creature" (v. 10).

Since God cares for birds (Matthew 6:26; 10:29), we can be assured He loves and cares for us, even when we don't understand our circumstances. Look around and learn of Him.

—*Alyson Kieda*

Lured Away

JAMES 1:5–6, 12–15

*But each person is tempted when he is lured
and enticed by his own desire.*
—JAMES 1:14 (ESV)

In the summer of 2016, my niece convinced me to play Pokémon Go—a game played on a smartphone, using the phone's camera. The object of the game is to capture little creatures called Pokémon, which are more easily caught when the gamer uses a lure to attract them.

Pokémon characters aren't the only ones who can be lured away. In his New Testament letter to believers, James, the brother of Jesus, reminds us that each person is "lured and enticed by his own desire" (1:14 ESV). In other words, our desires work with temptation to lure us down a wrong path. Though we may be tempted to blame God or even Satan for our problems, our real danger lies within.

But there is good news. We can escape the lure of temptation by talking to God about the things that tempt us. Although "God cannot be tempted by evil, nor does he tempt anyone," as James explains in 1:13, He understands our human desire to do what's wrong. We have only to ask for the wisdom God promised to provide (1:1–6).

—*Linda Washington*

What Can I Give Him?

PSALM 103:1–18

*Praise the LORD, my soul, and
forget not all his benefits.*
—PSALM 103:2

One year, the people responsible for decorating their church for Christmas gave each person a red or green tag instead of ornaments. On one side of the tag they were to write down the gift they would like from Jesus; and on the other, they were to list the gift they would give to Him.

What gift would you ask for and what would you offer? The Bible gives us lots of ideas. God promises to supply all our needs, so we might ask for a new job, help with finances, physical healing, or a restored relationship. We might be wondering what our spiritual gift is that equips us for God's service. Many of these are listed in Romans 12 and 1 Corinthians 12. Or we might desire to show more of the fruit of the Holy Spirit—to be more loving, joyful, peaceful, patient, kind and good, faithful, gentle and self-controlled (Galatians 5:22–23).

The most important gift we can receive is God's gift of His Son, our Savior, giving us forgiveness, restoration, and the promise of eternal life. And the most important gift we can ever give is to give Jesus our heart.

—*Marion Stroud*

Trial by Fire

JAMES 1:1–12

*Blessed is the one who perseveres under trial
because, having stood the test, that person
will receive the crown of life that the Lord has
promised to those who love him.*

—JAMES 1:12

Did you know that an entire grove of slender, white-trunked aspen trees can grow from a single seed and share the same root system? These root systems can exist for thousands of years whether or not they produce trees. They sleep underground, waiting for fire, flood, or avalanche to clear a space for them. After a natural disaster has cleared the land, aspen roots can sense the sun at last. The roots send up saplings, which become trees.

For aspens, new growth is made possible by the devastation of a natural disaster. James writes that our growth in faith is also made possible by difficulties. "Consider it pure joy," he writes, "whenever you face trials of many kinds, because you know that the testing of your faith produces perseverance" (James 1:2–4). And that leads to maturity.

It's difficult to be joyful during trials, but we can take hope from the fact that God will use difficult circumstances to help us reach maturity. Like aspen trees, faith can grow in times of trial when difficulty clears space in our hearts for the light of God to touch us.

—*Amy Peterson*

Spreading Joy

JOHN 16:16–24

*But the angel said to them, "Do not be afraid.
I bring you good news that will cause
great joy for all the people."*

—LUKE 2:10

When Janet went to teach English in a school overseas, she found the atmosphere gloomy and depressing. People did their jobs, but no one seemed happy. They didn't help or encourage one another. But Janet, grateful for what God had done for her, expressed it in everything she did. She smiled. She was friendly. She helped people. She hummed songs and hymns.

Little by little, as Janet shared her joy, the school's atmosphere changed. People began to smile and help each other. When a visiting administrator asked the principal why his school was so different, the principal, who was not a believer, responded, "Jesus brings joy."

It's true. The gospel of Luke tells us that when God sent an angel to ordinary shepherds to deliver an extraordinary birth announcement, he made the surprising proclamation that the newborn baby "will cause great joy for all the people" (Luke 2:10), which indeed He did.

This message has spread through the centuries to us, and now we are Christ's messengers of joy to the world. Let's keep spreading the joy of Jesus as we follow His example and serve others.

—*Julie Ackerman Link*

Trust Me

1 KINGS 17:7–16

"Do not worry about tomorrow."
—MATTHEW 6:34

After graduation from college, I had a low-paying job. Money was tight, and sometimes I didn't even have enough for my next meal. I learned to trust God for my daily provision.

It reminded me of the prophet Elijah's experience. During his prophetic ministry, he learned to trust God to meet his daily needs. Shortly after Elijah pronounced God's judgment of a drought in Israel, God sent him to a deserted place, Kerith Ravine, where He used the ravens to bring Elijah his daily meals and refresh him with water from the brook (1 Kings 17:1–4).

But when the brook dried up, God said: "Go at once to Zarephath. . . . I have directed a widow there to supply you with food" (v. 9). Zarephath was in Phoenicia, whose inhabitants were enemies of the Israelites. Would anyone offer Elijah shelter? And would a poor widow have food to share?

Our loving Father whispers, *Trust Me.* Just as He used ravens and a widow to provide for Elijah, nothing is impossible for Him. We can count on His love and power to meet our daily needs.

—*Poh Fang Chia*

I See You

PSALM 121

The LORD will watch over your coming and going both now and forevermore.

—PSALM 121:8

While I shopped for shoes, our two-year-old Xavier and my husband Alan played hide-and-seek behind stacks of shoeboxes. Suddenly, I saw Alan dash frantically from aisle to aisle, calling Xavier's name. We raced to the front of the store. Our child, still laughing, ran toward the open door leading to a busy street. Within seconds, Alan scooped him up. We embraced as I thanked God, sobbed, and kissed our toddler's chubby cheeks.

A year before I became pregnant with Xavier, I'd lost our first child during the pregnancy. When God blessed us with our son, I became a fearful parent. I knew I couldn't always protect him, but I discovered peace as I learned to turn to my only sure source of help—God—when I struggled with worry and fear.

Our heavenly Father never takes His eyes off us (Psalm 121:1–4). While we can't prevent trials, heartache, or loss, we can live with confident faith, relying on an ever-present Protector (vv. 5–8).

We may feel powerless when we can't shield loved ones. But we can trust that our all-knowing God never loses sight of us—His beloved children.

—*Xochitl Dixon*

Our Covering

ROMANS 3:21–26

Blessed is the one whose transgressions are forgiven, whose sins are covered.
—PSALM 32:1

When talking about faith in Jesus, we sometimes use words without understanding or explaining them. One of those words is *righteous*. We say that God has righteousness and that He makes people righteous, but this can be a tough concept to grasp.

The way the word *righteousness* is pictured in the Chinese language is helpful. It is a combination of two characters. The top word is *lamb*. The bottom word is *me*. The lamb covers or is above the person.

When Jesus came to this world, John the Baptist called Him "the Lamb of God, who takes away the sin of the world!" (John 1:29). We need our sin taken care of because it separates us from God, whose character and ways are always perfect and right. Because of His great love for us, God made His Son Jesus "who had no sin to be sin for us, so that in him we might become the righteousness of God" (2 Corinthians 5:21). Jesus, the Lamb, sacrificed himself and shed His blood. He became our "cover."

Being right with God is a gift from Him. Jesus, the Lamb, is God's way to cover us.

—*Anne Cetas*

What Kind of Savior Is He?

JOHN 6:47–51, 60–66

From this time many of his disciples turned
back and no longer followed him.
—JOHN 6:66

Last year, friends and I prayed for healing for three women battling cancer. We knew God had the power. We had seen Him work in the past and believed He could do it again. There were days in each one's battle when healing looked like it was a reality, and we rejoiced. But they all died that fall. The loss hurt deeply. We wanted Him to heal them all—here and now—but no miracle came.

Some people followed Jesus for the miracles He performed and to get their needs met (John 6:2, 26). Some simply saw Him as the carpenter's son (Matthew 13:55–58), and others expected Him to be their political leader (Luke 19:37–38). Some thought of Him as a great teacher (Matthew 7:28–29), while others quit following Him because His teaching was hard to understand (John 6:66).

Jesus still doesn't always meet our expectations. Yet He is so much more than we can imagine! He's the provider of eternal life (vv. 47–48). He is good and wise; and He loves, forgives, and brings us comfort. May we find rest in Jesus and keep following Him.

—*Anne Cetas*

Expect the Messiah

MATTHEW 13:53–58

"Isn't this the carpenter's son?
Isn't his mother's name Mary?"
—MATTHEW 13:55

The repairman looked young—too young to fix our problem, a car that wouldn't start. "He's just a kid," my husband, Dan, whispered to me. His disbelief sounded like the grumbling in Nazareth where citizens doubted who Jesus was.

"Isn't this the carpenter's son?" they asked (Matthew 13:55) when Jesus taught in the synagogue. Scoffing, they were surprised to hear that someone they knew was healing and teaching, and they asked, "Where did this man get this wisdom and these miraculous powers?" (v. 54). Instead of trusting in Jesus, they were offended by the authority he displayed (vv. 15, 58).

Similarly, we may struggle to trust our Savior's wisdom and power, especially in the mundane details of daily life. When we do, we may miss out on the wonder of His life transforming ours (v. 58).

The help Dan needed was right there. The young mechanic switched just one bolt and had the car running in seconds—engine humming and lights ablaze. "It lit up like Christmas," Dan said.

So too can we expect the Messiah to bring fresh light and help into our daily journey with Him.

—*Patricia Raybon*

Unlighted Paths

JOSHUA 1:1–9

"Have I not commanded you? Be strong and courageous. Do not be afraid; do not be discouraged, for the LORD your God will be with you wherever you go."

—JOSHUA 1:9

As we ventured home from a family vacation, the road took us through some desolate parts of central Oregon. For nearly two hours after dusk we drove through deep canyons and across desert plateaus. Eventually the moon rose on the horizon, visible to us when the road crested hills but eclipsed when we traveled through the lowlands. My daughter called the moon's light a reminder of God's presence. I asked whether she needed to see it to know He was there. She replied, "No, but it sure helps."

After Moses's death, Joshua was charged with leading the Israelites into the promised land. Despite his divine commission, Joshua must have felt challenged by the daunting nature of his task. God assured Joshua assurance that he would be with him on the journey (Joshua 1:9).

Life often travels through uncharted territory, and God's plan may not always be apparent to us. But He has promised to be with us "always, to the very end of the age" (Matthew 28:20). What greater assurance could we hope for, no matter what challenge we face? Even when the path is unlit, the Light is with us.

—*Kirsten Holmberg*

Many Gifts, One Purpose

1 CORINTHIANS 12:4–14

*Just as a body, though one, has many
parts, but all its many parts form
one body, so it is with Christ.*
—1 CORINTHIANS 12:12

Corn, also called maize, is the staple food in my home country of Mexico. There are so many different types. You can find yellow, brown, red, and black cobs, even spotted ones. But people in the cities usually won't eat the spotted cobs; they think uniformity means quality. Yet the spotted cobs taste good, and they make excellent tortillas.

The church of Christ is much more similar to a spotted ear of corn than to a cob of just one color. In the church, even though we are all one body of believers and have the same God, each of us has been given a different gift. Paul said, "There are different kinds of service, but the same Lord. There are different kinds of working, but . . . it is the same God at work" (1 Corinthians 12:5–6). Our diversity in the ways we help each other shows God's generosity and creativity.

As we embrace our diversity, may we also keep our unity in faith and purpose. We have different abilities, backgrounds, languages, and nationalities; but we have the same wonderful God. And He delights in so much variety.

—*Keila Ochoa*

Singing to the Firing Squad

MARK 14:16–26

I trusted in the LORD when I said,
"I am greatly afflicted."
—PSALM 116:10

While in prison two men convicted of drug trafficking learned of God's love for them in Jesus, and their lives were transformed. When it came time for them to be executed, they faced their fate reciting the Lord's Prayer and singing "Amazing Grace." Because of their faith in Christ, through the power of the Spirit they faced death with incredible courage.

They followed the example of faith set by their Savior. When Jesus knew His death was imminent, He spent part of the evening singing with friends. On that night, Jesus and His friends had a Passover meal, which ends with a series of Psalms known as the Hallel, Psalms 113–118. Facing death, Jesus sang about the "cords of death" entangling Him (Psalm 116:3). Yet He praised God's faithful love (117:2) and thanked Him for salvation (118:14). Surely these Psalms comforted Jesus on the night before His crucifixion.

Jesus's trust in God was so great that even as He approached His own death—a death He did not deserve—He chose to sing of God's love. Because of Jesus, we too can have confidence that whatever we face, God is with us.

—*Amy Peterson*

The Daily Prayer

EPHESIANS 6:18–19

*Pray in the Spirit on all occasions with
all kinds of prayers and requests.*
—EPHESIANS 6:18

Singer-songwriter Robert Hamlet wrote "Lady Who Prays for Me" as a tribute to his mother who made a point of praying for her boys each morning before they went to the bus stop. After a young mom heard Hamlet sing his song, she committed to praying with her own little boy before he left the house. The result was heartwarming! Five minutes later he returned—bringing kids from the bus stop with him! The boy explained to his mom, "Their moms didn't pray with them."

In the book of Ephesians, Paul urges us to pray "on all occasions with all kinds of prayers" (6:18). Demonstrating our daily dependence on God is essential in a family. Many children first learn to trust God as they observe genuine faith in the people closest to them (2 Timothy 1:5). There is no better way to teach the utmost importance of prayer than by praying for and with our children.

When we "start children off" by modeling a "sincere faith" in God (Proverbs 22:6; 2 Timothy 1:5), we give them a special gift, an assurance that God is an ever-present part of our lives.

—*Cindy Hess Kasper*

Our Powerful God

AMOS 4:12–13

*He who forms the mountains, who creates the
wind, and who reveals his thoughts to mankind,
. . . the LORD God Almighty is his name.*

—AMOS 4:13

One day by the seaside, I delighted in watching kite
surfers as they bounced along the water, moved by the
force of the wind. When one came to shore, I asked
him if the experience was as difficult as it looked.
"No," he said, "It's actually easier than regular surf-
ing because you harness the power of the wind."

Later, as I walked by the sea I paused to wonder
at our God the Creator. As we see in the Old Testament book of Amos, He who "forms the mountains"
and "creates the wind" can turn "dawn to darkness"
(v. 13).

Through this prophet, the Lord reminded His people of His power as He called them back to himself.
Because they had not obeyed Him, He said He would
reveal himself to them (v. 13). Although we see His
judgment here, we also know of His sacrificial love
in sending His Son to save us (see John 3:16).

This breezy day in the South of England reminded
me of the sheer immensity of the Lord. If you feel
the wind today, why not stop and ponder our all-
powerful God?

—*Amy Boucher Pye*

A Perfect World

REVELATION 21:1–5

He who was seated on the throne said,
"I am making everything new!"
—REVELATION 21:5

Katie was given a school assignment to write an essay entitled "My Perfect World." She wrote: "In my perfect world . . . ice cream is free, lollipops are everywhere, and the sky is blue all the time." Then her essay took a more serious turn. In that world, she continued, "No one will come home to bad news. And no one will have to be the one to deliver it."

"No one will come home to bad news." Sounds wonderful! Those words point to the confident hope we have in Jesus. He is "making everything new"—healing and transforming our world (Revelation 21:5).

Paradise is the place of "no more"—no more evil, death, mourning, pain, or tears (v. 4)! It is a place of perfect communion with God, who by His love has redeemed us (v. 3). What marvelous joy awaits us!

As we seek to fellowship with God daily, we experience the joy of His presence (Colossians 1:12–13). And even as we struggle against sin, we experience, in part, the victory that is ours in Christ (2:13–15), who will make everything new.

—*Poh Fang Chia*

Marvelous Maker

PSALM 104:24–34

How many are your works, LORD! In wisdom you
made them all; the earth is full of your creatures.
—PSALM 104:24

As an amateur photographer, I enjoy capturing glimpses of God's creativity with my camera. I see His fingerprints on each delicate flower petal, each vibrant sunrise and sunset, and each cloud-painted and star-speckled sky canvas.

My camera's powerful zoom option allows me to take photos of the Lord's creatures too. I've snapped shots of a chattering squirrel in a cherry blossom tree, a colorful butterfly flitting from bloom to bloom, and sea turtles sunning on a rocky black beach. Each one-of-a-kind image prompted me to worship my marvelous Maker.

I'm not alone in admiring His unique creations. The writer of Psalm 104 sings of the Lord's many works of art in nature (v. 24). He regards "the sea, vast and spacious, teeming with creatures beyond number" (v. 25) and rejoices in God for providing constant and complete care for His masterpieces (vv. 27–31).

While reflecting on the Lord's magnificent and immense creation, we can join the psalmist in singing to our Creator with thankful praise for how powerful, majestic, and loving He is and always will be. Hallelujah!

—*Xochitl Dixon*

Stories of Jesus

JOHN 21:24–25; 1 JOHN 1:1–4

Jesus did many other things as well.
—JOHN 21:25

As a girl I loved to visit my small local library. One day, I challenged myself to read every book in the young adult section. In my enthusiasm I forgot one important fact—new books were regularly added. Although I gave it a valiant effort, there were simply too many books.

The apostle John likely would be amazed with the availability of books today—especially since his five New Testament books, the gospel of John; 1, 2, and 3 John; and Revelation, were handwritten on parchment scrolls.

John wrote those scrolls because he felt compelled by the Holy Spirit to provide an eyewitness account of Jesus's life and ministry (1 John 1:1–4). But John's writings contained only a small fraction of what Jesus did and taught during His ministry. In fact, John said if everything Jesus did were written down "the whole world could not contain the books that would be written" (John 21:25 NLT).

The libraries of the world cannot contain every story of Jesus's love and grace. What a privilege to be able to proclaim that love forever! (Psalm 89:1).
—*Lisa Samra*

Breaking the Chains

EPHESIANS 1:3–14

In him we have redemption through
his blood, the forgiveness of sins.
—EPHESIANS 1:7

We found our visit to Christ Church Cathedral in Stone Town, Zanzibar, deeply moving, for it sits on the site of what was formerly the largest slave market in East Africa. The designers of this cathedral wanted to show through a physical symbol how the gospel breaks the chains of slavery. No longer would the location be a place of horrible atrocities, but it would become a picture of God's grace.

Those who built the cathedral wanted to express how Jesus's death on the cross provides freedom from sin—"In him we have redemption through his blood" (Paul in Ephesians 1:7). Here the word *redemption* points to the idea of the marketplace, with someone buying back a person or item. Jesus buys back a person from a life of slavery to sin and wrongdoing.

As Paul begins this letter (vv. 3–14), he bubbles over with joy at the thought of his freedom in Christ. He points to God's work of grace through Jesus's death, which sets us free from the penalty of sin. No longer are we slaves; we are set free to live for God and His glory.

—*Amy Boucher Pye*

Nobody Likes Me

PSALM 142

*No one is concerned for me. I have
no refuge; no one cares for my life.*
—PSALM 142:4

As a child, when I felt lonely, rejected, or sorry for myself, my mother would sometimes attempt to cheer me up by singing a popular ditty: "Nobody likes me, everybody hates me. I think I'll go eat worms." After a smile brightened my downcast face, she'd help me see the many special relationships and reasons for gratitude I truly did have.

When I read that David felt no one cared for him, that ditty rings in my ears. Yet David's pain wasn't at all exaggerated. Where I had feelings of loneliness typical for my age, David actually had good reason to feel abandoned. He wrote these words in the dark depths of a cave where he hid from Saul, who pursued him with murderous plans (1 Samuel 22:1; 24:3–10). In the midst of the loneliness David felt, he cried out to God as his "refuge" and "portion in the land of the living" (Psalm 142:5).

God never minimizes our loneliness. He wants to be our companion in the dark caves of our lives. Even when we think no one cares for our life, God cares!
—*Kirsten Holmberg*

God with Skin On

ROMANS 12:9–18

Share with the Lord's people who
are in need. Practice hospitality.
—ROMANS 12:13

My husband left for a month-long trip, and almost immediately I was overwhelmed by the needs of my job, our house, and our children. A writing deadline loomed. The lawn mower broke. My children were on school break and bored. How would I take care of all of these things on my own?

I soon realized I wasn't on my own. Friends from church showed up to help. Josh, John, Cassidy, and Abi all pitched in. They demonstrated the kind of community Paul describes in Romans 12. They loved sincerely (v. 9), considered the needs of others rather than their own (v. 10), shared with me when I was in need, and showed hospitality (v. 13).

Because of the love of my friends, I remained "joyful in hope" and "patient in affliction" (v. 12), even in the mild affliction of solo parenting for a month. My brothers and sisters in Christ became "God with skin on" for me. They showed me the kind of sincere love we ought to show to everyone, especially those in our community of faith (Galatians 6:10). I hope to be more like them.

—*Amy Peterson*

Gazing at the Horizon

HEBREWS 11:8–16

We are looking for the city that is to come.
—HEBREWS 13:14

Almost as soon as the ferryboat started to move, my little daughter said she felt ill. Seasickness had already begun to affect her. Soon I was feeling queasy myself. "Just stare at the horizon," I reminded myself. Sailors say this helps to regain a sense of perspective.

The Maker of the horizon (Job 26:10) knows that sometimes in life we may become fearful and restless. We can regain perspective by focusing on the distant but steady point of our destiny.

The writer of Hebrews understood this. He sensed discouragement in his readers. Persecution had driven many of them from their homes. So he reminded them that other people of faith had endured extreme trials and had been left homeless. They endured it all because they anticipated something better.

The writer asked his readers to focus on God's promise: "For here we do not have an enduring city, but we are looking for the city that is to come" (13:14).

We are "foreigners and strangers on earth" (11:13), but gazing at the horizon of God's promises provides the point of reference we need.

—*Keila Ochoa*

Can We Relax?

JOHN 14:25–31

*Do not let your hearts be troubled
and do not be afraid.*
—JOHN 14:27

Darnell entered the physical therapist's office knowing he would experience a lot of pain. The therapist stretched and bent his arm and held it in positions it hadn't been in for months since his injury. After holding each uncomfortable position for a few seconds, she gently told him: "Okay, you can relax." He said later, "I think I heard that at least fifty times in each therapy session: 'Okay, you can relax.'"

Thinking of those words, Darnell realized they could apply to the rest of his life as well. He could relax in God's goodness and faithfulness instead of worrying.

As Jesus neared His death, He wanted to encourage His disciples. So He said He would send the Holy Spirit to live with them and remind them of what He had taught (John 14:26). And so He could say, "Peace I leave with you; . . . Do not let your hearts be troubled and do not be afraid" (v. 27).

There's plenty we could be uptight about in our everyday lives. But as we draw on God's strength, we can hear Him in the therapist's words: "Okay, you can relax."

—*Anne Cetas*

When Morning Comes

HEBREWS 11:1-8

*Now faith is confidence in what we hope for
and assurance about what we do not see.*
—HEBREWS 11:1

It was very late when we stopped for the night at a country inn outside of Munich. We were delighted that our cozy room had a balcony, although an oppressive fog made it impossible to see anything. But when the sun rose a few hours later, the haze faded. Then we could see what had been shrouded earlier—an idyllic scene—peaceful and lush green meadow, sheep grazing, and fluffy white clouds in the sky.

Sometimes life can get clouded over by a heavy fog of despair. Our situation may look so dark that we begin to lose hope. But just as the sun burns away a fog, our faith in God can burn away the haze of doubt.

Hebrews 11 defines faith as "confidence in what we hope for and assurance about what we do not see" (v. 1). The passage goes on to remind us of the faith of Noah, who was "warned about things not yet seen," yet obeyed God (v. 7).

Although we have not seen Him and cannot always feel His presence, God is always present and will help us through our darkest nights.

—*Cindy Hess Kasper*

As Advertised

JOHN 16:25–33

"In this world you will have trouble. But take heart! I have overcome the world."
—JOHN 16:33

During a vacation, my husband and I signed up for a leisurely rafting tour down Georgia's Chattahoochee River. Dressed in sandals, a sundress, and a wide brimmed hat, I groaned when we discovered—contrary to the advertisement—that the trip included light rapids. After a trip downriver that provided more excitement than I wanted, I stepped onto the shore and dumped water from my purse as my husband helped me wring out the hem of my soaked dress. We enjoyed a good laugh, even though the trip had not turned out as advertised.

Unlike the tour brochure, which clearly left out a key detail, Jesus explicitly warned His disciples that rough waters were ahead. He told them they'd be persecuted and martyred and that He would die and be resurrected. He also guaranteed His trustworthiness, affirming that He would guide them toward undeniable triumph and everlasting hope (John 16:16–33).

Trials won't define, limit, or destroy God's plan for us, because Jesus's resurrection has already propelled us to eternal victory.

—*Xochitl Dixon*

The Prayer and the Chain Saws

NEHEMIAH 1

*"LORD, let your ear be attentive to
the prayer of this your servant."*
—NEHEMIAH 1:11

I respect my Aunt Gladys's intrepid spirit, although it concerns me sometimes. Once, the source of my concern came in the form of an email: "I cut down a walnut tree yesterday."

My chainsaw-wielding aunt is seventy-six years old! The tree had grown up behind her garage. When the roots threatened to burst through the concrete, it had to go. But she did tell us, "I always pray before I tackle a job like that."

While serving as butler to the king of Persia during the time of Israel's exile, Nehemiah heard news concerning the people who had returned to Jerusalem: "The wall of Jerusalem is broken down, and its gates have been burned with fire" (Nehemiah 1:3). Jerusalem was vulnerable to attack by enemies. Nehemiah wanted to get involved. But prayer came first, especially since a new king had intervened to stop the building efforts in Jerusalem (see Ezra 4). Nehemiah prayed for his people (Nehemiah 1:5–10), and then he asked God for help before requesting permission from the king to leave (v. 11).

Is prayer your response? It's always the best way to face any task or trial in life.

—*Linda Washington*

Think Before You Speak

PSALM 141

Set a guard over my mouth, LORD;
keep watch over the door of my lips.
—PSALM 141:3

Cheung and his family had planned to round out their holiday in Japan with a scrumptious meal before catching the flight home. But his wife failed to check directions to the restaurant, so they had to miss that meal. Frustrated, Cheung criticized his wife for her poor planning.

Later Cheung realized he had been too harsh, plus he realized he could have checked the directions himself. And he knew he should have thanked his wife for planning the entire vacation.

Many of us can identify with Cheung. When angry, we let words fly without control. That's why we need to pray as the psalmist did: "Set a guard over my mouth, LORD; keep watch over the door of my lips" (Psalm 141:3).

Here's a helpful tip: Think before you speak. Are your words good and helpful, gracious and kind? (See Ephesians 4:29–32.)

Setting a guard over our mouth requires that we stay quiet when we're irritated and that we seek the Lord's help to say the right words with the right tone. Thankfully, God is working in us, giving us "the desire and the power to do what pleases him" (Philippians 2:13 NLT).

—*Poh Fang Chia*

Seeing God

EXODUS 34:1–9

"The LORD is slow to anger, abounding in love and forgiving sin and rebellion."
—NUMBERS 14:18

Caricature artists set up their easels in public places and draw pictures of people who are willing to pay for a humorous image of themselves. Their drawings amuse us by exaggerating our physical features in a way that is recognizable but funny.

Caricatures of God, on the other hand, are not funny. Exaggerating one of His attributes presents a distorted view that people easily dismiss. A distorted view of God is not taken seriously. For instance, those who see God portrayed only as an angry and demanding judge are easily lured away by someone who emphasizes mercy. Those who see God as an intellectual idea rather than a living, loving being eventually find other ideas more appealing. Those who see God as a best friend often leave Him behind when they find human friends who are more to their liking.

God declares himself to be merciful and gracious, but He is also just in punishing the guilty (Exodus 34:6–7).

As we put our faith into action, we need to avoid portraying God as having only our favorite attributes. We must worship all of God, not just what we like.

—*Julie Ackerman Link*

Treasure in Heaven

MATTHEW 6:19–21

*"For where your treasure is,
there your heart will be also."*
—MATTHEW 6:21

When I was growing up, my two sisters and I liked to sit side-by-side on top of my mother's large cedar-lined chest. My mom kept our wool sweaters in it and handiwork created by my grandmother. She valued the contents of the chest and relied on the pungent odor of the cedar wood to discourage moths from destroying what was inside.

Most earthly possessions can easily be destroyed by insects or rust, or can even be stolen. Matthew 6 encourages us to place a special focus instead on things that have *eternal* value. When my mom died at fifty-seven, she had not accumulated a lot of earthly possessions, but I like to think about the treasure she stored in heaven (vv. 19–20).

I recall how much she loved God and served Him: caring faithfully for her family, teaching children in Sunday school, comforting a young mother who had lost her baby. And she *prayed*. . . . Even after she lost her sight and could no longer walk, she continued to love and pray for others.

What "treasures" are we storing up in heaven by serving and following Jesus?

—*Cindy Hess Kasper*

Healing Flood

PSALM 107:1–16, 35–36

*He turned the desert into pools of water and
the parched ground into flowing springs.*
—PSALM 107:35

I've always loved a good thunderstorm. As kids, whenever a storm was truly incredible—with booming thunder and buckets of heavy rain pounding down—my siblings and I would make a mad dash around the outside of our house, slipping and sliding along the way. When it was time to go back inside, we were soaked to the bone.

It was an exhilarating taste—for just a few minutes—of being immersed in something so powerful we couldn't quite tell whether we were having fun or terrified.

This picture comes to mind when, as in Psalm 107, Scripture compares God's restoration to a barren wilderness transformed into "pools of water" (v. 35). The kind of storm that transforms a desert into an oasis isn't a gentle shower—it's a downpour!

Isn't that the kind of restoration we long for? When we are "hungry and thirsty"—*starving*—for healing that never seems to arrive (vv. 4–5), we need more than a bit of hope.

Let's give our fears and shame to the One who's able to break our chains and flood our darkness with His light (vv. 13–14).

—*Monica Brands*

Righteous among the Nations

ESTHER 4:5–14

For such a time as this.
—ESTHER 4:14

At Yad Vashem, Israel's Holocaust museum, my husband and I went to the Righteous Among the Nations garden, which honors those who risked their lives to save Jewish people during the Holocaust. While looking at the memorial, we met a group from the Netherlands. One woman was there to see her grandparents' names listed on the large plaques. Intrigued, we asked about her family's story.

Members of a resistance network, the woman's grandparents Rev. Pieter and Adriana Müller took in a two-year-old Jewish boy and passed him off as the youngest of their eight children from 1943–1945.

Moved by the story, we asked, "Did the little boy survive?" An older gentleman in the group stepped forward and proclaimed, "I am that boy!"

The bravery of many to act on behalf of the Jewish people reminds me of Queen Esther. Perhaps she could have avoided death under King Xerxes's decree to annihilate the Jews around 475 BC by continuing to conceal her ethnicity. But she risked everything to confront her husband and win protection for her people.

If we are ever required to speak out against an injustice, may God grant us the courage He gave the Müllers and Queen Esther.

—Lisa Samra

Remembering My Father

JOB 38:1–11

Whatever you do, work at it with all your heart, as working for the Lord.
—COLOSSIANS 3:23

When I remember my dad, I picture him best outdoors hammering or gardening or downstairs working in his cluttered workroom, stuffed with fascinating tools and gadgets. His hands were always busy at a task or project—sometimes building (a garage or a deck or a birdhouse), sometimes locksmithing, and sometimes designing jewelry and stained-glass art.

Remembering my dad prompts me to think of my heavenly Father and Creator, who has always been busy at work. In the beginning, "[God] laid the earth's foundations . . . [and] marked off its dimensions . . . while the morning stars sang together and all the angels shouted for joy" (Job 38:4–7). Everything He created was a work of art, a masterpiece. He designed a breathtakingly beautiful world and pronounced it "very good" (Genesis 1:31).

That includes you and me. God designed us in intimate and intricate detail (Psalm 139:13–16); and He entrusted us with and instilled in us (His image bearers) the goal and desire to work, which includes ruling and caring for the Earth and its creatures (Genesis 1:26–28; 2:15).

In everything we do, may we do it to please Him.
—*Alyson Kieda*

Unseen Heroes

EXODUS 17:8–15

When Moses' hands grew tired, they took a stone and put it under him and he sat on it. Aaron and Hur held his hands up.

—EXODUS 17:12

Stories in the Bible can make us stop and wonder. For instance, when Moses led God's people into the promised land and the Amalekites attacked, we aren't told how he knew to go to the top of the hill and hold up God's staff (Exodus 17:8–15). All we know is that when Moses raised his hands, the Israelites would win the battle. When Moses got tired, his brother Aaron and another man, Hur, held up Moses's arms so the Israelites could triumph.

We aren't told much about Hur, but he played a crucial role.

Unseen heroes matter. Those who encourage leaders play a key and often overlooked role. Leaders may be the ones getting the glory, but the quiet, faithful witness of those who serve behind the scenes is not overlooked by the Lord. He sees the person who intercedes in prayer for friends and family. He sees the woman who puts away the chairs after Sunday school. He sees the neighbor who reaches out with a word of encouragement.

God is using us, even if our task feels insignificant. And may we notice and thank any unseen heroes who help us.

—*Amy Boucher Pye*

Let's Finish the Race

ECCLESIASTES 4:9–12

*Two are better than one, because they have a
good return for their labor; if either of them
falls down, one can help the other up.*
—ECCLESIASTES 4:9–10

In the 2016 Rio Olympics, two athletes in the 5,000-meter race caught the world's attention. About 3,200 meters into the race, New Zealander Nikki Hamblin and American Abbey D'Agostino collided and fell. Abbey was quickly up on her feet, but she stopped to help Nikki. Moments after the two athletes had started running again, Abbey began faltering, her right leg injured as a result of the fall. It was now Nikki's turn to stop and encourage her fellow athlete to finish the race. When Abbey eventually stumbled across the finish line, Nikki was waiting to embrace her. What a beautiful picture of mutual encouragement!

That sounds like Ecclesiastes 4: "Two are better than one . . . . If either of them falls down, one can help the other up." (vv. 9–10). As runners in a spiritual race, we need one another, perhaps even more so, for we are not competing. We are members of the same team.

The spiritual race is not to be run alone. Is God leading you to be a Nikki or Abbey in someone's life? Respond to His prompting today, and together let's finish the race!

—*Poh Fang Chia*

Dumb Sheep, Good Sheep

EZEKIEL 34:7–16

As a shepherd looks after his scattered flock when
he is with them, so will I look after my sheep.
—EZEKIEL 34:12

My friend Chad spent a year as a shepherd in Wyoming. "Sheep are so dumb that they'll only eat what is right in front of them," he told me. "Even if they've eaten all the grass in front of them, they won't turn to look for a fresh patch—they'll just start eating dirt!"

We laughed, and I couldn't help but think about how often the Bible compares humans to sheep. No wonder we need a shepherd! But not just any shepherd will do; sheep need a shepherd who cares about them. When the prophet Ezekiel wrote to God's people in exile in Babylon, he compared them to sheep led by bad shepherds. Instead of caring for the flock, Israel's leaders had left them for the wild animals to devour (v. 5).

But they were not without hope. God, the Good Shepherd, promised to rescue them—to bring them home. He would heal the injured and go after the lost (vv. 11–16) so that His flock would be safe (v. 28).

As members of God's flock, we are blessed to have a Shepherd who leads us to green pastures! (v.14).

—*Amy Peterson*

Hard Conversations

1 SAMUEL 25:21–25

If it is possible, as far as it depends on you,
live at peace with everyone.
—ROMANS 12:18

I once drove fifty miles to have a hard conversation with a remote staff person who had been presenting our company improperly to others.

In 1 Samuel 25, a woman named Abigail took great personal risk to confront a future king of Israel about a disastrous choice he was about to make. Abigail was married to Nabal, whose character matched the meaning of his name ("fool"; vv. 3, 25). Nabal had refused to pay David and his troops the customary wage for protecting his livestock (vv. 10–11). Hearing that David planned a murderous revenge on her household and knowing her foolish husband wouldn't listen to reason, Abigail prepared a peace offering, rode to meet David, and persuaded him to reconsider (vv. 18–31).

How did Abigail accomplish this? She spoke truth to David, reminding him of God's call on his life. If he resisted his desire for revenge, when God made him king he wouldn't "have on his conscience the staggering burden of needless bloodshed" (v. 31).

You might know someone dangerously close to a making a harmful mistake. Like Abigail, might God be calling you to a hard conversation?

—*Elisa Morgan*

Preserving the Peace

PSALM 3

I lie down and sleep; I wake again,
because the LORD sustains me.
—PSALM 3:5

As I continue trusting God through my struggles with chronic pain, even the simplest setback can feel like a fierce enemy attacker. Problem One jabs me from the right. Problem Two shoves me from behind. Problem Three punches me square in the nose. When my strength wanes and immediate relief evades me, hiding can seem like a good idea. But since I can't escape my pain, I'm learning to rely on God to carry me through.

When I need encouragement, comfort, and courage, I prayerfully read through the songs of the psalmists, who honestly bring their situations to God. In one of my favorite psalms, King David flees from Absalom, his son who wanted to take his kingdom. Although David lamented his painful situation (Psalm 3:1–2), he trusted God's protection. The king was able to rest because he trusted God to sustain and save him (vv. 5–8).

Physical and emotional pain can often feel like aggressive adversaries. We may be tempted to give up. But like David, we can learn to trust that God will hold us up and help us rest in His constant and loving presence.

—*Xochitl Dixon*

Table Rock

LUKE 6:46–49

*"Why do you call me, 'Lord, Lord,'
and do not do what I say?"*
—LUKE 6:46

A large, illuminated cross stands erect on Table Rock, a plateau overlooking my hometown. Several homes were built on neighboring land, but recently the owners have been forced to move out. Despite their close proximity to the firm bedrock of Table Rock, these homes aren't secure. They have been shifting atop their foundations—nearly three inches every day—and are in danger of collapsing.

Jesus compares those who hear and obey His words to those who build their homes on rock (Luke 6:47–48). These homes survive the storms. By contrast, He says homes built without a firm foundation—like people who don't heed His instruction—cannot weather the torrents.

I've often been tempted to ignore my conscience when I knew God asked more of me than I had given, thinking my response had been "close enough." Yet the homes in those shifting foothills have depicted for me that being "close" is nowhere near enough when it comes to obeying Him. To be like those who built their homes on a firm foundation and withstand the storms of life, we must heed the words of our Lord completely.

—*Kirsten Holmberg*

Power of Touch

MARK 1:40–45

Moved with compassion, Jesus
reached out and touched him.
—MARK 1:41 (NLT)

Dr. Paul Brand, twentieth-century pioneer medical missionary to India, saw firsthand the stigma associated with leprosy. During an appointment, he touched a patient to reassure him treatment was possible. Tears streamed down the man's face. An attendant said to Dr. Brand, "You touched him, and no one has done that for years. They are tears of joy."

Early in His ministry, Jesus was approached by a man with leprosy, an ancient label for all types of infectious skin diseases. The man was considered untouchable. If he found himself in close proximity to healthy people, he had to call out, "Unclean! Unclean!" so they could avoid him (Leviticus 13:45–46). The man may have gone years without human contact.

Filled with compassion, Jesus reached out and touched the man. Jesus had the power and authority to heal people with just a word (Mark 2:11–12). But His touch assured the man that he was not alone.

We can extend grace and show compassion to others with a gentle touch that conveys dignity and value. The healing power of human touch goes a long way to remind hurting people of our care and concern.

—*Lisa Samra*

Hovering over Us

DEUTERONOMY 32:7–12

In a desert land he found him, in a barren and howling waste. He shielded him and cared for him; he guarded him as the apple of his eye.
—DEUTERONOMY 32:10–11

Betty's daughter arrived home from an overseas trip feeling unwell. When her pain became unbearable, Betty and her husband took her to the emergency room. The doctors and nurses set to work, and after a few hours one of the nurses said to Betty, "She's going to be okay! We're going to take good care of her." In that moment, Betty felt peace and love flood over her. She realized that the Lord is the perfect parent who nurtures His children, comforting us in difficult times.

In the book of Deuteronomy, the Lord reminded His people how, when they were wandering in the desert, He cared for them: He never left them, but was like an eagle "that spreads its wings" to catch its children and "carries them aloft" (32:11). He wanted them to remember that although they experienced hardship and strife in the desert, He didn't abandon them.

We face many challenges, but we can take courage that our God will never leave us. When we feel that we are falling, the Lord, like an eagle, will spread His wings to catch us (v. 11).

—*Amy Boucher Pye*

Bring Your Boats

PROVERBS 3:21–31

*Do not withhold good from those to whom
it is due, when it is in your power to act.*
—PROVERBS 3:27

Hurricane Harvey brought catastrophic flooding to eastern Texas in 2017. The onslaught of rain and floodwaters stranded thousands of people in their homes. In what was dubbed the "Texas Navy," many private citizens brought boats from other parts of the state and nation to help evacuate stranded people.

The actions of these valiant, generous men and women call to mind the encouragement of Proverbs 3:27, which instructs us to help others when we can. Their actions demonstrate a willingness to use whatever resources they had at their disposal for the benefit of others.

We may not always feel adequate for the task at hand; often we become paralyzed by thinking we don't have the skills, experience, resources, or time to help others. In such instances, we're quick to sideline ourselves, discounting what we *do* have that might be of assistance to someone else. The Texas Navy couldn't stop the floodwaters from rising nor could they legislate government aid. But they used what they had—their boats—to assist their fellow man. May we all bring our "boats"—whatever they may be—to take the people in our paths to higher ground.

—*Kirsten Holmberg*

Terrible and Beautiful Things

PSALM 57

Awake, my soul! Awake, harp and lyre!
I will awaken the dawn.
—PSALM 57:8

Fear can leave us frozen. We know all the reasons to be afraid—everything that's hurt us in the past, everything that could easily do so again. So sometimes we're stuck—unable to go back; afraid to move forward. *I just can't. I'm not strong enough to handle being hurt like that again.*

I'm captivated by how author Frederick Buechner describes God's grace: like a gentle voice that says, "Here is the world. Terrible and beautiful things will happen. Don't be afraid. I am with you."

Terrible things will happen. Like the psalmist David, we carry our own stories of when evil surrounded us or when, like "ravenous beasts," others wounded us (Psalm 57:4). And we grieve; we cry out (vv. 1–2).

But because God is with us, beautiful things can happen. As we run to Him with our hurts and fears, we find ourselves carried by a love far greater than anyone's power to harm us (vv. 1–3). His love is a solid refuge where our hearts find healing (vv. 1, 7). Soon we'll find ourselves with renewed courage, ready to greet the day with a song of His faithfulness (vv. 8–10).

—*Monica Brands*

Hope in Darkness

JEREMIAH 31:16–26

I will refresh the weary and satisfy the faint.
—JEREMIAH 31:25

According to legend, Qu Yuan was a wise, patriotic Chinese government official during the time of the Warring States period (475–246 BC). He tried repeatedly to warn his king about a threat that would destroy the country, but the king rejected his advice. Eventually, Qu Yuan was exiled. When he learned about the fall of his beloved country to the foe he had warned about, he ended his life.

Qu Yuan's life resembles some aspects of the life of the prophet Jeremiah. He too served kings who scorned his warnings, and his country was ravaged. However, while Qu Yuan gave in to despair, Jeremiah found genuine hope. Why the difference?

Jeremiah knew the Lord who offers the only true hope. "There is hope for your descendants," God had assured His prophet. "Your children will return to their own land" (Jeremiah 31:17). Although Jerusalem was destroyed in 586 BC, it was later rebuilt (see Nehemiah 6:15).

We all find ourselves in dire situations. But when life knocks us down, we can look up. God is on the throne! He holds our days in His hands, and He holds us close to His heart.

—*Poh Fang Chia*

Riding the Rapids

ISAIAH 43:1–7

When you pass through the rivers,
they will not sweep over you.
—ISAIAH 43:2

The rafting guide escorted our group to the river's edge and directed us to put on life jackets and grab paddles. After highlighting the thrills the watery voyage ahead would hold for us, he detailed a series of directions we could expect to hear—and would need to follow—to steer the boat through the white water. He assured us that although there might be tense moments, our journey would be both exciting and safe.

Sometimes life feels like a white-water rafting trip, one that contains more rapids than we might like. God's promise to Israel through the prophet Isaiah can guide our feelings when we fear the worst is happening: "When you pass through the rivers, they will not sweep over you" (Isaiah 43:2). The Israelites faced an overwhelming fear of rejection by God as they went into exile. Instead, He affirms them and promises to be with them because He loves them (vv. 2, 4).

God won't abandon us in the rough waters. We can trust Him to guide us through the rapids—our fears and troubles—because He also loves us and promises to be with us.

—*Kirsten Holmberg*

Celebrate Freedom

ROMANS 6:15–23

The law of the Spirit who gives life has set you free from the law of sin and death.

—ROMANS 8:2

After being kidnapped, held hostage for thirteen days, and released, New Zealand news cameraman Olaf Wiig, with a broad smile on his face, announced, "I feel more alive now than I have in my entire life."

For reasons difficult to understand, being freed is more exhilarating than being free.

For those who enjoy freedom every day, Olaf's joy was a good reminder of how easily we forget how blessed we are. This is also true spiritually. Those of us who have been Christians for a long time often forget what it's like to be held hostage by sin. We can become complacent and even ungrateful. But then God lets us hear from a new believer who gives an exuberant testimony of what God has done. Once again we see the joy that comes when we are "free from the law of sin and death" (Romans 8:2).

In Christ, we are no longer slaves to sin; we are freed to be holy and to enjoy eternal life with Christ Jesus! (6:22).

Let's celebrate our freedom in Christ by taking the time to thank God for the things we are free to do as His servant.

—*Julie Ackerman Link*

Responding to God's Leading

EXODUS 3:7–14

At once they left their nets and followed him.
—MATTHEW 4:20

When preparing to attend a university a couple of hours from home, I realized I probably wouldn't move back home after graduation. My mind raced. *How can I leave home? Family? Church? What if God calls me to another state or country?*

Like Moses, when God told him to go "to Pharaoh to bring [His] people the Israelites out of Egypt" (Exodus 3:10), I was afraid. I didn't want to leave my comfort zone. Yes, Moses obeyed and followed God, but not before questioning Him and requesting that someone else go instead (vv. 11–13; 4:13).

A better example of what to do when we sense a clear call from God would be the disciples. When Jesus called them, they left everything and followed Him (Matthew 4:20–22; Luke 5:28).

Being away from home is still difficult. But as I continually seek God, He opens doors for me that confirm I am where I am supposed to be.

When we are led out of our comfort zone, we can either go reluctantly or willingly. But no matter how difficult it may be, following Jesus is worth it.

—*Julie Schwab*

Side by Side

NEHEMIAH 3:1–12

*Two are better than one, because they
have a good return for their labor.*
—ECCLESIASTES 4:9

In ancient times, a city with broken walls revealed a defeated people, exposed to danger and shame. That is why the Jews rebuilt the walls of Jerusalem by working side by side.

At first glance, Nehemiah 3 might appear to be a boring account of who did what in the reconstruction. However, a closer look highlights how people worked together. Priests were working alongside rulers. Perfume-makers were helping as well as goldsmiths. Some who lived in nearby towns came to give a hand. Others made repairs opposite their houses. Shallum's daughters, for example, worked alongside the men (3:12).

Two things stand out. First, they all worked together for a common goal. Second, all of them are commended for being part of the work, not for how much or little they did as compared to others.

We can help to rebuild our neighborhoods by showing others they can find hope and new life in Jesus. All of us have something to do. So let us work side by side and do our part—whether big or small—to create a community of love where people can find Jesus.

—*Keila Ochoa*

The Advocate

JOHN 16:7–15

*"But when he, the Spirit of truth, comes,
he will guide you into all the truth."*
—JOHN 16:13

As I boarded the airplane to study in a city a thousand miles from home, I felt nervous and alone—until I remembered that Jesus promised His disciples the comforting presence of the Holy Spirit.

Jesus's friends must have felt bewildered when He told them, "It is for your good that I am going away" (John 16:7). How could they be better off without Him? But Jesus told them that if He left, then the Advocate—the Holy Spirit—would come.

Jesus, nearing His last hours on earth, shared with His disciples (in John 14–17) words to help them understand His death and ascension. Central in this conversation was the coming Holy Spirit (14:16–17), who would be with them (15:15)—teaching (v. 26), testifying (v. 26), and guiding them (16:13).

We who have accepted God's offer of new life have been given this gift of His Spirit living within us. He convicts us of our sins and helps us to repent. He brings us comfort to help our pain, wisdom to understand God's teaching, hope and faith to believe, and love to share.

We can't be alone; we have the Advocate.

—*Amy Boucher Pye*

Apart, but Not Abandoned

ACTS 20:17–20, 35–38

"Now I commit you to God and to the word of his grace, which can build you up and give you an inheritance among all those who are sanctified."
—ACTS 20:32

I had a lump in my throat as I said goodbye to my niece who was moving 800 miles away for graduate school. Although she had been away four years as an undergraduate, she hadn't left our state. Now she was so far away we could longer meet regularly to talk. I had to trust that God would take care of her.

Paul likely felt the same way as he said goodbye to the elders of the church in Ephesus. Having established the church and taught them for three years, Paul considered these elders to be as close as family. Now that Paul was headed to Jerusalem, he would not see them again.

But Paul had parting advice for the Ephesians, who did not have to feel abandoned. God would continue to train them through "the word of his grace" (Acts 20:32). Unlike Paul, God would always be with them.

Saying goodbye is difficult when loved ones move beyond our influence. When we let go of their hands, we can trust that God has them in His. He can meet their real needs—more than we ever could.

—*Linda Washington*

It Takes Time to Grow

EPHESIANS 4:11–16

Speaking the truth in love, we will grow to become in every respect the mature body of him who is the head, that is, Christ.

—EPHESIANS 4:15

On her first day in preschool, young Charlotte was asked to draw a picture of herself. Her artwork featured a simple orb for a body, an oblong head, and two circle eyes. On her last day of preschool, Charlotte was again directed to draw a self-portrait. This one showed a little girl in a colorful dress, a smiling face with distinct features, and a cascade of beautiful red tresses. The school was demonstrating the difference time can make in the level of maturity.

We know maturity takes time, but we sometimes grow impatient with ourselves or fellow believers who show slow spiritual growth. The author of Hebrews spoke of this when he wrote to the church: "Though by this time you ought to be teachers, you need someone to teach you the elementary truths of God's word all over again" (Hebrews 5:12).

Let's pray for each other and patiently come alongside those who seem to struggle with spiritual growth. "Speaking the truth in love," let's encourage one another to "grow to become in every respect the mature body of him who is the head, that is, Christ" (Ephesians 4:15).

—*Cindy Hess Kasper*

The Release of Fear

MARK 6:45–53

"Take courage! It is I! Don't be afraid."
—MARK 6:50

Our bodies react to our feelings of dread and fear. A weight in the pit of our stomachs, along with our hearts pounding as we gulp for breath, signal our sense of anxiety. Our physical nature keeps us from ignoring these feelings of unease.

The disciples felt shockwaves of fear one night after Jesus had performed the miracle of feeding more than five thousand people. The Lord had sent them ahead to Bethsaida so He could be alone to pray. During the night, they were rowing against the wind when suddenly they saw Him walking on the water. Thinking He was a ghost, they were terrified (Mark 6:49–50).

But Jesus reassured them, telling them not to be afraid and to take courage. As He entered their vessel, the wind died down and they made it to the shore. I imagine that their feelings of dread calmed as they embraced the peace He bestowed.

When we're feeling anxious, we can rest in Jesus's power. He'll give us the gift of His peace that "transcends all understanding" (Philippians 4:7). As He releases us from our fears, we can return to a state of rest.

—*Amy Boucher Pye*

Age-Old Wisdom

1 KINGS 12:1-7, 12-17

Is not wisdom found among the aged?
Does not long life bring understanding?
—JOB 12:12

A Singapore newspaper published a report presenting life lessons from eight senior citizens. It said, "While aging brings challenges to mind and body, it can also lead to . . . an abundance of emotional and social knowledge; qualities which scientists are beginning to define as the wisdom of elders."

Indeed, wise older people have much to teach us about life.

In the Bible we meet a new king who failed to recognize this. King Solomon had just died, and "the whole assembly of Israel went to Rehoboam" with a petition (1 Kings 12:3). They asked the new king to lighten the harsh labor and heavy taxes his father Solomon had demanded of them. In return, they would loyally serve Rehoboam.

The young king consulted the elders (v. 6) but rejected their advice. He accepted the foolish counsel of younger men (v. 8)—making the burden on the people even greater, which cost him most of his kingdom.

We all need the counsel that comes with years of experience, especially from those who have walked with God and listened well to His counsel. Let's seek them out and listen to their wisdom.

—*Poh Fang Chia*

Lead Me to the Rock

PSALM 61

I call as my heart grows faint; lead me
to the rock that is higher than I.
—PSALM 61:2

While shopping one day, I struck up a conversation with an older woman. We began talking about a flu virus in our area, one that left her with a lingering cough and headache. Soon she launched into a bitter tirade—expressing her theory about the origin of the virus. I listened, unsure what to do. She soon left the store angry and frustrated. She had expressed her feelings, but I couldn't do anything to take away that pain.

King David wrote psalms to express his anger and frustration to God. David knew that God not only listened but He could also do something about his pain. In Psalm 61, he writes, "I call as my heart grows faint; lead me to the rock that is higher than I" (v. 2). God was his "refuge" (v. 3)—the "rock" to which David ran.

David's example is a good one to follow. We can head to "the rock that is higher" or lead someone there. While God may not take away all the pain, we can rest in the peace He provides and the assurance that He hears our cry.

—*Linda Washington*

Loving Perfectly

1 CORINTHIANS 13:4–8

[Love] always protects, always trusts, always hopes, always perseveres. Love never fails.
—1 CORINTHIANS 13:7–8

Her voice shook as she shared the problems she was having with her daughter. Worried about her teenager's questionable friends, this concerned mum confiscated her daughter's mobile phone and chaperoned her everywhere. Their relationship seemed only to go from bad to worse.

When I spoke with the daughter, I discovered that she loves her mum dearly but is suffocating under a smothering love. She longs to break free.

As imperfect beings, we all struggle in our relationships. We grapple with expressing love the right way, saying and doing the right thing at the right time. We grow in love throughout our lifetime.

In 1 Corinthians 13 the apostle Paul outlines what perfect love looks like. Putting that love into practice can be daunting. Thankfully, we have Jesus as our example. As He interacted with people with varying needs and issues, He showed us what perfect love looks like in action. As we walk with Him, keeping ourselves in His love and steeping our mind in His Word, we'll reflect more and more of His likeness. It's a love that "always protects" and it "never fails" (vv. 7–8).

—*Poh Fang Chia*

Enough

2 KINGS 4:42–44

*They ate and had some left over,
according to the word of the LORD.*
—2 KINGS 4:44

When my husband and I were first asked to host a Bible study group in our home, my immediate reaction was to decline. I felt inadequate. Our home was small and couldn't hold many people. I doubted that we had the skills to facilitate the discussion. I worried about preparing food, something for which I lacked both passion and funds. I didn't feel like we had "enough." But we wanted to give to God and our community, so despite our fears, we agreed. Over the next five years we found great joy in welcoming the group into our living room.

I observe similar doubt in the man who brought bread to God's servant, Elisha. When Elisha instructed him to give it to the people, the man questioned whether twenty loaves was enough. He seems to have been tempted to withhold the food because it didn't seem sufficient. Yet it was more than enough (2 Kings 4:44), because God took his obedient gift and made it enough.

When God asks us to give what we have, He is the one who makes it "enough."

—*Kirsten Holmberg*

A Good Daddy

PSALM 63

*On my bed I remember you; I think of you
through the watches of the night.*

—PSALM 63:6

When our son, Xavier, was younger, business trips often pulled my husband Alan away from home. Though Alan called often, there were rough nights when the calls alone didn't comfort Xavier. To help, I'd pull out our photo albums. I'd point out the images that showed the two spending time together and ask, "Do you remember this?"

Memory after memory encouraged our son, who often said, "I have a good daddy."

Whenever I'm going through lonely times, I too long to know I'm loved, especially by my heavenly Father.

David proclaimed his deep yearning for God as he hid from his enemies in the desert (Psalm 63:1). Remembering his personal encounters with God's satisfying love led him to praise (vv. 2–5). Through his most difficult nights, David could still rejoice in his dependable Father's loving care (vv. 6–8).

During our dark times, when we feel as if God's not there for us, we need reminders of God's love. Reflecting on our personal experiences with Him, as well as His actions recorded in Scripture, can affirm the countless ways our good Abba Father loves us (Romans 8:15).

—*Xochitl Dixon*

Gleaning the Fields

RUTH 2:1–12

Ruth the Moabite said to Naomi, "Let me go to the fields and pick up the leftover grain behind anyone in whose eyes I find favor."

—RUTH 2:2

A Tanzanian friend has a vision for redeeming a piece of desolate land in the capital city of Dodoma. Recognizing the needs of local widows, Ruth wants to transform these dusty acres into a place where they can keep chickens and grow crops. Her vision is rooted in her love for God and was inspired by her biblical namesake, Ruth.

God's laws allowed the poor or the foreigner to glean (harvest) from the edges of the fields (Leviticus 19:9–10). Ruth, a foreigner, was allowed to work in the fields, gathering food for her and her mother-in-law, Naomi. Gleaning in the field of Boaz, a close relative, led to Ruth and Naomi ultimately finding a home and protection. Ruth used her ingenuity and effort, and God blessed her.

The passion of my friend Ruth and the dedication of the biblical Ruth stir me to give thanks to God for how He cares for the poor and downtrodden. The two Ruths inspire me to seek ways to help others as a means of expressing my thanks to our giving God. In what ways can we worship God by extending His mercy to others?

—*Amy Boucher Pye*

Reason to Sing

PSALM 98

*Sing to the LORD a new song,
for he has done marvelous things.*
—PSALM 98:1

When I was thirteen, on my first day in choir, the instructor called the students to the piano individually to hear their voices and place them in the room according to their vocal range. During my turn at the piano, I sang the notes she played multiple times, but I wasn't directed to a section in the room. Instead, she sent me to the counseling office to find a different class to take. From that moment on, I felt I shouldn't sing at all.

I carried that thought with me until I read Psalm 98 as a young adult. The writer opens with an invitation to "sing to the LORD" (Psalm 98:1). This has nothing to do with the quality of our voices. God delights in our songs of thanksgiving and praise. We are invited to sing because God "has done marvelous things" (v. 1).

The psalmist points out two wonderful reasons to joyfully praise God in song and in attitude: His saving work in our lives and His ongoing faithfulness toward us. In God's choir, we're all invited to sing of the marvelous things He has done.

—*Kirsten Holmberg*

The Ultimate Good

JAMES 4:13–17

*If anyone, then, knows the good they ought
to do and doesn't do it, it is sin for them.*
—JAMES 4:17

In a *Peanuts* cartoon by Charles Schulz, Marcie gives her schoolteacher some flowers. Not to be outdone, Peppermint Patty says to the teacher, "I thought about doing the same thing, Ma'am, but I never got around to it. Could you use a vase full of good intentions?"

We've all had intentions of doing something good but failed to follow through: check up on a friend, visit a sick neighbor, or write a note of encouragement. But we don't take the time.

Some people know that Jesus is the only way to heaven, and they plan to trust in Him someday. Yet they keep putting it off. They may have good intentions, but that won't bring salvation.

As Christians, we may say we want to grow closer to the Lord, but we don't make the time to read the Word of God or pray.

James has some strong words about our inaction: "To him who knows to do good and does not do it, to him it is sin" (4:17 NKJV).

Is there something you've been putting off? It's not too late to act. A vase full of good intentions never brightened anyone's day.

—*Anne Cetas*

Keeping Close

DEUTERONOMY 6:1–9

*Tie them as symbols on your hands
and bind them on your foreheads.*
—DEUTERONOMY 6:8

My mile-long walk home from dropping off my daughter at her school gives me the opportunity to memorize some verses from the Bible—if I'm intentional about doing so. When I take those minutes to turn over God's Word in my mind, I often find them coming back to me later in the day, bringing me comfort and wisdom.

When Moses prepared the Israelites to enter the promised land, he urged them to hold close to God's commands and decrees (Deuteronomy 6:1–2). Wanting them to flourish, he said they should turn these instructions over in their minds and discuss them with their children (vv. 6–7). He didn't want them to forget God's instructions to live as people who honored the Lord and enjoyed His blessings.

How might you consider God's words today? One idea is to write out a verse from Scripture, and every time you wash your hands or take a drink, read the words and think about them. Or before you go to sleep, consider a short passage from the Bible as the last act of the day. Many are the ways of keeping God's Word close to our hearts!

—*Amy Boucher Pye*

Ring in a Dumpster

MATTHEW 13:44–46

*Seek and you will find; knock and
the door will be opened to you.*
—MATTHEW 7:7

In college, I woke up one morning to find Carol, my roommate, in a panic. Her signet ring was missing. We searched everywhere—even in a dumpster.

I ripped open a trash bag. "You're so dedicated to finding this!"

"I'm not losing a two-hundred-dollar ring!" she exclaimed.

Carol's determination reminds me of Jesus's parable about the kingdom of heaven, which "is like treasure hidden in a field. When a man found it, he hid it again, and then in his joy went and sold all he had and bought that field" (Matthew 13:44). Certain things are worth going great lengths to find.

God promises that those who seek Him will find Him. In Deuteronomy, He explained to the Israelites that they would find Him when they turned from their sin and sought Him with all their hearts (4:28–29). And in Jeremiah, God gave the same promise to the exiles, saying He would bring them back from captivity (29:13–14).

If we seek God through His Word, worship, and prayer, we will find Him and know Him. That's even better than the sweet moment when Carol pulled her ring out of that trash bag!

—*Julie Schwab*

Watchful Care

JEREMIAH 23:20–24

"Do not I fill heaven and earth?"
declares the LORD.
—JEREMIAH 23:24

Before my son raced out the door to school, I asked him if he had brushed his teeth. I reminded him of the importance of telling the truth. Unmoved by my gentle admonishment, he half-jokingly informed me that what I really needed was a security camera in the bathroom so he wouldn't be tempted to lie.

While the presence of a security camera may help remind us to follow the rules, we can still go undetected. But we fool ourselves if we think we are ever outside the gaze of God.

God asks, "Who can hide in secret places so that I cannot see them?" (Jeremiah 23:24). There is both an encouragement and a warning in His question.

The warning is that we cannot hide from God. We can't outrun or fool Him. Everything we do is visible to Him.

This is also an encouragement. We are never outside the watchful care of our heavenly Father. Even when we feel alone, God is with us. Let's allow that truth encourage us to choose obedience to His Word and receive His comfort.

—*Lisa Samra*

Jesus Knows Why

MARK 8:22–26

*When Jesus had finished saying these things,
the crowds were amazed at his teaching.*

—MATTHEW 7:28

As I think of friends who struggle with side effects of diseases they had or of others who overcame addictions but still feel inadequate, I have a question: *Why doesn't God heal them completely—once and for all?*

In Mark 8:22–26, we read the story of Jesus healing a blind man. Jesus spit on the man's eyes and "put his hands on him." The man said he saw people who looked "like trees walking around." Then Jesus touched the man's eyes again, and this time he saw "everything clearly."

In His ministry, Jesus's words and actions often amazed and baffled the crowd and His followers. No doubt this two-part miracle caused confusion. Why not *immediately* heal this man?

We don't know why. But Jesus knew what the man—and the disciples who viewed his healing—needed in that moment. And He knows what we need today to draw us closer to Him. Though we won't always understand, we can trust that God is working in our lives and the lives of our loved ones. And He will give us the strength, courage, and clarity we need to persevere in following Him.

—*Alyson Kieda*

Keep Up the Good Work

1 THESSALONIANS 4:1–12

We . . . urge you . . . to do this more and more.
—1 THESSALONIANS 4:1

My son loves to read. If he reads more books than what is required at school, he receives an award certificate. That bit of encouragement motivates him to keep up the good work.

When Paul wrote to the Thessalonians, he motivated them not with an award but with words of encouragement. He said, "We instructed you how to live in order to please God, as in fact you are living. Now we ask you and urge you in the Lord Jesus to do this more and more" (1 Thessalonians 4:1). These Christians were pleasing God through their lives, and Paul encouraged them to keep it up.

Maybe today you and I are giving our best to know and love and please our Father. Let's take Paul's words as an incentive to continue on in our faith.

But let's go one step further. Does someone come to mind who is diligent in following the Lord and seeking to please Him? Perhaps you can tell this person to keep up the good work! What you say may be just what they need to continue following and serving Jesus.

—*Keila Ochoa*

Perfect Imperfection

EPHESIANS 3:8–19

I pray that out of his glorious riches he
may strengthen you with power through
his Spirit in your inner being.
—EPHESIANS 3:16

A college professor, picking up on my perfectionism-induced procrastination, gave me some wise advice. "Don't let perfect be the enemy of good," he said. Accepting the reality that my work would always be imperfect would give me the freedom to keep growing.

Paul explained an even more profound reason to let go of our own efforts to perfect ourselves: it can blind us to our need for Christ.

Paul had learned this the hard way. After years striving to perfectly obey God's law, encountering Jesus changed everything (Galatians 1:11–16). Paul realized that if his own efforts were enough to be whole and right with God, "then there was no need for Christ to die" (2:21 NLT). Only by letting go of—*dying* to—self-reliance, could he experience Jesus living in him (v. 20). Only in his imperfection could he experience God's perfect power.

In this lifetime, we will always be works in progress. But as our hearts humbly accept our constant need for the only perfect One, Jesus makes His home there (Ephesians 3:17). Rooted in Him, we are free to grow ever deeper in His love.

—*Monica Brands*

Heart Hunger

JOHN 6:32–40

"I am the bread of life. Whoever comes to me will never go hungry, and whoever believes in me will never be thirsty."

—JOHN 6:35

Riding along with my husband on some errands, I scrolled through emails on my phone and was surprised at an incoming advertisement for a local donut shop, a shop we had just passed on the right side of the street. I marveled at how technology allows vendors to woo us into their establishments.

As I clicked off my email, I mused over God's constant yearning to draw me closer. He always knows where I am and longs to influence my choices. I wondered, *Does my heart long for Him the way I longed for a donut?*

In John 6, following the miraculous feeding of the five thousand, the disciples eagerly ask Jesus to give them "the bread that . . . gives life to the world" (vv. 33–34). Jesus responds in verse 35, "I am the bread of life. Whoever comes to me will never go hungry and whoever believes in me will never be thirsty." How amazing that a relationship with Jesus can provide constant nourishment!

God's continuous knowledge of my heart's condition invites me to recognize my ongoing need for Him and to receive the sustenance only He can provide.

—*Elisa Morgan*

Bound to Encourage

HEBREWS 10:19–25

*Let us consider how we may spur one another
on toward love and good deeds.*

—HEBREWS 10:24

The Steven Thompson Memorial Centipede is a cross-country meet unlike any other. Each seven- member team runs as a unit, holding a rope for the first two miles of a three-mile course. At the two-mile mark, the team drops the rope and the racers finish individually. Each person's time is a combination of the pace the team kept and his or her own speed.

This year, my daughter's team opted for this strategy: They put the fastest runner at the front and the slowest right behind her. Their goal was for the strongest runner to encourage the slowest runner.

Their plans depicted for me a passage from Hebrews. The writer urges us to "hold unswervingly to the hope we profess" (10:23) as we "spur one another on toward love and good deeds" (v. 24). One way of doing this: "not giving up meeting together, . . . but encouraging one another" (v. 25). Gathering together with other believers is a vital aspect of the life of faith.

The race of life can feel overwhelming. But as we run together, let's offer one another the encouragement to run strong!

—*Kirsten Holmberg*

Forsaken for Our Sake

MATTHEW 26:36–46

"Never will I leave you;
never will I forsake you."
—HEBREWS 13:5

Researchers at the University of Virginia wanted to see how the brain reacted to the prospect of pain, and whether it behaved differently if a person faced the threat of pain alone, holding a stranger's hand, or holding the hand of a close friend.

Researchers ran tests on dozens of pairs and found consistent results. When a person was alone or holding a stranger's hand while anticipating a shock, the regions of the brain that process danger lit up. But when holding the hand of a trusted person, the brain relaxed. The comfort of a friend's presence made the pain seem more bearable.

Jesus needed comfort as He prayed in the garden of Gethsemane. He asked His closest friends to stay and pray with Him, telling them that His soul was "overwhelmed with sorrow" (Matthew 26:38). But Peter, James, and John kept falling asleep.

Jesus faced the agony of the garden alone. But because He bore that pain, we know that God will never leave or forsake us (Hebrews 13:5). His companionship makes anything we endure more bearable.

—*Amy Peterson*

Jesus Reached Out

MATTHEW 14:22–33

Immediately Jesus reached out
his hand and caught him.
—MATTHEW 14:31

Sometimes life gets busy—classes are hard, work is exhausting, the bathroom needs to be cleaned, and a coffee date is on the day's schedule. It gets to the point where I force myself to read the Bible for a few minutes a day and tell myself I'll spend more time with God next week. But it doesn't take long before I'm distracted, drowning in the day's tasks, and forget to ask God for help of any kind.

When Peter was walking on water toward Jesus, he quickly became distracted by the wind and waves. He began to sink (Matthew 14:29–30). But as soon as Peter cried out, "immediately Jesus reached out his hand and caught him" (vv. 30–31).

We often feel as if we have to make it up to God after being distracted.

But that's not how God works. As soon as we turn to Him for help, Jesus reaches out without hesitation.

When we're unsettled by the chaos of life, it's easy to forget that God is with us in the middle of the storm. No matter what we're going through, He is there.

—*Julie Schwab*

A Constant Helper

JOHN 14:15–26

"[The Holy Spirit] will remind you
of everything I have said to you."
—JOHN 14:26

After a spinal injury left Marty paralyzed, he decided to go back to school to earn his MBA. Marty's mother, Judy, helped make his goal a reality. She sat with him through every lecture and study group, jotting notes and handling technology issues. She even assisted him onto the platform when he received his diploma. The unattainable became possible.

Jesus knew His followers would need strong support after He left the earth. When He told them about His upcoming absence, He said they would gain a new kind of connection with God through the Holy Spirit. This Spirit would be a moment-by-moment helper—a teacher and guide who would not only live with them but also be in them (John 14:17, 26).

The Spirit would provide Jesus's disciples with internal help from God, enabling them to endure what they couldn't handle on their own as they shared the good news.

Are you facing something that exceeds your own strength and ability? You can depend on the Spirit's constant help. God's Spirit working in you will bring Him the glory He deserves.

—*Jennifer Benson Schuldt*

Generous Givers

1 CHRONICLES 29:1–14

*Everything comes from you, and we have given
you only what comes from your hand.*
—1 CHRONICLES 29:14

Our church leaders presented the congregation with a proposal for a new gym to help us better serve our community. The leadership team announced they'd be the first to sign pledge notes to fund the construction. I initially prayed with a heart soured by selfishness, not wanting to offer more money than we had already committed to give. Still, my husband and I agreed to pray for the project. While considering God's provisions for us, we decided on a monthly offering. The combined gifts of our church family paid for the building.

Grateful for the many ways God has used that gym for community events since we opened its doors, I'm reminded of another generous giver—King David. David invested all his resources to the temple project (1 Chronicles 29:1–5). The leaders under him and the people they served gave generously too (vv. 6–9). The king acknowledged that all they contributed had first come from God (vv. 10–16).

When we recognize that God owns it all, we can commit to grateful, generous, and faithful giving for the benefit of others. And we can trust that the Lord will provide.

—*Xochitl Dixon*

Treasure in a Pumpkin

2 CORINTHIANS 4:7–18

We have this treasure in jars of clay to show that this all-surpassing power is from God and not from us.
—2 CORINTHIANS 4:7

In one of my favorite pictures of my daughter as an infant, she is gleefully sitting in the belly of a hollowed-out pumpkin. There she sat, the delight of my heart, contained in an overgrown squash. The pumpkin withered in the ensuing weeks, but my daughter continued to grow and thrive.

The way Paul describes knowing the truth of who Jesus is reminds me of that photo. He likens the knowledge of Jesus in our heart to a treasure stored in a clay pot. Remembering what Jesus did for us gives us the courage and strength to persevere through struggles in spite of being "hard pressed on every side" (2 Corinthians 4:8). Because of God's power in our lives, when we are "struck down, [we're] not destroyed" (v. 9).

We may feel the wear and tear of our trials. But the joy of Jesus in us continues to grow in spite of those challenges. Our knowledge of Him—His power at work in our lives—is the treasure stored in our frail clay bodies. We can flourish in the face of hardship because of His power at work within us.

—*Kirsten Holmberg*

The Burden of Waiting

PSALM 90

Teach us to number our days, that we may gain a heart of wisdom.

—PSALM 90:12

Over the last few years, two members of my family have faced life-threatening diagnoses. For me, the hardest part of supporting them through their treatments has been the constant uncertainty. Instead of being given clarity about their situations, we were often asked to wait.

It's hard to bear the burden of uncertainty, always wondering what the next test will reveal. Will we have weeks, months, years, or decades before death separates us? Things like cancer bring our mortality to the forefront instead of letting it hide in the recesses of our minds where we like to keep it.

Faced with sobering reminders of our mortality, I find myself praying words that Moses once prayed. Psalm 90 tells us that though our lives are like grass that withers and fades (vv. 5–6), we have an eternal home with God (v. 1). Like Moses, we can ask God to teach us to number our days so we can make wise decisions (v. 12) and make what we do for Him count (v. 17). Ultimately, our hope is not in a doctor's diagnosis, but in a God who is "from everlasting to everlasting" (v. 2).

—*Amy Peterson*

God Is Here

HOSEA 6:1–6

Let us acknowledge the LORD; let us
press on to acknowledge him.
—HOSEA 6:3

A plaque in our home states "Bidden or not bidden, God is present." A modern version might read, "Acknowledged or unacknowledged, God is here."

Hosea, a prophet who lived in the late eighth century BC (755–715), wrote similar words to the Hebrew nation. He encouraged the Israelites to "press on" (Hosea 6:3) to acknowledge God because they had forgotten Him (4:1). As the people forgot God's presence, they began to turn away from Him (v. 12). Hosea's simple but profound insight to acknowledge God reminds us He's near and at work in our lives, in both the joys and struggles.

To acknowledge God might mean that when we get a promotion at work, we recognize God gave us insight to finish our work on time and within budget.

If we don't make it into the college of our choice, we can acknowledge that God is with us and take comfort in His presence even in our disappointment. As we enjoy dinner, to acknowledge God is to remind ourselves of God's provision.

When we acknowledge God, we remember His presence in both the successes and sorrows, whether big or small, of our lives.

—*Lisa Samra*

Direct Instructions

1 KINGS 13:11–22

"I have been told by the word of the LORD . . ."
—1 KINGS 13:17

My second child was eager to sleep in a big-girl bed in her sister's room. Each night I tucked Britta in, warning her I'd return her to the crib if she didn't stay in bed. Night after night, I found her in the hallway and had to escort my discouraged darling back to her crib. Years later I learned her customarily sweet older sister wasn't excited about having a roommate and told Britta that she'd heard me calling for her. Britta heeded her sister's words, went looking for me, and landed herself back in the crib.

Listening to the wrong voice is a bad idea. When God sent a man to Bethel to speak on His behalf, He gave explicit instructions for him to not eat or drink while there (1 Kings 13:9). When an older prophet extended a dinner invitation, the man initially declined. But he relented when the man deceived him, saying an angel told him it was okay. I imagine God was saddened the man didn't heed His instructions.

We can trust God completely. His words are our path to life; we are wise to listen and obey.

—*Kirsten Holmberg*

Discovering My True Self

1 JOHN 2:28–3:3

*We know that when Christ appears, we shall
be like him, for we shall see him as he is.*
—1 JOHN 3:2

"Who am I?" That's the question a faded stuffed animal asks himself in the children's book *Nothing* by Mick Inkpen. Left in a dusty corner of an attic, the animal hears movers call him "nothing" and thinks that's his name: Nothing.

Encounters with other animals spark memories. Nothing realizes that he used to have a tail, whiskers, and stripes. But it's not until he meets a tabby cat who helps him find his way home that Nothing remembers who he truly is: a stuffed cat named Toby. His owner lovingly restores him, sewing on new ears, tail, whiskers, and stripes.

This book makes me think about my own identity. Who am I? John, writing to believers, said that God has called us His children (1 John 3:1). We don't fully understand that identity, but when we see Jesus, we will be like Him (v. 2). Just like Toby the cat, we will one day be restored to the identity intended for us. But for now, we have been marred by sin.

One day, when we see Jesus, we will be fully restored to the identity God intended for us. We will be made new.

—*Amy Peterson*

Honoring God with Thanks

PSALM 50:8–15

*Call on me in the day of trouble; I will
deliver you, and you will honor me.*
—PSALM 50:15

The doctor wasn't frowning, despite talking to my husband about his recent cancer diagnosis. Smiling, she offered a suggestion: start each day by giving thanks for at least three things.

Dan agreed, knowing that gratitude opens our hearts to find encouragement in God's goodness. Thus, Dan starts each day with words of praise. Thank you, God, for a good night's sleep. For my clean bed. For sunshine. For breakfast on the table. For a smile on my lips.

Does our praise in life's small details matter to Almighty God? In Psalm 50, Asaph offers a clear answer. God has "no need of a bull from your stall or of goats from your pens" (v. 9). Instead, God wants His people to give Him their hearts and lives in gratitude (vv. 14, 23), which helps our spirits flourish.

When we call on the Lord "in the day of trouble," He will "deliver" us (v. 15).

Does this mean Dan will be healed? We don't know. But for now, Dan delights in showing God he's grateful for His love, and for who God is: Redeemer. Healer. Friend. And friends delight to hear this: Thank you.

—*Patricia Raybon*

God Hears

ROMANS 12:9–21

*Be joyful in hope, patient in affliction,
faithful in prayer.*
—ROMANS 12:12

Diane listened as the others in the group asked for prayers for their family members and friends facing challenges or illness. She had a family member who had been struggling with an addiction for years. But Diane kept her request silent. She couldn't bear to see the looks on people's faces or hear the questions or advice that often followed whenever she spoke the words aloud.

Although Diane didn't share her request with that group, she did have a few trusted friends she asked to pray with her. Together they asked God to set her loved one free from the very real bondage of addiction that he might experience freedom in Christ—and that God would give Diane the peace and patience she needed. As she prayed, she found comfort and strength from her relationship with Him.

Many of us have earnest, persistent prayers that seem to go unanswered. But we can be assured that God does care, and He does hear all our requests. He urges us to continue to walk closely with Him, being "joyful in hope, patient in affliction, faithful in prayer" (Romans 12:12). We can lean on Him.

—*Alyson Kieda*

My Real Face

1 TIMOTHY 1:12–17

*I thank Christ Jesus our Lord, who has given
me strength, that he considered me trustworthy,
appointing me to his service.*

—1 TIMOTHY 1:12

For years, I struggled with feelings of unworthiness and shame over my less-than-godly past. What if others found out?

One day God gave me the courage to invite a ministry leader to lunch. Striving for perfection, I scrubbed my house, whipped up a three-course meal, and donned my best jeans and blouse.

Rushing outside to turn off the sprinklers, I was drenched by a gush of water. With towel-dried hair and smeared makeup, I changed into dry sweat pants and a T-shirt . . . just as the doorbell rang. Frustrated, I confessed my morning's antics and motives. My new friend shared her own fear, insecurity, and guilt over lunch. After prayer, she welcomed me to her team of God's imperfect servants.

Paul accepted his new life in Christ, refusing to deny his past or let it stop him from serving (1 Timothy 1:12–14). Paul knew Jesus's work on the cross saved and changed him. So he praised God and encouraged others to trust Him (vv. 15–17).

When we accept God's forgiveness, we're freed from our past. We have no reason to be ashamed of our real faces as we serve others.

—Xochitl Dixon

The Secret of Peace

2 THESSALONIANS 3:16–18

The Lord of peace himself give you peace.
—2 THESSALONIANS 3:16

Grace is a special lady—a woman of *peace*. The quiet, restful expression on her face has seldom changed in the six months I have known her, even though her husband was diagnosed with a rare disease and then hospitalized.

When I asked Grace the secret of her peace, she said, "It's not a secret, it's a person. It's Jesus in me. There is no other way I can explain the quietness I feel in the midst of this storm."

The secret of peace is our relationship to Jesus Christ. He is our peace. When He is our Savior, and as we become more like Him, peace becomes real. This peace reassures us that God holds our lives in His hands (Daniel 5:23), and we can trust that things will work together for good.

The inner confidence that God is in control gives us an indescribable peace. My wish for all of us echoes the words of the apostle Paul: "May the Lord of peace himself give you peace." And may we feel this peace "at all times and in every way" (2 Thessalonians 3:16).

—*Keila Ochoa*

Anywhere

JEREMIAH 2:1–8; 3:14–15

*I remember the devotion of your youth, how
as a bride you loved me and followed me
through the wilderness.* —JEREMIAH 2:2

As I flipped through a box of old wedding photographs, I stopped at a picture of my husband and me, newly christened "Mr. and Mrs." My dedication to Evan was obvious in my expression. I would go *anywhere* with him.

Nearly four decades later, our marriage is tightly threaded with love and a commitment that has carried us through both hard and good times. Year after year, I've recommitted my dedication to go *anywhere* with him.

In Jeremiah 2:2, God yearns for His beloved but wayward Israel, "I remember the devotion of your youth, how as a bride you loved me and followed me." The Hebrew word for *devotion* conveys the highest loyalty and commitment possible. At first, Israel expressed this unwavering devotion to God, but gradually she turned away.

Complacency can dull the sharp edge of love, and a lack of zeal can lead to unfaithfulness. In our love relationship with God, are we as devoted to Him now as we were when we first came to faith?

God faithfully allows His people to return (3:14–15). Today we can renew our vows to follow Him—anywhere.

—*Elisa Morgan*

Are You Being Prepared?

1 SAMUEL 17:8, 32–37, 48–50

The Lord who rescued me from the paw of the lion and . . . the bear will rescue me.
—1 SAMUEL 17:37

When I worked at a fast-food restaurant in high school, some aspects of the job were difficult. Customers verbalized their anger while I apologized for the unwanted slice of cheese on the sandwich I didn't make. Soon after I left, I applied for a computer job at my university. The employers were more interested in my fast-food experience than my computer skills. They wanted to know how I dealt with people. My unpleasant fast-food circumstances prepared me for a better job!

Young David persevered through a tough experience. When Israel was challenged to send someone to fight Goliath, no one was brave enough to step up. No one but David. King Saul was reluctant, but David explained that as a shepherd he had killed a lion and a bear (1 Samuel 17:34–36). Confidently he stated, "The Lord who rescued me from the paw of the lion . . . will rescue me from the hand of this Philistine" (v. 37).

Being a shepherd prepared David to fight Goliath. We may be in difficult circumstances, but through them God might be preparing us for something greater!

—*Julie Schwab*

When One Hurts, All Hurt

1 CORINTHIANS 12:14–26

If one part suffers, every part suffers with it; if one part is honored, every part rejoices with it.
—1 CORINTHIANS 12:26

When a coworker called in sick due to extreme pain, everyone at the office was concerned. After a trip to the hospital and a day of bed rest, he returned to work and showed us the source of that pain—a kidney stone. He'd asked his doctor to give him the stone as a souvenir. Looking at that stone, I winced in sympathy, remembering the gallstone I had passed years ago. The pain had been excruciating.

Isn't it interesting that something so small can cause a whole body so much agony? But in a way, that's what the apostle Paul alludes to in 1 Corinthians 12:26: "If one part suffers, every part suffers with it." Since as Christians we're all part of the same body, if one person hurts, we all hurt. When a fellow Christian faces persecution, grief, or trials, we hurt as if we're experiencing that pain.

In the body of Christ, someone's pain ignites our compassion and moves us toward action. We might pray, offer a word of encouragement, or do whatever it takes to aid the healing process. That's how the body works together.

—*Linda Washington*

Knowing Better

2 KINGS 22:1–4, 8–13

*Josiah was eight years old when he became king,
and he reigned in Jerusalem thirty-one years.*

—2 KINGS 22:1

When we brought our adoptive son home, I was eager to shower him with love and provide what he had lacked, especially quality food. But despite our best efforts, he grew very little. After nearly three years, we learned he had severe food intolerances. We removed those items from his diet, and he grew five inches in just a few months. I rejoiced at this surge in his health!

I suspect Josiah felt similarly when the Book of the Law was discovered after having been lost in the temple for years. Just as I grieved having unintentionally hindered my son's growth, Josiah grieved having ignorantly missed God's best intentions for His people (2 Kings 22:11). Although he is commended for doing what was right in God's eyes (v. 2), he learned better how to honor the Lord after finding the Law. He then led the people to worship as God had instructed (23:22–23).

As we learn through the Bible how to honor Him, we may grieve the ways we've fallen short of God's will for us. Yet He heals and restores us, and He leads us gently into deeper understanding.

—*Kirsten Holmberg*

Holy, Holy, Holy

REVELATION 4

Day and night they never stop saying:
"'Holy, holy, holy is the Lord God Almighty,'
who was, and is, and is to come."
—REVELATION 4:8

"Time flies when you're having fun." This cliché has no basis in fact, but experience makes it seem true.

When life is pleasant, time passes all too quickly. Give me a task that I enjoy, or a person whose company I love, and time seems irrelevant.

My experience of this "reality" has given me a new understanding of the scene described in Revelation 4. In the past, when I considered the four living creatures seated around God's throne who keep repeating the same few words, I thought, *What a boring existence!*

I don't think that anymore. I think of how amazed they are at God's wise and loving involvement with wayward earthlings. Then I think, *What better response could there be? What else is there to say but, "Holy, holy, holy"?*

Is it boring to say the same words over and over? Not when you're in the presence of the one you love. Not when you're doing exactly what you were designed to do.

Like the four creatures, we were designed to glorify God. Our lives will never be boring if we're focusing our attention on Him and fulfilling that purpose.

—*Julie Ackerman Link*

The Widow's Faith

2 KINGS 4:1–7

The pagans run after all these things, and your
heavenly Father knows that you need them.
—MATTHEW 6:32

It's dark when Ah-pi starts her day. Others in the village will wake up soon to make their way to the rubber plantation of Hongzhuang Village, China. To collect as much latex as possible, workers must tap the trees before daybreak. Ah-pi will be among the rubber tappers, but first she will spend time communing with God.

Ah-pi's father, husband, and only son have passed away, and she—with her daughter-in-law—is providing for an elderly mother and two young grandsons. Her story reminds me of another widow in the Bible who trusted God.

The widow's husband had died and left her in debt (2 Kings 4:1). In her distress, she looked to God for help by turning to His servant Elisha. God provided miraculously for the dire needs of this widow (vv. 5–6). This same God also provided for Ah-pi—though less miraculously—through the toil of her hands, the produce from the ground, and gifts from His people.

We can always draw strength from God, entrust our cares to Him, and do all we can. Then be amazed with what He can do with our situation.

—*Poh Fang Chia*

On-the-Job Training

2 TIMOTHY 1:6–14

*Of this gospel I was appointed a herald
and an apostle and a teacher.*
—2 TIMOTHY 1:11

When my son's teacher asked me to serve as a chaperone for their science camp, I hesitated. How could I be a role model when mistakes littered my past, when I still slipped into old bad habits? God helped me love and raise my son, but I often doubted He could use me to serve others.

Sometimes I fail to recognize that God transforms us over time. Then the Holy Spirit reminds me how Paul encouraged Timothy to embrace his on-the-job training, persevere in faith, and use the gifts God had given him (2 Timothy 1:6). Timothy could be courageous because God, his power source, would help him love and be disciplined as he continued to grow and serve others (v. 7).

Christ saves and empowers us to honor Him with our lives, not because we have special qualifications but because we're each valuable members of His family (v. 9).

We can persevere with confidence when we know our role is to simply love God and others. When we follow Jesus daily, He transforms us *while* using us to encourage others as we share His love and truth wherever He sends us.

—*Xochitl Dixon*

Enduring Hope

ROMANS 5:1–11

This hope will not lead to disappointment.
For we know how dearly God loves us,
because he has given us the Holy Spirit
to fill our hearts with his love.
—ROMANS 5:5 (NLT)

Heather Kampf is an exceptional runner with impressive credentials. She once took first place in a 600-meter race after falling flat on her face! In the final 200 meters, just as she took the lead, Heather tripped and fell hard. She could easily have become discouraged and accepted what everyone was thinking—her race was over. But she didn't stay down. Instead, Heather sprang up and raced on. To the amazement of everyone watching, she went on to *win* the race.

Kampf's comeback provides a reflection of the enduring hope we can experience in Jesus—a perspective she understands because of her own faith in Jesus. When we face a major setback, we are able to stand in the joy and confidence our Lord provides: "We have been made right in God's sight by faith, we have peace with God because of what Jesus Christ our Lord has done for us" (Romans 5:1–2 NLT). And "we can rejoice, too, when we run into problems and trials, for we know that they help us develop endurance" (Romans 5:3 NLT). This endurance develops character, which strengthens our confident hope of salvation.

In Jesus, our hope endures!

—*Ruth O'Reilly-Smith*

Don't Run Alone

EXODUS 17:8–13

Therefore, since we are surrounded by such a great cloud of witnesses, let us throw off everything that hinders and the sin that so easily entangles. And let us run with perseverance the race marked out for us.
—HEBREWS 12:1

My husband Jack was on mile twenty-five out of twenty-six when his strength failed him.

This was his first marathon, and he was running alone. After stopping for a drink of water, he sat down on the grass beside the course. Minutes passed, and he couldn't get up. He had resigned himself to quitting the race when two middle-aged schoolteachers from Kentucky came by. They noticed Jack and asked if he wanted to run with them. Suddenly, he found his strength restored. Accompanied by the two women, he finished the race.

Those women who encouraged Jack remind me of Aaron and Hur, two people who helped Moses, the leader of the Israelites, at a key point (Exodus 17:8–13). The Israelites were under attack, and they were winning only as long as Moses held his staff up (v. 11). When his strength began to fail, Aaron and Hur stood on either side of him, holding up his arms for him until sunset (v. 12).

God did not create us to run the race of life alone. Companions can help us persevere through difficulty as we do what God has called us to do.

—*Amy Peterson*

Free to Follow

MATTHEW 11:25–30

"Take my yoke upon you and learn from me,
for I am gentle and humble in heart,
and you will find rest for your souls."
—MATTHEW 11:29

My high school cross-country coach once advised me before a race, "Don't try to be in the lead. The leaders almost always burn out too quickly."

Leading can be exhausting; following can be freeing. Knowing this improved my running, but it took me a lot longer to realize how this applies to Christian discipleship. In my own life, I was prone to think being a believer in Jesus meant trying *really hard*. By pursuing my own exhausting expectations for what a Christian should be, I was inadvertently missing the joy and freedom found in simply following Him (John 8:32, 36).

Jesus promised that in seeking Him we will find the rest we long for (Matthew 11:25–28). Unlike many other religious teachers' emphasis on rigorous study of Scripture or an elaborate set of rules, Jesus taught that it's simply through knowing Him that we know God (v. 27). In seeking Him, we find our heavy burdens lifted (vv. 28–30) and our lives transformed.

Following Him, our gentle and humble Leader (v. 29), is never burdensome—it's the way of hope and healing. Resting in His love, we are free.

—*Monica Brands*

Our Safe Place

PSALM 91

*I will say of the LORD, "He is my refuge and
my fortress, my God, in whom I trust."*
—PSALM 91:2

My first job was at a fast-food restaurant. One Saturday evening, a guy kept hanging around, asking when I got out of work. I felt uneasy. As the hour grew later, he ordered fries, then a drink, so the manager wouldn't kick him out. Though I didn't live far, I was scared to walk home alone. Finally, at midnight, I went to the office and made a phone call.

Without a second thought, my dad got out of a warm bed and came to get me.

The certainty I had that my dad would help me that night reminds me of the assurance we read about in Psalm 91. Our Father in heaven is always with us, protecting and caring for us when we are confused or afraid or in need. He declares: "When they call on me, I will answer" (v. 15 NLT). He is not just a place we can run to for safety. He's our shelter (v. 1).

In times of uncertainty, we can trust God's promise that when we call on Him, He will hear and be with us in our trouble (vv. 14–15). God is our safe place.
                              —*Cindy Hess Kasper*

God Provides

DEUTERONOMY 24:19–22

*Those who work their land will have abundant
food, but those who chase fantasies have no sense.*
—PROVERBS 12:11

Outside my office window, the squirrels race against
winter to bury their acorns in a safe place. Their commotion amuses me. A herd of deer can go through
our back yard and not make a sound, but one squirrel
sounds like an invasion.

The two creatures are different in another way as
well. Deer don't prepare for winter. When the snow
comes, they eat whatever they can find along the way.
But squirrels would starve if they followed that example.

The deer and the squirrel represent ways God
cares for us. He enables us to work and save for the
future, and He also meets our need when resources
are scarce. God gives us seasons of plenty so we can
prepare for seasons of need (Proverbs 12:11). And
as Psalm 23 says, the Lord leads us through perilous
places to pleasant pastures.

God also provides by instructing those with plenty
to share with those in need (Deuteronomy 24:19). So
when it comes to provision, the message of the Bible
is this: Work while we can, save what we can, share
what we can, and trust God to meet our needs.

—*Julie Ackerman Link*

"I See You"

GENESIS 16:1–13

She gave this name to the LORD who spoke to her:
"You are the God who sees me," for she said,
"I have now seen the One who sees me."
—GENESIS 16:13

"I see you," a friend said in an online writers' group where we support and encourage each other. Having felt stressed and anxious, I experienced a sense of peace and well-being with her words. She "saw" me—my hopes, fears, struggles, and dreams—and loved me.

When I heard my friend's simple but powerful encouragement, I thought of Hagar, a slave in Abram's household. After many years of Sarai and Abram longing for an heir, Sarai followed the custom of the culture and told her husband to conceive through Hagar. But when Hagar became pregnant, the two women treated each other with contempt, and Hagar fled to the desert.

The Lord saw Hagar in her pain and confusion, and He blessed her with the promise that she would be the mother of many descendants. After the encounter, Hagar called the Lord "El Roi," which means "the God who sees me" (Genesis 16:13), for she knew she wasn't alone or abandoned.

As Hagar was seen—and loved—so are we. We might feel ignored or rejected by others, yet we know that our Father sees all of our secret feelings and fears.
—*Amy Boucher Pye*

The Right Way to Pray

MATTHEW 6:5–15

"When you pray, go into your room, close the door and pray to your Father, who is unseen."
—MATTHEW 6:6

I admire people who record prayer requests in journals, keeping track of every prayer and praise and then faithfully update their lists. I'm inspired by those who gather with others to pray and whose kneeling wears out the carpet at their bedsides. For years, I tried to copy their styles. I strived to unravel what I thought was a mystery as I longed to learn the right way to pray.

Eventually, I learned that our Lord desires prayer that begins and ends with humility (Matthew 6:5). He invites us into an intimate exchange through which He promises to listen (v. 6). He never requires fancy words or phrases (v. 7). He assures us that prayer is a gift, an opportunity to honor His majesty (vv. 9–10), to display our confidence in His provision (v. 11), and to affirm our security in His forgiveness and guidance (vv. 12–13).

God assures us He hears and cares about every single prayer. Praying with a humble heart that's surrendered to and dependent on Him is always the right way to pray.

—*Xochitl Dixon*

Earnestly Searching

ISAIAH 62:1–12

You will be called Sought After,
the City No Longer Deserted.
—ISAIAH 62:12

Every Saturday during high school cross-country season, our family lines the edges of the course to cheer on my daughter. After crossing the finish line, the athletes fan out to rejoin their teammates, coaches, and parents. Crowds engulf the finishers—often more than 300 of them—making it difficult to find one person. We scan the crowd excitedly until we spot her, eager to put our arms around the one athlete we came to watch: our much-loved daughter.

After the Jews spent seventy years of captivity in Babylon, God returned them to Jerusalem and Judah. Isaiah describes the delight God has in them. God reaffirms His calling of them as His holy people and restores their honor with a new name, "Sought After, the City No Longer Deserted" (Isaiah 62:12). He sought them from the scattered reaches of Babylon to bring them back to himself.

We too are God's beloved, earnestly sought-after children. Although our sin once isolated us from Him, Jesus's sacrifice paves our way back to Him. He searches for each of us intently, waiting expectantly to fold us into a heartfelt embrace.

—*Kirsten Holmberg*

Mosaic and Beauty

LUKE 1:46–55

"My soul glorifies the Lord and my spirit rejoices in God my Savior."

—LUKE 1:46–47

Sitting in the courtyard of the Church of the Visitation in Ein Karem, Israel, I was overwhelmed with the beautiful display of sixty-seven mosaics containing the words of Mary's Magnificat (Luke 1:46–55). These verses are Mary's joyous response to the announcement that she will be the mother of the Messiah.

Each plaque contains Mary's words, including: "My soul glorifies the Lord and my spirit rejoices in God my Savior. . . . For the Mighty One has done great things for me" (vv. 46–49). The biblical hymn etched in the tiles is a song of praise.

A grateful recipient of God's grace, Mary rejoices in her salvation (v. 47). She acknowledges that God's mercy and care (v. 50) and His powerful acts on behalf of His people (v. 51). She also thanks God, recognizing that her daily provision comes from His hand (v. 53).

Mary shows us the importance of praising God for the great things He has done for us. Let's consider God's goodness as we reflect on Him. In doing so, we may create a mosaic of great beauty with our words of praise.

—Lisa Samra

Following the Leader

LUKE 9:21–24

*"Whoever wants to be my disciple
must deny themselves and take up
their cross daily and follow me."*

—LUKE 9:23

Three fighter jets screamed over our house—flying in formation so close together they appear to be one. "Wow," I said to my husband, Dan. "Impressive," he agreed. We live near an Air Force base, and it's not unusual to see such sights.

Every time these jets fly over, however, I wonder: how can they fly so close together and not lose control? One reason, I learned, is humility. Trusting that the lead pilot is traveling at precisely the correct speed and trajectory, the wing pilots surrender any desire to switch directions or question their leader's path. Instead, they get in formation and closely follow. The result? A more powerful team.

It's no different for followers of Jesus. He says, "Whoever wants to be my disciple must deny themselves and take up their cross daily and follow me" (Luke 9:23).

It's quite a sight, this humbling, close walk with God. Following His lead, and staying so close, we can appear with Christ as one. Then others won't see us—they'll see Him. There's a simple word for what that looks like: "Wow!"

—*Patricia Raybon*

The Spirit's Wind

ACTS 2:1–12

Suddenly a sound like the blowing of a violent wind came from heaven and filled the whole house where they were sitting.

—ACTS 2:2

It was October, a month in my part of the world when temperatures begin to dip and the leaves of many types of trees turn brilliant colors. The trees dazzled me with their autumn glory. I plopped down in the middle of a grove of trees to soak it all in. Then I lay down in a bed of leaves and gazed up at the blue sky. I was within a natural cathedral that swayed to and fro in the chilly fall wind.

Luke's description in Acts 2:2 came to mind: "a sound like the blowing of a violent wind came from heaven and filled the whole house." In my pristine setting, I prayed that the Holy Spirit would blow into my life in a fresh way.

I desperately need the power of the Holy Spirit to do the work God has assigned to me—to guide and direct me—for I dare not try to do God's work in my own power. We are transformed as we submit to the Holy Spirit's work—allowing us to more perfectly love God and others.

—*Marlena Graves*

When the Bottom Drops Out

1 KINGS 17:15–24

*Let us then approach God's throne of grace with
confidence, so that we may receive mercy and
find grace to help us in our time of need.*

—HEBREWS 4:16

During the 1997 Asian Financial Crisis, I lost my job.
After nine anxious months, I landed employment as
a copywriter. But the company fell on bad times and
I was jobless again.

Ever been there? It seems like the worst is over
when suddenly the bottom drops out. The widow
at Zarephath could relate (1 Kings 17:12). Due to a
famine, she was preparing the last meal for herself
and her son when the prophet Elijah requested a bite
to eat. She reluctantly agreed and God provided a
continuous supply of flour and oil (vv. 10–16).

But then her son fell ill. His health declined until
he stopped breathing. The widow cried out, "What
do you have against me, man of God? Did you come
to remind me of my sin and kill my son?" (v. 18).

Elijah took the concern to God, praying earnestly
and honestly for the boy, and God raised him up!
(vv. 20–22).

When the bottom drops out, may we—like Elijah—realize that we can rest in God's purposes even
as we pray for understanding. He won't desert us.

—*Poh Fang Chia*

Courage to Be Faithful

1 PETER 3:3–18

Rather, it should be that of your inner self,
the unfading beauty of a gentle and quiet spirit,
which is of great worth in God's sight.

—1 PETER 3:4

Hadassah, a young Jewish girl living in the first century, is a fictional character in Francine Rivers's book *A Voice in the Wind*. After Hadassah becomes a slave in a Roman household, she fears persecution for her faith in Christ. She knows that Christians are despised, and many are sent to their execution or thrown to the lions in the arena. Will she have the courage to stand for the truth when she is tested?

When her worst fear becomes reality, her mistress and other Roman officials who hate Christianity confront her. She has two choices: recant her faith in Christ or be taken to the arena. Then, as she proclaims Jesus as the Christ, her fear falls away and she becomes bold even in the face of death.

The Bible reminds us that sometimes we will suffer for doing what is right. We are told not to be frightened (1 Peter 3:14), but to "revere Christ as Lord" in our hearts (v. 15).

When we make the decision to honor Christ, He will help us to be bold and to overcome our fears in the midst of opposition.

—*Keila Ochoa*

Quieting the Critic

NEHEMIAH 4:1–6

Hear us, our God, for we are despised.
Turn their insults back on their own heads.
—NEHEMIAH 4:4

I work with a team to put on an annual community event. We spend eleven months plotting details to ensure the event's success: Choosing a date, picking a venue, setting prices, selecting food vendors and sound techs. Then, once the event is over, we collect feedback. Some good. Some hard to hear. The negative feedback can be discouraging and sometimes tempts us to give up.

Nehemiah also had critics as he led a team to rebuild Jerusalem's wall. They actually mocked the workers, saying, "Even a fox climbing up on it would break down [your] wall of stones" (Nehemiah 4:3). His response to the critics helps me handle my own: Instead of feeling dejected or defensive, he turned to God for help—asking Him to hear the way His people were being treated and to defend them (v. 4). After entrusting those concerns to God, he and his co-laborers continued to work steadily on the wall.

We can learn from Nehemiah. When we're criticized, instead of responding to our critics out of hurt or anger, let's prayerfully ask God to protect us from discouragement so we can continue with a whole heart.

—*Kirsten Holmberg*

If I Knew Then

1 PETER 1:3–9

*In his great mercy [God] has given us new birth into
a living hope through the resurrection of Jesus.*
—1 PETER 1:3

On the way to work, I listened to the song "Dear
Younger Me," which asks: If you could go back,
knowing what you know now, what would you tell
your younger self? As I listened, I thought about the
wisdom I might give my younger, less-wise self. Most
of us have thought about how we might have done
things differently.

The song also illustrates that although we may
have regrets, our experiences have shaped who we
are. We can't change the consequences of our choices
or our sin. But because of what Jesus has done, we
don't have to carry the mistakes around with us. "In
his great mercy he has given us new birth into a living
hope through the resurrection of Jesus Christ from
the dead!" (1 Peter 1:3).

If we turn to Him in faith and sorrow for our sins,
He will forgive us. We are made brand-new and begin
the process of being spiritually transformed (2 Corinthians 5:17). No matter what we've done, we are
forgiven through Jesus's sacrifice. We can move forward, making the most of today and anticipating a
future with Him. In Christ, we're free!

—*Alyson Kieda*

From Wailing to Worship

PSALM 30

You turned my wailing into dancing;
you . . . clothed me with joy.
—PSALM 30:11

A few years ago, Kim began battling breast cancer. Four days after her treatment ended, doctors diagnosed her with a progressive lung disease and gave her three to five years to live. She spent the first year grieving before God. By the time I met Kim a year later, she had surrendered her situation to Him. Her joy and peace were contagious. God continues to transform her heart-wrenching suffering into a testimony of hope-filled praise.

Even in dire circumstances, God can turn our wailing into dancing. Though His healing won't always look or feel like we'd hoped or expected, we can be confident in God's ways (Psalm 30:1–3). No matter how tear-stained our path may be, we have countless reasons to praise Him (v. 4) for our confident faith (vv. 5–7) and His mercy (vv. 8–10).

Only God can transform wails of despair into vibrant joy despite our circumstances (vv. 11–12).

As our merciful God comforts us in our sorrow and envelops us in peace. Our loving, faithful Lord can and does turn our wailing into worship that can lead to heart-deep trust and praise.

—*Xochitl Dixon*

Algae and God's Creation

JOB 37:14–24

*"Listen to this, Job; stop and
consider God's wonders."*

—JOB 37:14

"What's a diatom?" I asked my friend. I was looking at pictures she had taken through a microscope. "Oh, it's like algae, but it's harder to see. Sometimes they have to be dead to see them," she explained. I was amazed. I couldn't stop thinking about the intricate detail God put into microscopic life!

God's creation and works are endless. In the book of Job, one of Job's friends, Elihu, points this out to Job as he struggles through his loss. Elihu said, "Stop and consider God's wonders. Do you know how God controls the clouds and makes his lightning flash? Do you know how the clouds hang poised, those wonders of him who has perfect knowledge?" (Job 37:14–16). We as humans can't begin to understand the complexity of God's creation.

Even the parts of creation we can't see reflect God's glory and power. His glory surrounds us. No matter what we're going through, God is working, even when we can't see it and don't understand. Let's praise Him today, for "He performs wonders that cannot be fathomed, miracles that cannot be counted" (Job 5:9).

—*Julie Schwab*

The Lord Rejoices

ZEPHANIAH 3:14–20

[God] will rejoice over you with singing.
—ZEPHANIAH 3:17

My grandmother sent me a folder full of old photographs, and as I thumbed through them, one caught my eye. In it, I'm two years old, and I'm sitting on one end of a hearth in front of a fireplace. On the other end, my dad has his arm around my mom's shoulders. Both are gazing at me with love and delight.

I pinned this photo to my dresser, where I see it every morning. It's a wonderful reminder of their love for me. The truth is, though, that even the love of good parents is imperfect. I saved this photo because it reminds me that although human love may fail, God's love never fails—and according to Scripture, God looks at me the way my parents are looking at me in this picture.

Zephaniah described this love in a way that astounds me: God rejoicing over His people with singing. God's people had not earned this love. They had failed to obey Him or to treat each other with compassion. But Zephaniah promised that in the end, God's love would prevail.

That's a love worth reflecting on every morning.
—*Amy Peterson*

Many Beautiful Things

MARK 14:1–9

She has done a beautiful thing to me.
—MARK 14:6

Just before her death, artist and missionary Lilias Trotter looked out a window and saw a vision of a heavenly chariot. According to her biographer, a friend asked, "Are you seeing many beautiful things?" She answered, "Yes, many, many beautiful things."

Trotter's final words reflect God's work in her life. Throughout her life, He revealed much beauty to her and through her. A talented artist, she chose to serve Jesus as a missionary in Algeria. John Ruskin, a famous painter who tutored her, is said to have commented, "What a waste," when she chose mission work over art.

Similarly, when a woman came to Simon the Leper's house with an alabaster jar and poured perfume on Jesus's head, those present saw it as a waste. Some thought the expensive perfume could have been used to help the poor. However, Jesus said, "She has done a beautiful thing to me" (Mark 14:6).

When we let Christ's life shine in our lives and display His beauty to others, some will say it's a waste. But we prefer to hear Jesus say that we have done many beautiful things for Him.

—*Keila Ochoa*

The Last Word

ECCLESIASTES 5:1–7

Do not be quick with your mouth,
do not be hasty in your heart.
—ECCLESIASTES 5:2

During a university philosophy class, a student made inflammatory remarks about the professor's views. Surprisingly, the teacher thanked him and moved on. When he was asked later why he didn't respond to the student, he said, "I'm practicing the discipline of not having to have the last word."

This teacher loved and honored God, and he wanted to embody a humble spirit as he reflected this love. His words remind me of another Teacher—the one who wrote Ecclesiastes. In addressing how we should approach the Lord, he said we should guard our steps and "go near to listen" rather than being quick with our mouths and hasty in our hearts. By doing so we acknowledge that God is the Lord, and we are those He has created (Ecclesiastes 5:1–2).

How do you approach God? If you need an attitude adjustment, why not spend time considering the majesty and greatness of the Lord? When we ponder His unending wisdom, power, and presence, we can feel awed by His overflowing love for us. With this posture of humility, we won't need to have the last word.

—*Amy Boucher Pye*

What We Want to Hear

2 CHRONICLES 18:5–27

I hate him because he never prophesies anything good about me, but always bad.
—2 CHRONICLES 18:7

We are prone to seek information that supports our opinions. When we're committed to our own way of thinking, we avoid being challenged.

Such was the case in King Ahab's rule over Israel. When he and Jehoshaphat, the king of Judah, discussed whether to go to war against Ramoth Gilead, Ahab gathered 400 prophets—"yes men," all of them—to help them decide. Each replied he should go.

Jehoshaphat then asked whether there was a God-chosen prophet they could consult. Ahab responded reluctantly because God's prophet, Micaiah, "never prophesies anything good about [him], but always bad" (v. 7). Indeed, Micaiah indicated they *wouldn't* be victorious, and the people would be "scattered on the hills" (v. 16).

In reading their story, I see how I too tend to avoid wise advice if it isn't what I want to hear. In Ahab's case, the result of listening to his "yes men" was disastrous (v. 34). May we be willing to seek and listen to the voice of truth, God's words in the Bible, even when it contradicts our personal preferences.

—*Kirsten Holmberg*

Work and Play

ECCLESIASTES 9:4–12

Whatever your hand finds to do,
do it with all your might.
—ECCLESIASTES 9:10

I've always wanted to learn how to play the cello. But I've never found the time to enroll in a class. Or, perhaps more accurately, I haven't *made* the time for it. I wanted to focus on using my time in the ways God has called me to serve Him now.

Life is short, and we often feel the pressure to make the most of our time before it slips away. But what does that really mean?

As King Solomon contemplated life, he offered two recommendations. First, live in the most meaningful way we can—fully enjoying the good things God allows us to experience in life and all of God's good gifts. This might include learning how to play the cello!

Second, work with diligence (v. 10). Life is full of opportunities, and there is always more work to do. We're to take advantage of the opportunities God gives us, seeking His wisdom on how to prioritize work and play to serve Him.

Life is a wonderful gift from the Lord. We honor Him when we take pleasure both in His daily blessings and in meaningful service.

—*Poh Fang Chia*

Before the Beginning

MATTHEW 3:13–17

"You loved me before the creation of the world."
—JOHN 17:24

"But if God has no beginning and no end, and has always existed, what was He doing before He created us?" Some precocious Sunday school student always asks this question when we talk about God's eternal nature. I used to respond that this was a bit of a mystery. But recently I learned that the Bible gives us an answer to this question.

When Jesus prays to His Father in John 17, He says "Father, . . . you loved me before the creation of the world" (v. 24). This is God as revealed to us by Jesus: Before the world was ever created, God was a trinity (Father, Son, and Holy Spirit)—all loving each other and being loved.

What a lovely and encouraging truth this is about our God! The mutual, outgoing love expressed by each member of the Trinity—Father, Son, and Holy Spirit—is key to understanding the nature of God. What was God doing before the beginning of time? What He always does: He was loving because He is love (1 John 4:8).

—*Amy Peterson*

Tossing and Turning
PSALM 4

*In peace I will lie down and sleep, for you alone,
LORD, make me dwell in safety.*
—PSALM 4:8

What keeps you awake at night?

Troubled relationships? An uncertain future? We all give in to worry at one point or another.

King David was clearly in distress when he penned Psalm 4. People were ruining his reputation with groundless accusations (v. 2). And some were questioning his competency to rule (v. 6). Surely he could have spent nights stewing about it. Yet we read these remarkable words: "In peace I will lie down and sleep" (v. 8).

Charles Spurgeon explains verse 8 beautifully: "In thus lying down, . . . [David] resigned himself into the hands of another; he did so completely, for in the absence of all care, he slept; there was here a perfect trust."

What inspired this trust? From the start, David was confident that God would answer his prayers (v. 3). And he was sure that since God had chosen to love him, He would lovingly meet his needs.

May God help us to rest in His power and presence when worries threaten. In His sovereign and loving arms, we can "lie down and sleep."
—*Poh Fang Chia*

Unexpected Kindness

EPHESIANS 2:1–10

*For we are God's handiwork, created
in Christ Jesus to do good works.*
—EPHESIANS 2:10

My friend was waiting to pay for her groceries when the man in front of her handed her a voucher for £10 ($14) off her bill. This unexpected kindness touched her heart and gave her hope during a period of exhaustion. She thanked the Lord for His goodness extended through another person.

In his letter to gentile Christians in Ephesus, Paul wrote about giving. He called the people to leave their old lives and embrace the new, saying that they were saved by grace. Out of this saving grace, he explained, flows our desire to "do good works," for we have been created in God's image and are His "handiwork" (2:10). We, like the man at the supermarket, can spread God's love through our everyday actions.

Of course, we don't have to give material things to share God's grace. We can take the time to listen to someone when she speaks to us. We can ask someone who is serving us how he is doing. We can stop to help someone in need. As we give to others, we'll receive joy in return (Acts 20:35).

—*Amy Boucher Pye*

Mercy Over Judgment

JAMES 2:1–13

Speak and act as those who are going to be judged by the law that gives freedom.

—JAMES 2:12

When my squabbling children tattled on one another, I took each child aside separately to hear his and her account of the problem. Since both were guilty, I asked them what they felt would be an appropriate, fair consequence for their sibling's actions. Both suggested swift punishment. To their surprise, I gave them each the consequence they had intended for the other. Suddenly, they lamented how "unfair" the sentence seemed—despite having deemed it appropriate when it was intended for the other.

My kids had shown the kind of "judgment without mercy" that God warns against (James 2:13). James reminds us that instead of showing favoritism to the wealthy, or even to one's self, God desires that we love others as we love ourselves (v. 8). Instead of using others for selfish gain, or disregarding anyone whose position doesn't benefit us, James instructs us to act as people who know how much we've been given and forgiven—and to extend that mercy to others.

God has given generously of His mercy. In all our dealings with others, let's remember the mercy He's shown us and extend it to others.

—*Kirsten Holmberg*

Home Sweet Home

JOHN 14:1–14

"I am going there to prepare a place for you."
—JOHN 14:2

"Why do we have to leave our home and move?" my son asked. It's difficult to explain what a home is, especially to a five-year-old. We were leaving a house, but not our home, in the sense that home is where our loved ones are. It's the place where we long to return after a long trip or after a full day's work.

When Jesus was in the upper room just hours before He died, He told His disciples, "Do not let your hearts be troubled" (John 14:1). The disciples were uncertain of their future because Jesus had predicted His death. But Jesus reassured them of His presence and reminded them they would see Him again. He told them, "My Father's house has many rooms . . . . I am going there to prepare a place for you" (v. 2). To describe heaven He chose words that describe a place where Jesus, our loved One, would be.

We can thank God for the homes we enjoy, but let's remember that our real home is in heaven where we "will be with the Lord forever" (1 Thessalonians 4:17).
—*Keila Ochoa*

Help from Heaven

JOSHUA 10:6–15

Surely the Lord was fighting for Israel!
—JOSHUA 10:14

The Morse code signal SOS was created in 1905 because sailors needed a way to indicate extreme distress. The signal gained renown in 1910 when used by the sinking steamship *Kentucky*, saving all forty-six people aboard.

While SOS may be a relatively recent invention, the urgent cry for help is as old as humanity. We hear it often in the Old Testament story of Joshua, who faced opposition from fellow Israelites (Joshua 9:18) and challenging terrain (3:15–17) as the Israelites conquered and settled the land God had promised them. During this struggle "the Lord was with Joshua" (6:27).

In Joshua 10, the Israelites went to the aid of the Gibeonites, who were being attacked by five kings. Joshua knew he needed the Lord's help (v. 12). God responded with a hailstorm, even stopping the sun briefly to give Israel more time to defeat the enemy. Joshua 10:14 recounts, "Surely the Lord was fighting for Israel!"

Are you in the midst of a challenging situation? Send out an SOS to God. Be encouraged that God will respond to your call for help in the way that is best for His glory.

—Lisa Samra

Infinite Dimensions

EPHESIANS 3:16–21

I pray that you . . . [will] grasp how wide and long
and high and deep is the love of Christ.
—EPHESIANS 3:17–18

I lay still on the vinyl-covered mat and held my breath as the machine whirred and clicked. Lots of folks have endured MRIs, but for claustrophobic me, the experience required focused concentration on something—Someone—much bigger than myself.

A phrase from Scripture—"how wide and long and high and deep is the love of Christ" (Ephesians 3:18)—moved in rhythm with the machine's hum to remind me of those four dimensions of God's love.

Enduring the MRI provided a new image for my understanding. *Wide*: the six inches on either side of my arms. *Long*: the distance between the cylinder's two openings. *High*: the six inches from my nose up to the "ceiling" of the tube. *Deep*: the support of the tube anchored to the floor, holding me up. Four dimensions illustrating God's presence surrounding and holding me in the MRI tube—and in every life.

God's love is all around us. *Wide*: He extends His arms to reach us. *Long*: His love never ends. *High*: He lifts us up. *Deep*: He dips down, holding us in all situations. Nothing can separate us from Him! (Romans 8:38–39).

—*Elisa Morgan*

Getting a Grip on Gratitude

NUMBERS 11:1–14

*Would they have enough if all the fish
in the sea were caught for them?*
—NUMBERS 11:22

The years of weariness caused by chronic pain and frustrations with my limited mobility had finally caught up with me. In my discontent, I became demanding and ungrateful. I began complaining about my husband's caregiving skills. When he finally shared that my grumbling hurt his feelings, I was resentful. He had no idea what I was going through. Eventually, God helped me see my wrongs, and I asked my husband and the Lord for forgiveness.

Longing for different circumstances can lead to complaining and even a form of relationship damaging self-centeredness. The Israelites were familiar with this dilemma. It seems they were never satisfied and always griping about God's provision (Exodus 17:1–3). Instead of rejoicing over the daily miracles of God's faithful and loving care, the Israelites wanted something more, something better, something different, or even something they used to have (Numbers 11:4–6). They took out their frustrations on Moses (vv. 10–14).

Trusting God's goodness and faithfulness can help us get a good grip on gratitude. Today we can thank Him for the countless ways He cares for us.

—*Xochitl Dixon*

Life and Death

GENESIS 50:22–26

Then Joseph said to his brothers, "I am about to die. But God will surely come to your aid and take you up out of this land to the land he promised on oath to Abraham, Isaac and Jacob."

—GENESIS 50:24

I'll never forget sitting at the bedside of my friend's brother when he died; it was the ordinary visited by the extraordinary. When we realized that Richard's breathing was becoming more labored, we gathered around him, watching, waiting, and praying. When he took his last breath, it felt like a holy moment; the presence of God enveloped us in the midst of our tears over a wonderful man dying in his forties.

Many of the heroes of our faith experienced God's faithfulness at death. For instance, Jacob announced he would soon be "gathered to [his] people" (Genesis 49:29–33). Jacob's son Joseph also announced his impending death: "I am about to die," he said to his brothers while instructing them how to hold firm in their faith. He seems to be at peace, yet eager that his brothers trust the Lord (50:24).

None of us knows when or how we will breathe our last breath, but we can ask God to assure us that He will be with us. And we know that Jesus will prepare a place for us in His Father's house (John 14:2–3).

—*Amy Boucher Pye*

A Solid Foundation

MATTHEW 7:24–27

*"Everyone who hears these words of mine
and puts them into practice is like a wise
man who built his house on the rock."*
—MATTHEW 7:24

One summer my husband and I toured Fallingwater, a house in rural Pennsylvania designed by architect Frank Lloyd Wright in 1935. I've never seen anything quite like it. Wright wanted to create a home that rose organically out of the landscape, as if it could have grown there—and he accomplished his goal. He built the house around an existing waterfall, and its style mirrors the neighboring rock ledges. Our tour guide explained what made the construction safe: "The whole vertical core of the house," she said, "rests on boulders."

Hearing her words, I couldn't help but think of Jesus's words to His disciples. Jesus told them that what He was teaching would be the sure foundation for their lives. If they heard His words and put them into practice, they would be able to withstand any storms. Those who heard but didn't obey, in contrast, would be like a house built on sand (Matthew 7:24–27).

When we listen to the words of Jesus and obey them, we're building our lives on a steady, rock-solid foundation. Maybe our lives can look a little like Fallingwater—beautiful and built to last on the Rock.
—*Amy Peterson*

Muscling Through

2 CHRONICLES 20:2–3, 14–22

Alarmed, Jehoshaphat resolved to inquire of the
LORD, *and he proclaimed a fast for all Judah.*
—2 CHRONICLES 20:3

Competitive bodybuilders endure a rigorous training cycle. During the initial months, they emphasize gaining size and strength. As the competition nears, the focus shifts to losing any fat that hides the muscle. In the final days, they consume less water than normal so their muscle tissue is easily visible. Bodybuilders are actually at their weakest on the day of competition, despite appearing strong.

In 2 Chronicles 20, we read of the opposite reality: acknowledging weakness in order to experience God's strength. "A vast army is coming against you," people told King Jehoshaphat. So "he proclaimed a fast for all Judah" (v. 3), depriving himself and all his people of nourishment. Then they asked God for help. Jehoshaphat placed singers at the front of his army (v. 21). As they began to sing praises, the Lord "set ambushes against the men . . . who were invading Judah, and they were defeated" (v. 22).

Jehoshaphat's decision demonstrated deep faith in God. He chose not to depend on self but instead to lean on God. Rather than trying to muscle our way through our trials, may we allow Him to be our strength.

—*Kirsten Holmberg*

From Shame to Honor

LUKE 1:18–25

"[The Lord] has shown his favor and taken away my disgrace among the people."
—LUKE 1:25

Imagine the plight of Elizabeth, who was childless despite being married for many years. In her culture, that was seen as a sign of God's disfavor (see 1 Samuel 1:5–6) and could actually be considered shameful. So while Elizabeth had been living righteously (Luke 1:6), her neighbors and relatives may have suspected otherwise.

Nonetheless, Elizabeth and her husband continued to serve the Lord faithfully. Then, when both were well advanced in years, a miracle occurred. God heard her prayer (v. 13). He loves to show us His favor (v. 25). And though He may seem to delay, His timing is always right and His wisdom always perfect. For Elizabeth and her husband, God had a special gift: a child who would become the Messiah's forerunner (Isaiah 40:3–5).

Do you feel inadequate because you seem to lack something—a university degree, a spouse, a child, a job, a house? Keep living for Him faithfully and waiting patiently for Him and His plan, just as Elizabeth did. No matter our circumstances, God is working in and through us. He knows your heart. He hears your prayers.

—*Poh Fang Chia*

A New Community

ACTS 2:1–12, 42–47

*All the believers were together and
had everything in common.*

—ACTS 2:44

My friend Carrie's five-year-old daughter, Maija, has an interesting approach to playtime. She loves mixing together dolls from different playsets to come up with a new community. She believes her people are happiest when they're together, despite being different sizes and shapes.

This reminds me of God's purpose for the church. On the day of Pentecost, "there were staying in Jerusalem God-fearing Jews from every nation under heaven" (Acts 2:5). Though these people were from different cultures and spoke different languages, the Holy Spirit's arrival made them a new community: the church. From then on, they would be considered one body, unified by the death and resurrection of Jesus.

The leaders of this new body were Jesus's disciples. If Jesus hadn't united them, more than likely they would never have come together. And now more people—"about three thousand" (v. 41)—had become Christ-followers. Thanks to the Holy Spirit, this once divided group "had everything in common" (v. 44). They were willing to share what they had with each other.

The Holy Spirit continues to bridge the gaps between people groups of various origins and languages. As believers in Christ, we belong together.

—*Linda Washington*

Reason to Sing

2 CHRONICLES 20:14–22

Sing praises to God, sing praises.
—PSALM 47:6

The apostle Paul's writing encourages the church to speak to one another with psalms, hymns, and spiritual songs (Ephesians 5:19). And the Bible repeats, "Sing praise" more than fifty times.

In 2 Chronicles 20, we read a story of God's people demonstrating their trust in God by singing as they marched into battle. Enemies were heading toward the people of Judah. Alarmed, King Jehoshaphat called everyone together. He led the community in intense prayer. They didn't eat or drink, but only prayed, "We don't know what to do, but our eyes are on you" (v. 12). The next day, they set out. They weren't led by their fiercest warriors, but by their choir. They believed God's promise that they would be delivered without having to fight at all (v. 17).

While they sang and walked toward the conflict, their enemies fought each other! By the time God's people reached the battlefield, the fighting had ended. God saved His people as they marched by faith, singing His praises.

God encourages us to praise Him. Praising God has power to change our thoughts, our hearts, and our lives.

—*Amy Peterson*

Following Where He Leads

1 KINGS 19:19–21

Then [Elisha] set out to follow
Elijah and became his servant.
—1 KINGS 19:21

As a child, I looked forward to our church's Sunday evening services. They were exciting. Sunday night often meant we got to hear from missionaries and other guest speakers. Their messages inspired me because of their willingness to leave family and friends—and at times, homes, possessions, and careers—to go off to strange, unfamiliar, and sometimes dangerous places to serve God.

Like those missionaries, Elisha left many things behind to follow God (1 Kings 19:19–21). When God called him into service through Elijah, he was a farmer. The prophet Elijah met him in the field where he was plowing, threw his cloak over Elisha's shoulders (the symbol of his role as prophet), and called him to follow. After giving his mother a kiss and saying goodbye to his father, Elisha sacrificed his oxen, burned his plowing equipment, and followed Elijah.

God wants all of us to follow Him and to "live as a believer in whatever situation the Lord has assigned to [us], just as God has called [us]" (1 Corinthians 7:17). Serving God can be thrilling and challenging no matter where we are—even if we never leave home.

—*Alyson Kieda*

How to Change a Life

PROVERBS 15:4, 16:24, 18:21

*Gracious words are a honeycomb, sweet to
the soul and healing to the bones.*
—PROVERBS 16:24

Sometimes our lives can change through the powerful impact of others. For rock 'n' roll legend Bruce Springsteen, it was the work of musical artists who helped him through a difficult childhood and a persistent struggle with depression. He expressed meaning in his own work this way: "You can change someone's life in three minutes with the right song."

Like a compelling song, others' well-chosen words can also give us hope, even change the course of our lives. I'm sure most of us could share stories of a conversation that forever impacted our lives.

The book of Proverbs emphasizes our responsibility to treasure words and use them wisely. Scripture never treats speech as if it's "just talk." Instead, we are taught that our words can have life-or-death consequences (18:21). In just a few words we could crush someone's spirit. Or, through words of wisdom and hope, we can nourish and strengthen others (15:4).

Not all of us have the ability to create powerful music. But we each can serve others through our speech (Psalm 141:3). With just a few well-chosen words, God can use us to change a life.

—*Monica Brands*

Only by Prayer

MARK 9:14–29

"Everything is possible for one who believes."
—MARK 9:23

My friend called me late one night during her cancer treatment. Grieved by her uncontrollable sobs, I added my own tears and a silent prayer. *What am I supposed to do, Lord?*

Her wails squeezed my heart. I couldn't stop her pain, but I knew who could help. As I wept with my friend, stumbling through a prayer, I whispered repeatedly, "Jesus. Jesus. Jesus." Her cries quieted to whimpers. Her husband's voice startled me. "She's asleep," he said. "We'll call tomorrow." I hung up, weeping prayers into my pillow.

The gospel of Mark shares the story of a desperate father bringing his suffering son to Jesus for help (Mark 9:17). Doubt clung to his plea as he explained their dire circumstances (vv. 20–22) and acknowledged his need for Jesus's help (v. 24). They experienced freedom, hope, and peace when Jesus stepped in and took control (vv. 25–27).

When loved ones are hurting, we want to do the right things and say the perfect words. But Christ is the only One who can truly help. When we call on His name, He can enable us to believe and rely on Him.

—*Xochitl Dixon*

Unlocked

COLOSSIANS 1:13–23

Once you were alienated from God. . . .
But now he has reconciled you.
—COLOSSIANS 1:21–22

A boy born with cerebral palsy was unable to speak or communicate. But his mother, Chantal Bryan, never gave up. When he was ten years old, she figured out how to communicate with him through his eyes and a letter board. After this breakthrough, she said, "He was unlocked, and we could ask him anything." Now Jonathan reads and writes, including poetry, by communicating through his eyes. When asked what it's like to "talk" with his family and friends, he said, "It is wonderful to tell them I love them."

Jonathan's story leads me to consider how God unlocks us from the prison of sin. Paul wrote to the Christians at Colossae that once we were "alienated from God" (Colossians 1:21), our evil behavior making us His enemy. But through Christ's death on the cross we are now presented to God as "holy in his sight" (v. 22). We may now "live a life worthy of the Lord."

We are no longer locked to a life of sin. As we continue in our faith, we can hold firm to our hope in Christ.

—*Amy Boucher Pye*

Pictures of Love

2 JOHN 1:1–6

*I am not writing you a new command but
one we have had from the beginning.
I ask that we love one another.*
—2 JOHN 1:5

My children and I have started a new practice. Every night at bedtime, we gather colored pencils and light a candle. Asking God to light our way, we get out our journals and draw or write answers to two questions: *When did I show love today?* and *When did I withhold love today?*

Loving our neighbors has been an important part of the Christian life "from the beginning" (2 John 1:5). John asked the people in his congregation to love one another in obedience to God (2 John 1:5–6). Practicing real love is one way to know that we "belong to the truth" (1 John 3:18–19).

When my kids and I reflect, we find that love takes shape in simple actions: sharing an umbrella, encouraging someone, or cooking a favorite meal. The moments when we're withholding love are equally practical: we gossip, refuse to share, or satisfy our own desires first.

Paying attention each night helps us be more aware each day—more tuned in to what the Spirit might be showing us. With the Spirit's help, we're learning to walk in love (2 John 1:6).

—*Amy Peterson*

Thanks Living

PSALM 23

*Surely your goodness and love will follow
me all the days of my life, and I will dwell
in the house of the LORD forever.*
—PSALM 23:6

Wanting to mature in her spiritual life and become more thankful, Sue started what she called a Thanks-Living jar. Each evening she wrote on a small piece of paper one thing she thanked God for and dropped it in the jar. Some days she had many praises; other difficult days she struggled to find one. At the end of the year she emptied her jar and read through all of the notes. She found herself thanking God again for everything He had done.

Sue's discovery reminded me of what the psalmist David says he experienced (Psalm 23). God refreshed him with "green pastures" and "quiet waters" (vv. 2–3). He gave him guidance, protection, and comfort (vv. 3–4). David concluded: "Surely your goodness and love will follow me all the days of my life" (v. 6).

Recently, I made a Thanks-Living jar. Maybe you'd like to as well. Let's see how many reasons we have to thank God—His gifts of friends and family and His provisions for our physical, spiritual, and emotional needs. We'll be reminded that the goodness and love of God follow us all the days of our lives.

—*Anne Cetas*

Going First

1 JOHN 4:7–21

We love because he first loved us.
—1 JOHN 4:19

We worked patiently to help our son heal and adjust to his new life with our family. Trauma from his early days in an orphanage was fueling some negative behaviors. While I had enormous compassion for those earlier hardships, I felt myself begin to withdraw from him emotionally. Ashamed, I shared my struggle with his therapist. Her gentle reply hit home: "He needs you to go first . . . to show him he's worthy of love before he'll be able to act like it."

John pushes the recipients of his letter to an incredible depth of love, citing God's love as both the source and the reason for loving one another (1 John 4:7, 11). I admit I often fail to show such love to others—whether strangers, friends, or my own children. Yet John's words spark in me renewed desire and ability to do so. God went first: He sent His Son to demonstrate the fullness of His love for us.

God is unwavering in offering His love to us (Romans 5:8). His "go-first" love compels us to love one another as a reflection of that love.

—*Kirsten Holmberg*

What About You?

EPHESIANS 4:25–32

The tongue has the power of life and death,
and those who love it will eat its fruit.
—PROVERBS 18:21

Emily listened as a group of friends talked about their Thanksgiving traditions with family. "We go around the room and each one tells what he or she is thankful to God for," Gary said.

Another friend mentioned his family's Thanksgiving meal and prayer time. He recalled time with his dad before he had died: "Even though Dad had dementia, his prayer of thanks to the Lord was clear." Emily's sadness and jealousy grew as she thought of her own family, and she complained: "Our traditions are to eat turkey, watch television, and never mention anything about God or giving thanks."

Right away Emily felt uneasy with her attitude. *What could you do differently to change the day?* she asked herself. When the day arrived, she expressed her thankfulness for her family members one by one, and they all felt loved. It wasn't easy, but she experienced joy as she shared her love.

"Let everything you say be good and helpful," wrote the apostle Paul, "so that your words will be an encouragement to those who hear them" (Ephesians 4:29 NLT). Our words of thanks can remind others of their value to us and to God.

—*Anne Cetas*

Best Deal Ever!

ECCLESIASTES 5:10–20

As goods increase, so do those who consume them.
And what benefit are they to the owners?
—ECCLESIASTES 5:11

How much is enough? We might ask this simple question as we face the prospects of another Black Friday. The day after the US Thanksgiving holiday has become a time for stores to offer cut-price deals and help some shoppers with limited resources to purchase something at a price they can afford. But sadly, greed sometimes overtakes people and violence has erupted as people fight over bargains.

The wisdom of the Old Testament writer known as "the Teacher" (Ecclesiastes 1:1) provides an antidote to the frenzy of consumerism we may face in the shops—and in our hearts. He points out that those who love money never will have enough and will be ruled by their possessions. And yet, they will die with nothing: "As everyone comes, so they depart" (5:15). The apostle Paul echoes this idea when he says that the love of money is a root of all kinds of evil, and that we should strive for "godliness with contentment" (1 Timothy 6:6–10).

Consumerism cannot create contentment. When we look to the Lord for our sense of peace and well-being, He will fill us with His goodness and love.

—*Amy Boucher Pye*

What We Can Do

PHILIPPIANS 2:1–11

In your relationships with one another,
have the same mindset as Christ Jesus.
—PHILIPPIANS 2:5

Even though confined to his bed, ninety-two-year-old Morrie Boogaart knit hats for the homeless in Michigan. He had reportedly made more than 8,000 hats in fifteen years. He declared that his work made him feel good and gave him a purpose. He said, "I'm going to do this until I go home to the Lord"—which happened in 2018. Morrie's simple act of persevering love is still inspiring people.

We too can look past our struggles, place others before ourselves, and imitate our loving and compassionate Savior, Jesus Christ (Philippians 2:1–5). God in the flesh—the King of Kings—took on the "very nature of a servant" in genuine humility (vv. 6–7). Giving His life—the ultimate sacrifice—He took our place on the cross (v. 8). Jesus gave everything for us . . . all for the glory of God the Father (vv. 9–11).

As believers in Jesus, it's our privilege to show love and demonstrate concern for others through acts of kindness. We can actively seek opportunities to make a difference in people's lives by simply doing what we can.

—*Xochitl Dixon*

The Highest Place

COLOSSIANS 1:15–23

*He is before all things, and in him
all things hold together.*
—COLOSSIANS 1:17

My husband invited a friend to church. After the service his friend said, "I liked the songs and the atmosphere, but I don't get it. Why do you give Jesus such a high place of honor?" My husband explained that Christianity is a relationship with Christ. Without Him, Christianity would be meaningless. It's because of what Jesus has done that we meet together and praise Him.

Who is Jesus and what has He done? The apostle Paul answered this question in Colossians 1. No one has seen God, but Jesus came to reflect and reveal Him (v. 15). Jesus, as the Son of God, came to die for us and free us from sin. Sin has separated us from God's holiness, so peace could only be made through someone perfect. That was Jesus (vv. 14, 20). In other words, Jesus has given us what no one else could— access to God and eternal life (John 17:3).

Why does He deserve such a place of honor? He conquered death. He won our hearts by His love and sacrifice. He is everything to us!

Let's give Him the highest place in our hearts.

—*Keila Ochoa*

Living in the Light

1 JOHN 2:3–11

The darkness is passing and the true light
is already shining.
—1 JOHN 2:8

It was a dark morning. Low, steel-colored clouds filled the sky, and the atmosphere was so dim that I needed to turn on the lights in order to read a book. I had just settled in when the room suddenly filled with light. I looked up and saw that the wind was pushing the clouds to the east, clearing the sky and revealing the sun.

As I went to the window to get a better look at the drama, a thought came to mind: "The darkness is passing and the true light is already shining" (1 John 2:8). The apostle John wrote these words to believers as a message of encouragement. He went on to say, "Anyone who loves their brother and sister lives in the light, and there is nothing in them to make them stumble" (v. 10). By contrast, he equated hating people with roaming around in darkness.

When we choose love instead of hate, we are showing our relationship with Him and reflecting His radiance to the world around us. "God is light; in him there is no darkness at all" (1 John 1:5).

—*Jennifer Benson Schuldt*

God at Work

HEBREWS 13:20–21

May he work in us what is pleasing to him,
through Jesus Christ.
—HEBREWS 13:21

"How have you seen God at work lately?" I asked some friends. One replied, "I see Him at work as I read the Scriptures each morning; I see Him at work as He helps me face each new day; I see Him at work when I realize how He has helped me to face challenges while giving me joy." I love his answer. It reflects how through God's Word and the indwelling presence of the Holy Spirit, God works in those who love Him.

God working in His followers is a wonderful mystery that the writer to the Hebrews addresses: "May he work in us what is pleasing to him, through Jesus Christ" (13:21). The writer reinforces the essential message of his letter—that God will equip His people to follow Him and that God will work in and through them for His glory.

The gift of God working in us can take us by surprise; perhaps we forgive someone who wrongs us or show patience to someone we find difficult. How have you seen God at work lately?

—*Amy Boucher Pye*

What Can't You Give Up?

HOSEA 11:8–11

*[Nothing] will be able to separate
us from the love of God.*
—ROMANS 8:39

"What's one thing you can't give up?" the radio host asked. Listeners called in with interesting answers. Some mentioned their families, including a husband who shared memories of a deceased wife. Others shared they can't give up on their dreams. All of us have something we treasure dearly—a person, a passion, a possession.

In the book of Hosea, God tells us that He won't give up on Israel, His treasured possession. As Israel's loving husband, God provided her with everything she needed: land, food, drink, clothing, and security. Yet like an adulterous spouse, Israel rejected God and sought her happiness and security elsewhere. However, though she had hurt Him deeply, He would not give her up (v. 8). He would discipline Israel so as to redeem her; His desire was to re-establish His relationship with her (v. 11).

Today, all God's children can have the same assurance: His love for us will never let us go (Romans 8:37–39). If we've wandered from Him, He yearns for our return. We are His treasure; He won't give up on us.

—*Poh Fang Chia*

Not Enough?

2 CORINTHIANS 9:10–15

Do not forget to do good and to share with others.
—HEBREWS 13:16

On the way home from church, my daughter sat in the backseat enjoying Goldfish crackers as my other children implored her to share. I asked the hoarder of snacks, "What did you do in class today?" She said they made a basket of bread and fish because a child gave Jesus five loaves and two fish that Jesus used to feed more than 5,000 people (John 6:1–13).

"That was very kind of the little boy to share. Do you think maybe God is asking you to share your fish?" I asked. "No, Momma," she replied.

When I tried to encourage her not to keep all the crackers to herself, she concluded, "There's not enough for everyone!"

Sharing is hard. The assumption is that if I give, I will be left wanting.

Paul reminds us that all we have comes from God, who wants to enrich us "in every way so that [we] can be generous" (2 Corinthians 9:10–11). We can share joyfully because God promises to care for us even as we are generous to others.

—*Lisa Samra*

Sharing Slices

PROVERBS 11:23–31

A generous person will prosper; whoever
refreshes others will be refreshed.
—PROVERBS 11:25

Steve, a sixty-two-year-old homeless military veteran, made his way to a warm climate where sleeping outdoors was tolerable year-round. One evening, as he displayed his hand-drawn art—his attempt to earn some money—a young woman approached and offered him several slices of pizza. Steve gratefully accepted. Moments later, Steve shared his bounty with another hungry, homeless person. Almost immediately, the same young woman resurfaced with another plate of food, acknowledging that he had been generous with what he'd been given.

Steve's story illustrates the principle found in Proverbs 11:25 that when we're generous with others, we're likely to experience generosity as well. We give to help others in loving response to God's instruction to do so (Philippians 2:3–4; 1 John 3:17). When we do, God is pleased. He often finds a way to refresh us—in His own matchless way.

Steve shared his second plate of pizza too with a smile and open hands. He's an example of what it means to live generously, willing to cheerfully share what we have with others. As God leads and empowers us, may the same be said of us.

—*Kirsten Holmberg*

Waiting

MICAH 5:2–4

"But you, Bethlehem Ephrathah, though you are small among the clans of Judah, out of you will come for me one who will be ruler over Israel."

—MICAH 5:2

"How much longer until Christmas?" When my children were little, they asked this question repeatedly. Although we used a daily Advent calendar to count down the days, they still found the waiting excruciating.

Waiting is a challenge for all of us. Consider, for instance, those who received the message of the prophet Micah, who promised that out of Bethlehem would come a "ruler over Israel" (5:2) who would "shepherd his flock in the strength of the LORD" (v. 4). The initial fulfillment of this prophecy came 700 years later when Jesus was born in Bethlehem (Matthew 2:1). But some of the prophecy's fulfillment is yet to come. We wait in hope for Jesus's return, when "his greatness will reach to the ends of the earth" (Micah 5:4). Then we will rejoice, for our long wait will be over.

We may not find waiting easy, but God promises to be with us as we wait (Matthew 28:20). When Jesus was born in Bethlehem, He ushered in life in all its fullness (see John 10:10)—life without condemnation. We enjoy His presence with us today while we eagerly await His return.

—*Amy Boucher Pye*

White as Snow

ISAIAH 1:16–20

Though yours sins are like scarlet,
they shall be as white as snow.
—ISAIAH 1:18

One December, my family and I went to the mountains. We had lived in a tropical climate all our lives, so it was the first time we could see snow in all its magnificence. As we contemplated the white mantle covering the fields, my husband quoted Isaiah, "Though your sins are like scarlet, they shall be as white as snow" (Isaiah 1:18).

After asking about the meaning of scarlet, our three-year-old daughter asked, "Is the color red bad?" She knows sins are things God dislikes, but this verse is not talking about colors. The prophet was describing a pigment that was double-dyed in clothes so the color became fixed. Neither rain nor washing would remove it. Sin is like that. No human effort can take it away. It's rooted in the heart.

Only God can cleanse a heart from sin. Peter taught, "Repent, then, and turn to God, so that your sins may be wiped out" (Acts 3:19), God forgives us and gives us a new life. Only through Jesus's sacrifice can we receive what no one else can give—a pure heart. What a wonderful gift!

—*Keila Ochoa*

Behind the Scenes

DANIEL 10:1–14

*"Your words were heard, and I have
come in response to them."*
—DANIEL 10:12

My daughter texted a friend, hoping to have a question answered quickly. Her phone indicated that the recipient had read the message, so she waited anxiously. Mere moments passed, yet she grew frustrated at the delay. Irritation eroded into worry; she wondered whether there might be a problem between them. Eventually a reply came, and my daughter was relieved that their relationship was fine. Her friend had simply been seeking an answer.

The prophet Daniel also anxiously awaited a reply. After receiving a frightening vision, Daniel fasted and sought God through prayer (10:3, 12). Finally, after three weeks (vv. 2, 13), an angel arrived and assured Daniel his prayers had been heard "since the first day," and he had been battling on behalf of those prayers. God was at work during each of the twenty-one days that elapsed between Daniel's first prayer and the angel's coming.

We can grow anxious when God's reply doesn't come when we want it to. We're prone to wonder whether He cares. Yet Daniel's experience reminds us that God is at work on behalf of those He loves even when it isn't obvious to us.

—*Kirsten Holmberg*

Impaired Judgment

MATTHEW 7:1–6

"Do not judge, or you too will be judged."
—MATTHEW 7:1

I've been quick to judge people walking in the street while staring at their phones. *How could they be so oblivious to the traffic?* I've told myself. *Don't they care about their own safety?* But one day, while crossing the entrance to an alleyway, I was so engrossed in a text message that I missed seeing a car at my left. Thankfully, the driver saw me and came to an abrupt stop. But I felt ashamed. My self-righteous finger-pointing came back to haunt me. I had judged others, only to do the same thing myself.

My hypocrisy is the kind of thinking Jesus addressed in the Sermon on the Mount: "First take the plank out of your own eye, and then you will see clearly to remove the speck from your brother's eye" (Matthew 7:5). I had a huge "plank"—a blind spot through which I judged others with my own impaired judgment.

"For in the same way you judge others, you will be judged," Jesus also said (7:2).

None of us is perfect. Sometimes I forget that in my haste to judge others. We all need God's grace.

—*Linda Washington*

A Big Deal

ISAIAH 58:6–9

"This is the kind of fasting I want: . . .
Let the oppressed go free, and remove
the chains that bind people."
—ISAIAH 58:6 (NLT)

A family member needed help with his December rent. To his family, the request felt like a burden—especially with their own unexpected expenses at year's end. But they dug into their savings, grateful for God's provision and blessed by their relative's gratitude, and they provided the much-needed assistance.

Later, the recipient handed them a thank-you card filled with grateful words. "There you go again . . . doing nice things, probably passing it off as no big deal."

Helping others is a big deal, however, to God. The prophet Isaiah made that point to the nation of Israel. The people were fasting but still quarreling and fighting. In Isaiah 58, the prophet mentioned several ways to help, including, "Share your food with the hungry, and give shelter to the homeless" (v. 7 NLT).

Such a sacrifice, said Isaiah, shares God's light but also heals our own brokenness (v. 8). This was God's promise for being generous: "Your godliness will lead you forward, and the glory of the LORD will protect you from behind" (v. 8 NLT). Giving to others blesses us more.

—*Patricia Raybon*

Made Clean

EZEKIEL 36:24–32

"I will sprinkle clean water on you,
and you will be clean."
—EZEKIEL 36:25

When I opened our dishwasher, I wondered what had gone wrong. Instead of seeing sparkling clean dishes, I removed plates and glasses covered in a chalky dust.

God's cleansing, unlike that faulty dishwasher, washes away all impurities. We see in Ezekiel that God is calling His people back to himself as the prophet shared God's message of love and forgiveness. The Israelites had sinned as they proclaimed their allegiance to other gods and other nations. The Lord, however, was merciful in welcoming them back to himself. He promised to cleanse them "from all [their] impurities and all [their] idols" (36:25). As He placed His Spirit in them (v. 27), He would bring them to a place of fruitfulness, not famine (v. 30).

As in the days of Ezekiel, today the Lord welcomes us back if we go astray. When we submit to His will and His ways, He transforms us as He washes us clean from our sins. With His Holy Spirit dwelling within us, we have all we need to follow Him each day.

—*Amy Boucher Pye*

A Blessing Bowl

ROMANS 1:1–10

I thank my God every time I remember you.
—PHILIPPIANS 1:3

The familiar bing of an arriving email caught my attention while I wrote at my computer. Usually I try to resist the temptation to check every email, but the subject line was too enticing: "You are a blessing."

Eagerly, I opened it to discover a faraway friend telling me she was praying for my family. Each week, she displays one Christmas card photo in her kitchen table "Blessing Bowl" and prays for that family. She wrote, "I thank my God every time I remember you" (Philippians 1:3).

Through my friend's gesture, Paul's words to the Philippians came trickling into my inbox, creating the same joy in my heart I suspect readers received from his first-century thank-you note. Paul made it a habit to speak his gratitude to those who worked alongside him. A similar phrase opens many of his letters: "I thank my God through Jesus Christ for all of you" (Romans 1:8).

In the first century, Paul blessed his co-laborers with a thank-you note of prayerfulness. In the twenty-first century, my friend used a Blessing Bowl to bring joy into my day. How might we thank someone today?

—*Elisa Morgan*

Blessing in the Mess

GENESIS 28:10–22

*He who began a good work in you will carry it on
to completion until the day of Christ Jesus.*
—PHILIPPIANS 1:6

God's first encounter with Jacob is a beautiful illustration of His grace. Jacob had spent a lifetime trying to alter his destiny. He'd been born second at a time when firstborn sons typically received their father's blessing—believed to guarantee future prosperity.

So Jacob decided to do whatever it would take to get his father's blessing anyway. Eventually, he succeeded—through deceit—obtaining the blessing intended for his brother (Genesis 27:19–29).

But the price was a divided family, and Jacob fled from his furious brother (vv. 41–43). As night descended (28:11), Jacob must have felt as far from a life of blessing as ever.

But it was there, in the middle of his trail of deception, that Jacob met God. God showed him he didn't need desperate schemes to be blessed; he *already was*. His destiny was held securely by the One who would never leave him (v. 15).

It was a lesson Jacob would spend his whole life learning.

And so will we. No matter how many regrets we carry or how distant God seems, He is still there—gently guiding us out of our mess into *His* blessing.
—*Monica Brands*

December 9

Return on Investment

DEUTERONOMY 1:2; MARK 10:1–31

*Peter [said to Jesus], "We have left
everything to follow you!"*
—MARK 10:28

In 1995 US stock market investors received record-high returns—on average, a whopping 37.6 percent return. Then in 2008 investors lost almost exactly as much: a negative 37.0 percent. The years between had varying returns, causing those with money in the market to wonder—sometimes with fear—what would become of their investment.

Jesus assured His followers they would have an incredible return on investing their lives in Him. They "left everything to follow [Him]"—leaving their homes, jobs, status, and families to put their lives on deposit (v. 28). But they grew concerned about their investment after watching a wealthy man struggle with the grip worldly goods had on him. Jesus replied that anyone willing to sacrifice for Him would "receive a hundred times as much in this present age . . . and in the age to come eternal life" (v. 30).

We don't have to be concerned about the "interest rate" on our spiritual investment. With God, it's an unmatched certainty not measured in dollars and cents but in the joy that comes from knowing Him now and forever—and sharing that joy with others!
—*Kirsten Holmberg*

Wounds from a Friend

PROVERBS 27:5-10

Wounds from a friend can be trusted.
—PROVERBS 27:6

Charles Lowery complained to his friend about lower back pain. He was seeking a sympathetic ear, but what he got was an honest assessment. His friend told him, "I don't think your back pain is your problem; it's your stomach. Your stomach is so big it's pulling on your back."

In his column for *REV! Magazine*, Charles shared that he resisted the temptation to be offended. He lost the weight, and his back problem went away. Charles recognized that "Better is open rebuke than hidden love. Wounds from a friend can be trusted" (Proverbs 27:5–6).

True friends don't find pleasure in hurting us. Rather, they love us too much to deceive us. They are people who, with loving courage, point out what we may already know but find hard to truly accept and live by. They tell us not only what we like to hear but also what we need to hear.

Solomon honored such friendship in his proverbs. Jesus went further—He endured the wounds of our rejection not only to tell us the truth about ourselves but also to show us how much we are loved.

—*Poh Fang Chia*

Listeners and Doers

JAMES 1:22–27

*Look after orphans and widows
in their distress.*
—JAMES 1:27

The phone rang in the night for my husband, a minister. One of the prayer warriors in our church, a woman in her seventies who lived alone, was being taken to the hospital. Not knowing if she would live or die, we asked God for His help and mercy, feeling particularly concerned for her welfare. The church sprang into action with a round-the-clock schedule of visitors who not only ministered to her but also showed Christian love to the other patients, visitors, and medical staff.

James's letter to the early Jewish Christians encouraged the church to care for the needy. James wanted the believers to go beyond just listening to the Word of God and to put their beliefs into action (1:22–25). By citing the need to care for orphans and widows (v. 27), he named a vulnerable group, for in the ancient world the family would have been responsible for their care.

Do we see caring for the widows and orphans as a vital part of the exercise of our faith? May God open our eyes to the opportunities to serve people in need everywhere.

—*Amy Boucher Pye*

A Fitting Time

ECCLESIASTES 3:1–4

He has made everything beautiful in its time.
—ECCLESIASTES 3:11

When I purchased an airline ticket to send our first-born child to college, I was surprised the keyboard on my computer still functioned—given the waterworks my eyes unleashed on it during the flight selection process. I so enjoyed my eighteen years of daily life with her that I was saddened by the prospect of her departure. Yet I wouldn't rob her of this opportunity simply because I was going to miss her. It was fitting for her to embark on a new journey to discover adulthood and explore another part of the country.

As this season of parenting drew to a close, another one began. It will undoubtedly bring both new challenges and new delights. Solomon wrote that God appoints "a time for everything, and a season for every activity under the heavens" (Ecclesiastes 3:1). We have little control over the events of our lives, but God, in His mighty power, makes "everything beautiful in its time" (v. 11).

Our comforts and joys come and go, but God's works "will endure forever" (v. 14). We may not relish every season—some are quite painful—yet He can bring beauty to them all.

—*Kirsten Holmberg*

God's Doing Something New

1 THESSALONIANS 3:6–13

May the Lord make your love increase
and overflow for each other and for
everyone else, just as ours does for you.
—1 THESSALONIANS 3:12

"Is God doing something new in your life?" was the question the leader asked in a group I was in recently. My friend Mindy told of needing patience with aging parents, stamina for her husband's health issues, and understanding of her children and grandchildren who have not yet chosen to follow Jesus. Then she said something surprising: "I believe the new thing God is doing is He's expanding my capacity and opportunities to love."

That fits nicely with Paul's prayer for new believers in Thessalonica: "May the Lord make your love increase and overflow for each other and for everyone else" (1 Thessalonians 3:12). He had taught them about Jesus but had to leave abruptly because of rioting (Acts 17:1–9). Now he is encouraging them to stand firm in their faith (1 Thessalonians 3:7–8). And he prayed that the Lord would increase their love for all.

During difficulties we often complain and ask, Why? Or we wonder, Why me? A better way to handle those times could be to ask the Lord to expand His love in our hearts and to help us take new opportunities to love others.

—Anne Cetas

Hurry Not

ISAIAH 26:1–4

*You will keep in perfect peace those whose minds
are steadfast, because they trust in you.*
—ISAIAH 26:3

"Ruthlessly eliminate hurry." When two friends repeated that adage by the wise Dallas Willard, I knew I needed to consider it. Where was I rushing ahead and not looking to God for guidance and help? In the weeks and months that followed, I remembered those words and reoriented myself back to the Lord and His wisdom. I reminded myself to trust in Him rather than leaning on my own ways.

After all, rushing around frantically seems to be the opposite of the "perfect peace" the prophet Isaiah speaks of. The Lord gives this gift to "those whose minds are steadfast," because they trust in Him (v. 3). And He is worthy of being trusted today, tomorrow, and forever, for he is "the Rock eternal" (v. 4). Trusting God with our minds fixed on Him is the antidote to a hurried life.

Do we sense that we're hurried or even hasty? Maybe, in contrast, we often experience a sense of peace.

Wherever we may be, I pray today that we'll be able to put aside any hurry as we trust the Lord, who will never fail us and who gives us His peace.

—*Amy Boucher Pye*

Hand Made for You

EPHESIANS 2:4–10

We are God's handiwork, created in
Christ Jesus to do good works, which
God prepared in advance for us to do.
—EPHESIANS 2:10

My grandmother was a talented, award-winning seamstress in her native Texas. Throughout my life, she celebrated hallmark occasions with a hand-sewn gift. A burgundy mohair sweater for my high school graduation. A turquoise quilt for my marriage. Each had a signature tag reading, "Handmade for you by Munna." I sensed my grandmother's love for me and received a powerful statement of her faith in my future.

Paul wrote to the Ephesians of their purpose in this world, describing them as "God's handiwork, created in Christ Jesus to do good works" (2:10). Paul went on to describe that God's handiwork in creating us would result in our handiwork of creating good works for His glory in our world. When God "hand makes" us for His purposes, He can use us to bring others toward His great love.

With her head bowed over her needle, my Munna hand made items to communicate her love for me and her passion that I discover my purpose. And with His fingers shaping the details of our days, God stitches His love and purposes in our hearts that we might experience Him for ourselves and demonstrate His handiwork to others.

—*Elisa Morgan*

The Best Strategy for Life

ECCLESIASTES 4:1–12

*Though one may be overpowered,
two can defend themselves.*
—ECCLESIASTES 4:12

As we watched my daughter's basketball game from the bleachers, I heard the coach utter a single word to the girls on the court: "Doubles." Immediately, their defensive strategy shifted from one-on-one to two of their players teaming against their tallest opponent. They were successful in thwarting her efforts to shoot and score.

When Solomon, the writer of Ecclesiastes, grapples with the toils and frustrations of the world, he too acknowledges that having a companion in our labors yields "a good return" (Ecclesiastes 4:9). While a person battling alone "may be overpowered, two can defend themselves" (v. 12). A friend nearby can help us up when we fall down (v. 10).

Solomon's words encourage us to share our journey with others. For some, that requires a level of uncomfortable or unfamiliar vulnerability. Others crave that kind of intimacy and struggle to find friends with whom to share it. Whatever the case, we mustn't give up.

Solomon and basketball coaches agree: having teammates around us is the best strategy for facing the struggles on the court and in life.

Lord, thank you for the people you empower to encourage and support us. —Kirsten Holmberg

God's Hidden Hand

PSALM 139:13–18

All the days ordained for me were written in your book before one of them came to be.
—PSALM 139:16

My friend was the son of a missionary couple from the United States and grew up in Ghana. After his family moved back to the US, he began college but had to drop out. Later, he signed on with the military, which eventually helped him pay for college and took him all over the world. Through it all, God was preparing him for his current role writing and editing Christian literature for an international audience.

His wife also has an interesting story. She failed her chemistry exams during her first year of college because of strong epilepsy medication. She eventually switched her studies from science to American Sign Language, which had a more manageable workload. She says, "God was redirecting my life for a greater purpose." Today, she makes God's Word accessible to the hearing-impaired.

Do you sometimes wonder where God is leading you? Psalm 139:16 acknowledges God's sovereign hand in our lives: "All the days ordained for me were written in your book before one of them came to be." We don't know how God will use our circumstances, but we can be certain He is directing us with His sovereign hand.

—*Poh Fang Chia*

Everlasting Hope

PSALM 146

Blessed are those whose help is the God of Jacob,
*whose hope is in the L*ORD *their God.*
—PSALM 146:5

The week before Christmas, two months after my mom died, holiday shopping and decorating sat at the bottom of my priority list. I resisted my husband's attempts to comfort me as I grieved the loss of our family's faith-filled matriarch. I sulked as our son, Xavier, attached strands of Christmas lights onto the inside walls of our home. Without a word, he plugged in the cord before he and his dad left for work.

As the colorful bulbs blinked, God drew me out of my darkness. No matter how painful the circumstances, my hope remained secure in the light of God's truth.

Psalm 146 affirms what God reminded me on that difficult morning: My endless "hope is in the LORD," my mighty and merciful God (v. 5). As Creator, He "remains faithful forever" (v. 6). He "upholds the cause of the oppressed," protecting us and providing for us (v. 7). "The LORD lifts up those who are bowed down" (v. 8).

Sometimes, even at Christmas, we face loss, experience hurt, or feel alone. But at all times, God promises to be our light in the darkness, offering tangible help and everlasting hope.

—*Xochitl Dixon*

The "Hope for a Baby" Tree

LAMENTATIONS 3:1–3, 13–24

His compassions never fail. They are new every morning; great is your faithfulness.
—LAMENTATIONS 3:22–23

After wrapping the tree with clear twinkle lights, I tied pink and blue bows on its branches and christened it our "Hope for a Baby" Christmas tree. My husband and I had been waiting for a baby through adoption for more than four years. Surely by Christmas!

Every morning I stopped at the tree and prayed, reminding myself of God's faithfulness. On December 21 we received the news: no baby by Christmas. Devastated, I wondered: *Was God still faithful? Was I doing something wrong?*

At times, God's apparent withholding results from His loving discipline. And other times God lovingly delays to renew our trust. In Lamentations, Jeremiah describes God's correction of Israel. The pain is palpable: "He pierced my heart with arrows from his quiver" (3:13). Through it all, Jeremiah expresses ultimate trust in God's faithfulness: "his compassions never fail. They are new every morning; great is your faithfulness" (vv. 22–23).

I left the tree standing and continued my morning prayer. At last, on Easter weekend, we received our baby girl. God is always faithful.

Each year I set up a miniature version of the tree, reminding myself and others to hope in God's faithfulness.

—*Elisa Morgan*

Christmas at MacPherson

LUKE 1:68–75

*"Praise be to the Lord, the God of Israel, because
he has come to his people and redeemed them."*
—LUKE 1:68

About 230 people live at MacPherson Gardens, Block 72 in my neighborhood. Each person has a story. There's the elderly woman whose children have grown up, married, and moved out. She's by herself now. Then there's the young couple with two kids—a boy and a girl. And the young man serving in the army. He has been to church before; maybe he'll visit again. I met these people last Christmas when our church went caroling.

Every Christmas—as on the first Christmas—there are many people who do not know that God has entered our world as a baby named Jesus (Luke 1:68; 2:21). Or they do not know that event's significance: "good news that will cause great joy for all the people" (2:10). Yes, all people! Regardless of our life situation, Jesus came to die for us and offer forgiveness so we can enjoy His love, joy, peace, and hope. All people, from the woman next door to the colleagues we have lunch with, need to hear this wonderful news!

On the first Christmas, the angels were the bearers of this joyous news. Now it's our turn.

—*Poh Fang Chia*

God with Us

MATTHEW 1:18–23

"The virgin will conceive and give birth
to a son, and they will call him Immanuel"
(which means "God with us").
—MATTHEW 1:23

"Christ with me, Christ before me, Christ behind me, Christ within me, Christ beneath me, Christ above me, Christ at my right, Christ at my left . . ." These hymn lyrics, written by fifth-century Celtic Christian St. Patrick, echo in my mind when I read Matthew's account of Jesus's birth. They feel like a warm embrace, reminding me that I'm never alone.

The reality of God dwelling with His people is at the heart of Christmas. Quoting Isaiah's prophecy of a child to be called Immanuel, meaning "God with us" (7:14), Matthew points to the ultimate fulfillment of that prophecy—Jesus. This truth is so central that Matthew begins and ends his gospel with it, concluding with Jesus's words to His disciples: "And surely I am with you always, to the very end of the age" (Matthew 28:20).

St. Patrick's lyrics remind me that Christ is always with believers through His indwelling Spirit. When I'm afraid, I can cling to His promise that He will never leave me. When I'm filled with joy, I can thank Him for His gracious work in my life.

Jesus, Immanuel—God with us.

—*Amy Boucher Pye*

Winter Snow

ISAIAH 42:1–4

*He will not shout or cry out, or raise his voice in
the streets. A bruised reed he will not break.*

—ISAIAH 42:2–3

In winter, I often wake to the beautiful surprise of a
world blanketed in the peace and quiet of an early
morning snow. Not loudly like a spring thunderstorm
that announces its presence in the night, snow comes
softly.

In "Winter Snow Song," Audrey Assad sings that
Jesus could have come to earth in power like a hurricane, but instead He came quietly and slowly like
the winter snow falling softly in the night outside
my window.

Jesus's arrival took many by quiet surprise. Instead
of being born in a palace, He was born in an unlikely
place, a humble dwelling outside Bethlehem. And He
slept in the only bed available, a manger (Luke 2:7).
Instead of being attended by royalty and government
officials, Jesus was welcomed by lowly shepherds
(vv. 15–16). Instead of having wealth, Jesus's parents
could only afford the inexpensive sacrifice of two
birds when they presented Him at the temple (v. 24).

Jesus came gently in order to draw us to himself
with His offer of peace with God—a peace still available to anyone who believes the unexpected story of
a Savior born in a manger.

—*Lisa Samra*

Now Is the Time

LUKE 2:8–20

"Glory to God in the highest!"
—LUKE 2:14

During our church's Christmas celebration, I watched the choir members assemble in front of the congregation while the music director rifled through papers on a slim black stand. The instruments began, and the singers launched into a well-known song that started with these words: "Come, now is the time to worship."

Although I expected to hear a time-honored Christmas carol, I smiled at the appropriate choice of music. Earlier that week I'd been reading Luke's account of Jesus's birth, and I noticed that the first Christmas lacked our modern-day trappings—but it did include worship.

After the angel announced Jesus's birth to some wide-eyed shepherds, a chorus of angels began "praising God and saying: 'Glory to God in the highest!'" (Luke 2:13–14). The shepherds responded by running to Bethlehem where they found the newborn King. They returned to their fields "glorifying and praising God for all the things that they had heard and seen" (v. 20). Coming face to face with the Son inspired the shepherds to worship the Father.

Today, consider your response to Jesus's arrival. Is there room for worship in your heart as we celebrate His birth?

—*Jennifer Benson Schuldt*

A Thrill of Hope

LUKE 2:11–30

"Today in the town of David a Savior has been
born to you; he is the Messiah, the Lord."
—LUKE 2:11

Reginald Fessenden, who worked for years to achieve wireless radio communication, claimed that on December 24, 1906, he became the first person to play music over the radio.

Fessenden held a contract with a fruit company that had installed wireless systems on a dozen boats to communicate about the harvesting and marketing of bananas. That Christmas Eve, Fessenden told the wireless operators on board all ships to pay attention. At 9 o'clock they heard his voice.

He reportedly played a record of an operatic aria, and then he pulled out his violin and played "O Holy Night." Finally, he offered Christmas greetings and read from the nativity story of Luke 2.

Both the shepherds in Bethlehem over two thousand years ago and the sailors on board the United Fruit Company ships in 1906 heard an unexpected, surprising message of hope on a dark night. God still speaks that same message of hope to us today. A Savior has been born for us—Christ the Lord! (Luke 2:11). "Glory to God in the highest heaven, and on earth peace to those on whom his favor rests" (v. 14).
—*Amy Peterson*

A Fragile Gift

LUKE 2:1–7

Thanks be to God for his indescribable gift!
—2 CORINTHIANS 9:15

When we give a fragile gift, the word *fragile* is written with big letters on the box because we don't want anyone to damage what is inside.

God's gift to us came in the most fragile package: a baby. Sometimes we imagine Christmas day as a beautiful scene on a postcard, but any mother can tell you it wasn't so. Mary was tired, probably insecure. It was her first child, and He was born in the most unsanitary conditions. She "wrapped Him in swaddling cloths, and laid Him in a manger, because there was no room for them in the inn" (Luke 2:7 NKJV).

A baby needs constant care. Babies cry, eat, sleep, and depend on their caregivers. They cannot make decisions. In Mary's day, infant mortality was high, and mothers often died in childbirth.

Why did God choose such a fragile way to send His Son to earth? Because Jesus had to be like us in order to save us. God's greatest gift came in the fragile body of a baby, but God took the risk because He loves us. Let us be thankful today for such a gift!

—*Keila Ochoa*

A Christmas Letter

JOHN 1:1–14

The Word became flesh and made his dwelling among us. We have seen his glory, the glory of the one and only Son, who came from the Father.
—JOHN 1:14

Every Christmas, a friend of mine writes letters to his wife and daughters, reviewing the events of the year and dreaming about the future. His words of love make an unforgettable Christmas present.

We could say that the original Christmas love letter was Jesus, the Word made flesh. John highlights this truth in his gospel: "In the beginning was the Word, and the Word was with God, and the Word was God" (John 1:1). In ancient philosophy, the Greek for *Word* is *logos*, suggesting a divine order that unites reality. But John expands the definition to reveal the Word as a person: Jesus, the Son of God who was "with God in the beginning" (v. 2). This Word, the Father's "one and only Son," "became flesh and made his dwelling among us" (v. 14). Through Jesus the Word, God reveals himself perfectly.

Jesus as the Word gives light to our dark world (v. 9). If we believe in Him, we can experience the gift of being God's beloved children (v. 12).

Jesus, God's love letter to us, has come and made His home among us. Now, that's an amazing Christmas gift!

—*Amy Boucher Pye*

What We Have

2 CORINTHIANS 8:1–12

For if the willingness is there, the gift is acceptable according to what one has, not according to what one does not have.
—2 CORINTHIANS 8:12

My friend was eager to gather her family and friends for a festive holiday celebration at her home. Each guest looked forward to the event and wanted to help defray the expense of feeding so many. So some would bring bread; others, salad or a side dish. One guest, however, felt she couldn't afford to purchase food. Instead, she offered to clean the host's home as her gift.

She would have been welcome at the table had she come empty-handed. Yet she looked at what she did have to offer—her time and skills—and brought them to the gathering with her whole heart. That's precisely the spirit of Paul's words in 2 Corinthians 8. The people of Corinth had been eager to give to help some fellow Christians, and Paul urged them to follow through on that effort. He commended them for their desire and their willingness, saying their motivation to give is what makes a gift of any size or amount acceptable (v. 12).

We're often quick to compare our giving to that of others. But God views our giving differently: it's our willingness to give what we have that He loves.

—*Kirsten Holmberg*

The Messenger

MALACHI 3:1–5

"I will send my messenger, who will prepare the way before me."
—MALACHI 3:1

"I have a message for you!" A woman working at the conference I was attending handed me a piece of paper, and I wondered if I should be nervous or excited. But when I read, "You have a nephew!" I knew I could rejoice.

Messages can bring good news, bad news, or words that challenge. In the Old Testament, God used His prophets to communicate messages of hope or judgment. But we also see that even His words of judgment could lead to restoration.

Both types of messages appear in Malachi 3 when the Lord promised to send someone to prepare the way for Him. John the Baptist announced the coming of the true Messenger, Jesus (see Matthew 3:11)—"the messenger of the covenant" (Malachi 3:1) who will fulfill God's promises. But He will act "like a refiner's fire " (v. 2), for He will purify those who believe in His word.

God's message is one of love, hope, and freedom. He sent His Son to be a messenger who speaks our language—sometimes with correction, but always with hope. We can trust His message.

—*Amy Boucher Pye*

Thanks for Being You!

PSALM 100

Enter his gates with thanksgiving.
—PSALM 100:4

When I served as my mom's live-in caregiver at a cancer center, I got to know Lori, another caregiver who lived down the hallway from us with her husband, Frank. I would chat, laugh, vent, cry, and pray with Lori in the shared living areas. We enjoyed supporting each other as we cared for our loved ones.

One day, I missed the shuttle that took residents to buy groceries. Lori offered to drive me to the store later that evening, so I said, "Thanks for being you." I truly appreciated her for who she was as a person, not just for what she did for me as a friend.

Psalm 100 demonstrates an appreciation of God for who He is, not simply for all He does. The psalmist invites "all the earth" (v. 1) to "worship the LORD with gladness" (v. 2), being confident in knowing "the LORD is God" (v. 3). The Lord remains worthy of our ongoing thankfulness because He "is good," His "love endures forever," and His "faithfulness continues through all generations" (v. 5).

Our intimately loving Father deserves our genuine joy-filled gratitude.

—*Xochitl Dixon*

Beginning Again

EZRA 1:1-11

Then the family heads of Judah and Benjamin,
and the priests and Levites—everyone whose heart
God had moved—prepared to go up and build
the house of the LORD in Jerusalem. —EZRA 1:5

After Christmas festivities conclude, my thoughts often turn to the coming year. While my children are out of school and our daily rhythms are slow, I reflect on where the last year has brought me and where I hope the next will take me. The prospect of starting a new year fills me with expectancy, no matter what the last year held.

This anticipation of a fresh start pales in comparison to the sense of hope the Israelites must have felt when Cyrus, the king of Persia, released them to return to their homeland in Judah after seventy long years of captivity. The previous king, Nebuchadnezzar, had deported the Israelites from their homeland. But the Lord prompted Cyrus to send the captives home to Jerusalem to rebuild God's temple (Ezra 1:2–3). Cyrus also returned to them treasures taken from the temple. Their return to life in the land God had appointed to them would begin afresh after a long season of hardship in Babylon as a consequence for their sin.

No matter what lies in our past, God's forgiveness and mercy gives us a fresh start. What great cause for hope!

—*Kirsten Holmberg*

Faith-Building Memories

LAMENTATIONS 3:19–26

Great is your faithfulness.
—LAMENTATIONS 3:23

As I stepped into the music-filled sanctuary, I looked around at the crowd that had gathered for a New Year's Eve party. Joy lifted my heart with hope as I recalled the previous year. Our congregation had collectively grieved over wayward children, deaths of loved ones, job losses, and broken relationships. But we'd also experienced God's grace as we recalled changed hearts and healed personal connections. We'd celebrated victories, weddings, graduations, and baptisms. We'd welcomed children born, adopted, or dedicated to the Lord.

Reflecting over the history of trials our church family faced, much like Jeremiah remembered his "affliction" and his "wandering" (Lamentations 3:19), I believed that "because of the LORD's great love we are not consumed, for his compassions never fail" (v. 22). As the prophet reassured himself of God's past faithfulness, his words comforted me: "The LORD is good to those whose hope is in him" (v. 25).

That night, each person in our congregation represented an expression of God's life-transforming love. As we continue to seek Him and support one another, we can, as did Jeremiah, find our hope being ratified by faith-building memories of God's unchanging character and dependability.

—*Xochitl Dixon*

The Writers

Alyson Kieda has been an editor for Our Daily Bread Ministries for over a decade and has more than thirty-five years of editing experience. Alyson has loved writing since she was a child and is thrilled to be writing for *Our Daily Bread*. She is married with three adult children and a growing number of grandchildren. Alyson loves reading, walking in the woods, and being with family. She feels blessed to be following in her mother's footsteps—she wrote articles many years ago for another devotional.

Amy Peterson works with the honors program at Taylor University. She has a BA in English literature from Texas A&M, an MA in intercultural studies from Wheaton College, and is completing an MFA through Seattle Pacific University. Amy taught English as a second language for two years in Southeast Asia before returning stateside to teach in California, Arkansas, Washington, and Indiana. She is the author of *Dangerous Territory: My Misguided Quest to Save the World*. Amy enjoys reading, quilting, hiking, and experimenting in sustainable living practices.

Amy Boucher Pye is a writer, editor, and speaker. The author of *Finding Myself in Britain: Our Search for Faith, Home, and True Identity*, she runs the Woman Alive book club in the United Kingdom and enjoys life with her family in their English vicarage.

Anne Cetas became a follower of Jesus in her late teens. At nineteen, she was given a copy of *Our Daily Bread* by a friend to help her read the Bible consistently. She also devoured Discovery Series topical study booklets from Our Daily Bread Ministries. Several years later, she joined the editorial staff of *Our Daily Bread* as a proofreader. Anne began writing for the devotional booklet in September 2004 and is senior content editor for the publication. Anne and her husband, Carl, enjoy walking and bicycling together, and working as mentors in an urban ministry.

Cindy Hess Kasper served for more than forty years at Our Daily Bread Ministries. An experienced writer, she has penned youth devotional articles for more than a decade. She is a daughter of longtime senior editor Clair Hess, from whom she learned a love for singing and working with words. Cindy and her husband, Tom, have three grown children and seven grandchildren, in whom they take great delight.

Elisa Morgan has authored over fifteen books on mothering, spiritual formation, and evangelism, including *The NIV Mom's Devotional Bible* and *Hello, Beauty Full: Seeing Yourself as God Sees You*. She currently authors a blog under the title, *Really* (elisamorgan.com). For twenty years, Elisa served as CEO of MOPS International. Elisa is married to Evan (longtime senior vice president of global ministry efforts for Our Daily Bread Ministries), and they have two grown children and two grandchildren who live near them in Denver, Colorado.

Estera Pirosca Escobar is a Romanian with a heart for the world. After coming to the US as a college student, she experienced what it means to be lonely and homesick, but she also experienced the Christian community's love for internationals. She saw many international students become followers of Jesus as a result of the hospitality and love they received. In her role as National Field Director for International Friendships, Inc. (IFI), Estera helps IFI ministry leaders around the US strengthen and grow their local ministry. Estera and her Chilean-born husband, Francisco, live in Grand Rapids, Michigan.

Jennifer Benson Schuldt has been writing professionally since 1997 when she graduated from Cedarville University and began her career as a technical writer. A contributing writer for *Our Daily Bread*, Jennifer lives in the Chicago suburbs with her husband, Bob, and their two children. When she isn't writing or serving at home and church, she enjoys painting, reading poetry and fiction, and taking walks with her family.

Jolene Philo, a teacher for twenty-five years, now writes and speaks about caregiving. She is the author of *The Caregivers Notebook*, and she hosts a thriving online community for parents of children with special needs at DifferentDream.com. She and her husband have two children and live in Iowa.

Julie Ackerman Link, after a lengthy battle with cancer, went to be with the Lord on April 10, 2015. Julie began writing articles each month for *Our Daily Bread* in 2000. She was popular with readers, and her insightful and inspiring articles have touched millions of lives around the world. Julie also wrote the books *Above All, Love* and *A Heart for God.* Her book *100 Prayers Inspired by the Psalms* was published posthumously in 2017.

Julie Schwab lives in Michigan where she grew up exploring the woods in her backyard and attending tractor shows with her family. She received her BA in creative writing from Cornerstone University in 2017 and her MA in theological studies from Liberty University in 2018. She loves playing the guitar, learning to cook, and doing anything creative. She's passionate about God's Word, writing (both fiction and nonfiction), editing, reading about writing and grammar, and talking to others about writing and life in Christ. She also continually finds herself in awe of God and His love.

Karen Wolfe is a native of Jamaica who now lives in the US. She became a follower of Christ at age twenty-six, and one of the first devotionals she read was *Our Daily Bread.* Karen enjoys teaching and writing so she can share the truths she learns from Scripture. Her desire is to see men and women walk in the freedom that Christ has given and to see lives transformed by the Word of God. She completed her biblical studies degree at New Orleans Baptist Theological Seminary. She and her husband, Joey, live in Georgia.

Keila Ochoa and her husband have two young children. She helps Media Associates International with their training ministry for writers around the world and has written several books in Spanish for children, teens, and women. She serves in her church in the areas of youth, missions, and women's ministry.

Kirsten Holmberg is a speaker, author, and coach based in the Pacific Northwest. She's the author of *Advent with the Word: Approaching Christmas Through the Inspired Language of God* and several Bible studies. She speaks regularly at business, church, and community events, encouraging others to step closer to Jesus and better know His love for them through His Word. Find her online at kirstenholmberg.com or on Facebook, Twitter, and Instagram (@kirholmberg).

Linda Washington received a BA in English/Writing from Northwestern University in Evanston, Illinois, and an MFA from Vermont College of Fine Arts in Montpelier, Vermont. She has authored or coauthored fiction and nonfiction books for kids, teens, and adults, including *God and Me* (ages 10–12—Rainbow/Legacy Press/Rose Publishing) and *The Soul of C.S. Lewis* (with Jerry Root, Wayne Martindale, and others for Tyndale House).

Lisa Samra desires to see Christ glorified in her life and in the ministries she serves. Born and raised in Texas, Lisa is always on the lookout for sweet tea and brisket. She graduated with a BA in journalism from the University of Texas and earned a Master of Biblical Studies degree from Dallas Theological Seminary. Lisa now lives in Grand Rapids, Michigan, with her husband, Jim, and their four children. In addition to writing, she is passionate about facilitating mentoring relationships for women and developing groups focused on spiritual formation and leadership development.

Marion Stroud went to be with her Savior on August 8, 2015, after a battle with cancer. In 2014 Marion began writing *Our Daily Bread* devotional articles that touched the lives of readers around the world. Two of her popular books of prayers include *Dear God, It's Me and It's Urgent* and *It's Just You and Me, Lord*. Marion worked as a cross-cultural trainer for Media Associates International, helping writers produce books for their own culture. Marion is survived by her husband, Gordon, and their five children and sixteen grandchildren.

Marlena Graves is a bylined contributor for Her .meneutics, Gifted For Leadership, and Missio Alliance. She is married to her favorite person in existence, Shawn Graves. He's a philosophy professor at the University of Findlay in Ohio. Together they have three little girls. They enjoy their life together and always desire to welcome others into it. She's on staff at her church—offering and coordinating pastoral care for their beloved seniors. Her first book, *A Beautiful Disaster: Finding Hope in the Midst of Brokenness,* released in June 2014.

Monica Brands, an editor at Our Daily Bread Ministries, is from Edgerton, Minnesota, where she grew up on a farm with seven siblings. She studied English and theology at Trinity Christian College in Palos Heights, Illinois, and worked with children with special needs at Elim Christian Services before completing a Master of Theological Studies degree at Calvin

Seminary in Grand Rapids. She treasures time with friends, family, and her awesome nieces and nephews.

Patricia Raybon, a former *Sunday Magazine* editor at *The Denver Post* and former associate professor of journalism at the University of Colorado at Boulder, now writes bridge-building books "to inspire people to love God and each other." Passionate for God's Word, she also supports Bible-translation projects worldwide. Her award-winning books include *My First White Friend* and *I Told the Mountain to Move.* A mother of two and grandmother of five, she and her husband Dan live in Colorado where they enjoy movies, popcorn, cozy mysteries, and soapy PBS dramas. Find her at patriciaraybon.com or on Facebook or Twitter @patriciaraybon.

Poh Fang Chia never dreamed of being in a language-related profession; chemistry was her first love. The turning point came when she received Jesus as her Savior as a fifteen-year-old and expressed to Jesus that she would like to create books that touch lives. She serves with Our Daily Bread Ministries at the Singapore office as an editor and is also a member of the Chinese editorial review committee.

Regina Franklin is a mom at heart, and she teaches God's Word with passion. Regina teaches full-time at Westminster Schools of Augusta, Georgia, serves alongside her husband in ministry, and also freelances in writing. Married since 1995, Scott and Regina believe the greatest calling on their lives is that of pastoring their two children, Charis and Micah. After more than twenty years of youth ministry at New

Hope Worship Center, Scott and Regina felt the Lord directing them to step out into church planting—a dream they had carried in their hearts since their dating years. With the support of their home church and many others, they launched inMotion Church in September 2013.

Remi Oyedele is a finance professional and freelance writer with twin passions for God's Word and children's books. Her ultimate life goal is to shape scriptural truths into stories for children and children at heart. C. S. Lewis is a major inspiration for her. Remi has an MA in writing for children and has completed correspondence courses with the Christian Writer's Guild and the Institute of Children's Literature. A native of Nigeria, she currently resides in Central Florida where she spends her spare time reading and blogging at wordzpread.com. Remi is married to David, her number one blog fan.

Ruth O'Reilly-Smith is a qualified secondary school teacher with very little teaching experience and twenty years of radio broadcasting experience. Her brief stint on university radio got her hooked to what has become her vocation. Ruth has worked in community radio in South Africa and on FM and shortwave radio across Central and Southern Africa from the United Kingdom. She currently hosts a weekend radio show, broadcasting across the UK on UCB Inspirational. Ruth is married to an Englishman, and they have been blessed with twins.

Shelly Beach is a freelance writer, public speaker, and author of many books, including *Ambushed*

By Grace; *Precious Lord, Take My Hand*; *It Is Well with My Soul*; and the 2008 Christy Award–winning novel, *Hallie's Heart*. She is the founder of the Cedar Falls Christian Writers' Workshop in Cedar Falls, Iowa. Shelly and her husband, Dan, recently moved from Michigan to Iowa to be closer to their grandchildren.

Xochitl (soh-cheel) Dixon equips and encourages readers to embrace God's grace and grow deeper in their personal relationships with Christ and others. Serving as an author, speaker, and blogger at xedixon.com, she enjoys singing, reading, photography, motherhood, and being married to her best friend Dr. W. Alan Dixon Sr., a college professor. Her devotional book, *Waiting for God*, released in 2019.

ALSO AVAILABLE

Experience the peace of God in everyday moments with this collection of devotions from the writers of *Our Daily Bread*.

momentsofpeaceformoms.org

ALSO AVAILABLE

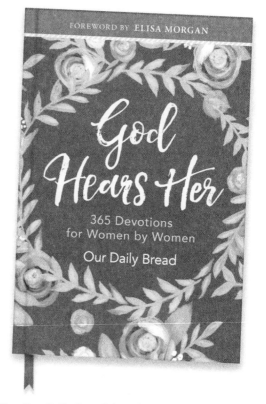

The *Our Daily Bread* devotionals selected for this collection are all written by women and offer the assurance that God is always with you and hears you.

u appreciated *God Sees Her*, please let others know.

- Pick up another copy to give as a gift.
- Share a link to the book or mention it on social media.
- Write a review on your blog, on a book-seller's website, or at our own site (ourdailybreadpublishing.org).
- Recommend this book for your church, book club, or small group.

Contact us to share your thoughts.

godhearsher.org

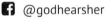 @godhearsher

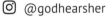 @godhearsher

Our Daily Bread Publishing
PO Box 3566
Grand Rapids, Michigan 49501 USA

✉ books@odb.org